FLOWERS FROM THE GARDEN OF EVIL

ALSO BY AENGUS SONG

On the Principles of Authoritarian Logic

Foundations of Authoritarian Thought

FLOWERS FROM THE GARDEN OF EVIL

EVERYONE'S GUIDE TO THE ELEMENTS OF AUTHORITARIAN DOGMA

By

AENGUS SONG

WHITE ROSE PUBLISHERS

This book is a publication of

WHITE ROSE PUBLISHERS

© 2016 by Aengus Song

ISBN-13: 978-0-9796329-3-8

Library of Congress Control Number: 2015951940

White Rose Publishers; Anacortes WA USA

Printed in the United States of America

For Pamela, Ken, Konrad, Herta, and Sophie

CONTENTS

INTRODUCTION

"IDEAS GOVERN THE WORLD," said the French philosopher Auguste Comte. If this is true then it behooves us to understand the ideas which govern the world's political life. But these ideas can be difficult to understand, in part because they are logically sophisticated, in part because the manner in which they are expressed is often sophistical. How are people to grasp the ideas which, as Comte suggests, govern the whole of world history, and, by implication, the people themselves, without dropping everything they are doing to study these ideas? This book was written to address this issue.

Comte himself was an "authoritarian" philosopher; he spent his life, to paraphrase Byron on Lord Castlereagh, cobbling at ideological manacles for all mankind. For while many of the ideas which have governed the world's history have had a liberating effect upon the human race, many also have had the effect which Comte intended: that of binding people in political and economic chains. It would be wonderful if these enslaving ideas were easy to identify and rebut but if they were they would not be politically dangerous.

Because such ideas are presented to us duplicitously and seductively, like flowers from a garden of evil, we must find a way to protect ourselves from them.

And the protection we need is to be found in the form of knowledge. Yet most of the books which offer knowledge about authoritarian ideas are written, not for the regular citizens who are the intended victims of these ideas, but for graduate students who become professors who write books for graduate students. The result is that only a scholarly elite really understands why religion has been so useful to tyrants, or why the philosophy of Karl Marx is not, as its fanciers frequently insist, a good idea which has tragically been betrayed. This book, however, was not written for an elite; it was written for you.

But would you have time to read a book like this? As was implied one of the most significant advantages that ideological manipulators have over their victims is that of time. For while the intellectual victims sweat in the fields or toil in the factories the intellectual manipulators, often enjoying the patronage of the most powerful people in society, and sometimes being those people, tinker at their leisure with the doctrines which permit them to "govern the world." This study, though, by identifying, compiling in one volume, and concisely explaining these doctrines, provides the information you need to protect yourself in a format you will have time to make use of.

But perhaps you think that you are too smart to require protection from authoritarian ideas. Perhaps you believe that evil ideas are easy to identify because they come impressed with infamous titles like *Mein Kampf*, *Das Capital*, or *The Prince* by Machiavelli. The dogmas of Adolf Hitler and Karl Marx, however, are just the obvious tendrils of ideological weeds that have much deeper roots in the loam of religious and philosophic thought. By teaching you to recognize the fundamental logic that is common to all authoritarian doctrines this survey makes it possible for you to identify and so defend yourself against destructive ideas even when they are manifested in the form of reputable theologies and respectable philosophies.

And this volume is generously illustrated with examples of such inadvisably venerated philosophic and religious doctrines, which are then deconstructed to reveal their relationship to the authoritarian tradition of argument. For if readers are apprised of the fact that many of the ideologies they have been taught to reflexively revere are in fact aspects of a malevolent intellectual heritage they will be less likely to uncritically accept these dogmas, and so unintentionally absorb pernicious concepts. Crucial tenets of the authoritarian intellectual canon are excerpted from such well-known authoritarian tracts as Benito Mussolini's *The Doctrine of Fascism* and then systematically compared with identical concepts as they appear in the works of eminent philosophers and theologians, so that the reader learns to recognize malicious ideas even when they are hidden in culturally accredited credos. And toward the end of this study, in the chapter entitled *The Gardeners of Evil*, the accredited institutions which propagate these creeds are themselves scrutinized, along with their motives.

And finally, in the concluding section, the reader is introduced to the tenets of the opposing tradition of political thought: the one upon which free or "liberal" societies are established. Every major aspect of the philosophic grounds of free societies is briefly but clearly contrasted with those of authoritarian societies so that the reader may make an informed choice between conflicting ideologies. Fundamental theories about the nature of reality and humanity: *metaphysics*; truth and knowledge: *epistemology*; morality: *ethics*; and human rights: *political* philosophy, are explained and compared, making the intellectual pathways that lead to freedom or to oppression clear. And at the back of the book an extensive glossary is provided to ensure that the meaning of philosophic terminology is clear to the reader as well.

Philosophic scholar Holmes Rolston, III noted that "without the widespread voluntary compliance of citizens" it is impossible for any government to rule, because "there are never enough enforcement officers to compel everybody." But why would people voluntarily comply with the rule of Adolf Hitler, Joseph Stalin, or the despots of Medieval Europe? The answer is that they fell under the spell of the world-governing ideas of philosophers like Auguste Comte, Karl Marx, and other intellectual manipulators. Those who thus succumbed were not evil, or stupid, or corrupt—*they were just like you*. By teaching you to recognize evil ideas when they are presented to you in the guise of good this survey will permit you to escape their fate.

—Aengus Song

A stupid despot may constrain his slaves with iron chains; but a true politician binds them even more strongly by the chain of their own ideas; it is at the stable point of reason that he secures the end of the chain; this link is all the stronger in that we do not know of what it is made and we believe it to be our own work; despair and time eat away the bonds of iron and steel, but they are powerless against the habitual union of ideas, they can only tighten it still more; and on the soft fibers of the brain is founded the soundest of Empires.

–Servan

CHAPTER ONE

A DISEASE OF IDEAS

The purpose of this book is to inoculate you against a disease. The disease is intellectual—a disease of ideas. The ideas are those which authoritarian ideologues—apostles of tyranny and dictatorship—teach to the people they intend to subjugate. Vaccines inoculate people against disease by teaching the body's immune system to recognize dangerous bacilli, the better to resist them. This book will teach you to recognize dangerous ideas so that your mind can reject them.

But you may think: I would recognize such ideas. I would recognize the ideas that fascist and communist and theocratic regimes are based upon without any help from a book. I am an intelligent person and I've been to college and I am not vulnerable to the vicious ideas that swindle weaker minds. But in fact you have probably already accepted many or even most of the ideas that provided the logical foundations for the political systems of feudal Europe, Nazi Germany, and Soviet Russia. And because, like most people, you are inclined to accept conclusions which are logically based on principles you already agree with, you may already be inclined to accept similar political systems.

But how can this be so? How can a decent, well-educated person like yourself be bamboozled into embracing the principles upon which the most irrational political ideologies and the most immoral political regimes have been established? The answer is that most of these principles are not readily recognizable as politically irrational or immoral. The reason for this is that most of them are not even political.

Most of the principles which provide the logical foundations for fascist, communist, and theocratic ideologies are *metaphysical*, *epistemological*, and *ethical* in nature, rather than political. These foundational ideas can be dangerous because they establish philosophic and theological premises in your mind which can lead you logically to authoritarian conclusions about politics. Once you've accepted these premises the political conclusions that follow logically from them can seem perfectly reasonable, so you must not accept them in the first place. This book tells you what these premises are and explains how they manipulate your thinking about politics.

Now, if you are new to the study of political philosophy words like metaphysical and epistemological can seem dauntingly abstruse and abstract. You may be intimidated by the technical sound of these terms and wonder why you must be familiar with their meanings before you can move on to the discussion of political theory. But philosophy generally and political philosophy as an aspect of philosophy are hierarchical structures of logic with "ground floors" and other "floors" established logically on top of the lower floors. You can no more understand political philosophy without first understanding metaphysical and epistemological philosophy than you can understand why a building stands without first understanding its structural geometry.

Political philosophy is the branch of philosophy that considers what is just in our relationships with other people and als[?] the nature of human rights. Such concepts are in turn based on theories about the nature of the world we live in, the nature of people, and broad theories about how people are supposed to live their lives. *Metaphysics, epistemology,* and *ethics* are the branches of philosophy that address these issues, so these branches of philosophy must be understood before we can have an intelligent conversation about political philosophy. The eighteenth century Scottish philosopher David Hume observed that, "as Force is always on the side of the governed, the governors have nothing to support them but opinion."[1] Because nothing so profoundly influences our opinions about politics and government as do our opinions about metaphysics, epistemology, and ethics, manipulating our opinions about these subjects has always been an imperative for those who would govern us.

Metaphysics is the branch of philosophy which studies the general nature of reality, and by implication the general nature of people. Epistemology is the branch of philosophy which discusses the nature of knowledge and how we are supposed to get it. And ethics is the branch which answers questions about the general nature of morality, including questions about how we are supposed to behave and what we are supposed to value. Because the particular theories of metaphysics, epistemology, and ethics we embrace tend to lead us logically to particular conclusions about politics people who want us to embrace authoritarian politics are determined that we should embrace certain specific concepts of metaphysics, epistemology, and ethics.

But how does a theory about the general nature of reality determine the nature of our politics? Well, consider a well-known theory of reality which says that the whole of reality is just one thing rather than many different things—the metaphysical theory known as *Monism*. This doctrine implies that transfers of wealth between people are really just transfers between the different parts of one entity rather than between two or more independent entities. If you embraced this theory of reality you might be led logically to the conclusion that transferring someone else's property to yourself without their permission would be perfectly moral because you and he or she were not really separate individuals. The value of monistic theories of metaphysics to an advocate of authoritarian redistributionist schemes is obvious.

And consider how theories about the nature of knowledge—epistemological theories—could affect your view of politics. The theories of human mental functioning sometimes referred to as *Reductive* and *Eliminative Materialism* suggest that human beings do not have intellectual free will, but rather think automatically, like machines. If this was true then people would not be able to think reliably about theories of political morality and political rights because they would not be able to conform their thinking to the facts which relate to these issues. How would you expect that someone who embraced such a doctrine would behave politically? The usefulness of this idea to a philosopher like Karl Marx, who employed it to dismiss considerations of political morality and human rights from practical politics,[2] is unmistakable.

And what about ethics? A famous ethical theory, *Hedonism*, says that pleasure is the highest good and that the moral value of any human action is determined exclusively by whether or not it results in pleasure. But what if the person who embraces this ethic gets his kicks by ruthlessly working to establish Adolf Hitler's Third Reich? Might not such a person assume that what is moral in the realm of ethics must be rightful in the realm of politics? Because our ideas about what is moral in the realm of ethics can affect our ideas about what is just in the province of politics authoritarian ideologists have always sought to manipulate our thinking about ethics.

But intellectual manipulation does not work nearly so well if the victim realizes that he or she is being manipulated. One way to hide intellectual manipulation is to permit the victim to arrive at conclusions through the agency of their own intellectual initiative rather than seeming to push the victim toward particular beliefs. Because such manipulation allows the manipulated person to come to conclusions through the exercise of their own intellectual free will it can seem as though the convictions being arrived at are exclusively the victim's own rather than following logically from premises suggested by a clever manipulator. This hides from the victim the fact that manipulation is occurring.

Also hiding authoritarian intellectual manipulation is the fact that the distinction between authoritarian and what we think of as normal or legitimate philosophy is not always apparent. Prior to the Constitutional establishment of the United States in 1789 almost all governments were institutionally authoritarian, and because it was in their interest to use metaphysical, epistemological, and ethical ideas to legitimize their authority these governments promoted philosophic and theological concepts that validated their sovereignty and suppressed the ideas which supported free societies. As a result, many of the ideas that survived to become what we think of today as the venerable Western tradition of classical philosophy and theology actually reflect the intellectual machinations of past authoritarian governments. This is why many of the doctrines this survey identifies as aspects of authoritarian theory are also aspects of what readers may think of as history's heritage of "legitimate" philosophical and theological concepts.

Really legitimate philosophy may be defined as the science of the most fundamental knowledge about ourselves and the universe we live in. Such fundamental knowledge represents humanity's broadest and most general understanding of reality, and as such is the foundation upon which all other human knowledge is established. Human knowledge needs such a foundation or else all of our knowledge would seem to be disconnected from reality in a fundamental way. Like a house without a foundation, human knowledge would seem to float in mid-air, disconnected from the underlying facts of the universe.

But philosophy itself has a foundation and that foundation is the branch of philosophy which we've already identified as metaphysics. Metaphysics, again, is the specific branch of philosophy that is concerned to discover reality's fundamental nature. Because philosophic theories are hierarchical structures of logic a false theory about reality's fundamental nature will lead logically to false theories about everything else, so authoritarian lying about politics begins with lying about metaphysics. The first part of our study, therefore, begins with a discussion of metaphysical lying.

But it is impossible to lie successfully about the general nature of reality without lying also about methods of acquiring knowledge. This is because people will soon discover the truth about reality's general nature if they discover reliable methods of getting information. To prevent people from making such discoveries authoritarian philosophers lie steadfastly about the branch of philosophy which addresses methods of attaining knowledge—the branch of philosophy known as epistemology. Because lying successfully about the nature of knowledge is so crucial to lying successfully about the nature of reality, a detailed examination of the authoritarian tradition of lying about epistemology is featured in the second part of this study.

And, finally, because philosophies of human *inter*action—politics—are based logically upon philosophies of human *action*—ethics—it is also possible to lead people astray with regard to political morality by leading them astray with regard to ethical morality. Ethics, to repeat, is the branch of philosophy that is concerned to discover what is moral in the realm of human behavior and prescribe what is good in the realm of human values. To protect readers from being misled about ethical morality, and thereby about political morality, the third part of this book introduces the subject of authoritarian ethics. But now let us begin our exploration of authoritarian philosophy where philosophy itself begins: with metaphysics.

PART ONE

AUTHORITARIAN METAPHYSICS

CHAPTER TWO

AUTHORITARIAN THEORIES
OF REALITY

Because philosophic beliefs provide the logical foundations for all our other beliefs when we get philosophy wrong we risk getting everything else wrong thereafter. And because philosophy itself starts out with metaphysics, when we get metaphysics wrong we risk getting everything about philosophy wrong as a logical consequence. Authoritarian philosophers want us to come to incorrect conclusions about the branch of philosophy which is politics so they try to get us to come to incorrect conclusions about the branch of philosophy which is metaphysics. Authoritarian philosophical manipulation, therefore, begins with metaphysical manipulation.

Metaphysics, once again, is the specific branch of philosophy which addresses the fundamental nature of reality, including human nature. Authoritarians offer not one, but rather three theories about reality's nature, which are known by the names *Idealism*, *Materialism*, and *Heracliteanism*. It might seem reasonable that because all three of these theories are used as supports for authoritarian political doctrines that they would all be fundamentally consistent, but in fact they are utterly contradictory. The reasons for this will be discussed at several points in this exposition but first these theories will be briefly defined.

Idealism, in the realm of metaphysics, says that reality is the product of some mind, or minds, and thus is fundamentally spiritual or immaterial in nature, like an idea. The modern, secular version of this doctrine says that reality is in some sense a manifestation of the mind of a human being, or of the minds of groups of human beings. The older, religious version says it is the embodiment of the mind of God.

Materialism, in contradistinction to Idealism, says that reality is exclusively physical or material, and that all events in nature, including the operations of the human mind, are governed by the mechanical forces which regulate the physical universe. In some of its applications this theory provides a metaphysical foundation for science, and even for political philosophies which are anti-authoritarian—or in the classical sense "liberal." But in its most common representation it provides premises for ideologies which say that human behavior is determined by the cause-and-effect laws which rule crude matter, such as Marxism.

And lastly, there is Heracliteanism, which is named after the Greek philosopher Heraclitus of Ephesus. This philosophy says that reality has no nature whatsoever, either spiritual or material. Nothing is anything in particular, Heraclitus said, because like the water in a river, everything is constantly changing. Heracliteanism, as seems apparent, contradicts both Idealism and Materialism.

IDEALISM

Of the three theories of reality employed as premises for authoritarian political doctrines by far the most significant is Idealism. This is primarily because Idealism subsumes religion, which has historically been the most prevalent instrument of authoritarian intellectual manipulation. Idealism offers several important arguments that facilitate authoritarian purposes, but before we look into these arguments we should note why Idealism is called "Idealism."

Metaphysical Idealism says that reality, like the ideas in a human mind, is a product of, or is of the nature of, thought, or consciousness, or spirit. The term Idealism, as it is employed to designate metaphysical theories, came into broad use in the early nineteenth century to refer to systems such as those of Plato, which say that reality is the embodiment of supernatural ideas ("Forms"), and Immanuel Kant, who said that reality is a product of human consciousness. The reader is asked to distinguish between the use of the terms Idealism and Materialism to refer to metaphysical theories and the popular use of the same terms to refer to ethical attitudes about abstract as opposed to concrete values.

Now, the idea that reality is a product of a consciousness, or a mind, or a spirit, implies that reality is an aspect of or is part of that mind or spirit, just as a person's thoughts may be said to be part of that person. Implied further is that if reality is of the nature of thought, or mind, or spirit, it may be construed that the material and physical reality we see around us isn't real, because it isn't spiritual, and so is of the nature of a hallucination or delusion. Although these notions may seem to be merely harmless, phantasmagorical speculations they have and do provide crucial argumentative supports for authoritarian political ideologies; but how?

The idea that reality has been or is being created by some mind can be used to underpin the notion that this mind, whether it is conceived of in a religious or a secular sense, owns reality, on the grounds that a sentient being owns the things that it creates. And the idea that reality is a part of the mind that creates it suggests that this mind has a right to control reality, on the grounds that a being has the right to control the various parts of itself. These ideas may seem innocuous when considered in the abstract, but what if this mind decides that among the parts of reality it has a right to own and control are you and your property?

And what if the material and physical reality we perceive around us is some sort of hallucination or delusion? In order to dispute the idea that reality is created by and is part of some omnipotent mind that owns and has a right to control everything we must appeal to the physical facts of the universe, which testify that this isn't so. But if reality is mental rather than physical then there are no such facts, and suddenly the most fantastic dogmas, which are themselves products of the human mind, become plausible. No wonder authoritarian dogmatists are fond of the idea that reality is mental rather than physical!

But who are these dogmatists? And what are the specific ideologies which they have developed to introduce the strange logic known as metaphysical Idealism into the minds of the human race? At this point we will begin to examine these specifics in greater detail.

RELIGIOUS IDEALISM

Historically, the earliest representations of metaphysical Idealism have been religious. Although most religions are not unequivocally idealist—that is, they do not categorically and unambivalently state that reality is exclusively mental or spiritual—they do proffer the idea that reality is created and/or sustained in existence by a mind or a spirit which is God. Beyond this, some religious doctrines, notably including the Christian, assert that human beings themselves can, through the agency of their faith, so profoundly alter reality that they in a sense create it.[1] Please note that while most religions are not exclusively idealist they all include tenets which either state or simply imply that reality is spiritual rather than material. This inconsistency is an instance of what is known as metaphysical *Dualism*, the theory that reality has two completely different natures. Dualism may be contrasted with metaphysical *Monism*, which says that reality is just one thing and has but one nature, and with metaphysical *Pluralism*, which says that reality is many things and has many natures.

The principal use that religious authoritarians have made of idealist concepts is that of premises for claims on political power. The most significant of these premises says that there is a God who has created the universe, and equally significant is another premise which says that God is the universe and the universe is God. The idea that there is a God is called *Theism*; the idea that God created the universe is called *Creationism*; and the idea that God is the universe (and the universe is God) is called *Pantheism*.

Religious authoritarians use the idea that there is a God who created the universe by saying that because God created the universe he therefore owns it. They then represent themselves as God's viceroys here on earth, His "property managers" so to speak, and claim a right to control everything which God owns. They use the idea that God *is* the universe by saying that because the universe is part of God that God has a right to control the universe—including that part of it which is the authoritarian state. Religious authoritarians then say that anything the state does is rightful because it represents God's exercise of His authority over Himself.

But why should people believe such things when everything their senses report denies them? Herein lies the profoundest import of Idealism. Metaphysical Idealism replaces the physical world perceived by the senses with a mental, "spiritual" world conceivable only by the mind. Religious idealists usually describe this world as either a supernatural other-world such as "heaven," or as an inner-world that exists in the hearts of the faithful. But whether described as a transcendent "above" or an immanent "within" it is always depicted as beyond the ken of humanity's faculties of sense-perception. Hence Jesus says of the coming of the Kingdom of God in the Gospel According To Luke that, "[t]he kingdom of God does not come with your careful observation, nor will people say, 'Here it is,' or 'There it is,' because the kingdom of God is within you" (Luke 17:20, 21, *New International Version*).

And because God's Kingdom is "within you," you cannot discern its coming by "careful observation"—that is, through the use of your sense-faculties. Although this passage has no obvious authoritarian implications in itself it nevertheless lays the groundwork for subsequent authoritarian arguments by legitimizing the whole notion of an unobservable reality which can be apprehended only by looking "within." For because human beings can make up anything they want within their own imaginations, legitimizing the within as being equal to the material can help to substantiate the premises of the divine regency—the Kingdom of God—which Christians wanted to establish here on earth. In his various Epistles Saint Paul reiterates Christ's assertion of the reality of the unobservable and then uses this to legitimize two crucial premises of the Christian kingdom.

"[W]e fix our eyes not on what is seen, but on what is unseen," Paul testifies in Second Corinthians, "[f]or what is seen is temporary, but what is unseen is eternal" (2 Cor. 4:18, NIV). Paul then tells us to look away from the visible and toward the invisible by asking us to "[s]et your minds on things above, not on earthly things" (Col. 3:2, NIV). Because faith "is being sure of what we hope for and certain of what we do not see," Paul enjoins us to use faith to "understand that the universe was formed at God's command, so that what is seen was not made out of what was visible" (Heb. 11:1, 3, NIV). Having then established the reality of the invisible through faith Paul succeeds in bolstering two principal pillars of religious tyranny: Theism, the idea that there is a god, and Creationism, the idea that "the universe was formed at God's command."

But it is not only Christianity which asks us to dismiss the "temporary" world of the material and fix our eyes on the "eternal" Ideal. All of the major religions make this same request of the faithful and use "unseen" evidence to substantiate the foundational assertions of their doctrines. Like Christianity the other major religions go back and forth between describing the unseen world as an immanent "within" the hearts and minds of the faithful and depicting it as the transcendent "above" of heaven, Valhalla, etc. Some religions, including Christianity, place greater emphasis on the reality of these transcendent, heavenly other-worlds, while others, like Buddhism, stress the reality of the ideal realms within the private mind of the believer. In William Theodore de Bary's *The Buddhist Tradition in India, China and Japan* A.L. Basham cites this passage from the Buddhist Sūtras to illustrate "the idealism of Mahayana [Buddhist] thought":[2]

> All phenomenon originate in the mind, and when the mind is fully known all phenomena are fully known. For by the mind the world is led....The mind...rears up like a wave...like a great flood the mind bears all things away. The bodhisattva [enlightened person]...dwells in everpresent mindfulness of the activity of the mind....And with the mind under his control all phenomena are under his control.[3]

The idea that with the mind under one's control all phenomena are under one's control is a reference to a compelling promise which many schools of Buddhist theology make to the religion's disciples. Devotees are told that if they believe fervently enough in Buddhism's *dhamma* [dharma], or virtues, they can supernaturally leave this material world of woe for a realm of heavenly bliss which is created by or which otherwise exists within their own heads. The dhammas teach that to enter this ideal world adherents must sever their emotional attachment to the material values and sensual pleasures of the illusionary and delusive material world in which they appear to live. The political effect of these teachings is to make it easier for those governments in which Buddhism is the state religion to confiscate such values. These excerpts from Buddhism's *Dhammapada* texts illustrate the use of idealist metaphysical arguments to convince believers to abandon the material world for the Ideal:

167. To lowly quality one should not resort;
    With heedlessness one should not live.
    To an improper view one should not resort.
    And one should not be a "world augmenter."

168. One should stand up, not be neglectful,
    Follow dhamma, which is good conduct.
    One who lives dhamma, sleeps at ease
    In this world and also in the next.

    ....

170. As upon a bubble one would look,
    As one would look upon a mirage,
    The one considering the world thus,
    King death does not see.

171. Come ye, look at this world—
    Like an adorned royal chariot—
    Wherein childish ones are immersed;

No clinging there is among those who really know.

....

174. This world has become blinded, as it were.
     Few here see insightfully.
     Like a bird set free from a net,
     Few to heaven go.
175. Swans go along the path of the sun.
     And in the air they go with psychic power.
     The wise ones are led from the world,
     Having conquered Māra [the devil] and his cohorts.

     ....

177. Truly, no misers get to the world of the gods.
     Certainly, childish ones do not applaud giving.
     The wise one gladly approves giving;
     Hence indeed is he at ease in the hereafter.

     ....

186. Not even with a rain of golden coins
     Is contentment found among sensual pleasures.
     "Sensual pleasures are of little delight, are a misery."
     Knowing so, the wise one
187. Takes no delight
     Even for heavenly sensual pleasures.
     One who delights in the end of craving
     Is a disciple of the Fully Enlightened One.
188. Many for refuge go
     To mountains and to forests....

     ....

189. But this is not a refuge secure,
     This refuge is not the highest....

     ....

190. But who to the Buddha, Dhamma [Buddhist teachings],
     And Saṅgha [Buddhist monastery] as refuge

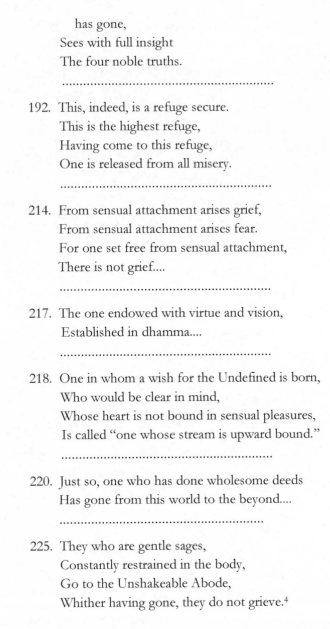

has gone,
Sees with full insight
The four noble truths.

....

192. This, indeed, is a refuge secure.
This is the highest refuge,
Having come to this refuge,
One is released from all misery.

....

214. From sensual attachment arises grief,
From sensual attachment arises fear.
For one set free from sensual attachment,
There is not grief....

....

217. The one endowed with virtue and vision,
Established in dhamma....

....

218. One in whom a wish for the Undefined is born,
Who would be clear in mind,
Whose heart is not bound in sensual pleasures,
Is called "one whose stream is upward bound."

....

220. Just so, one who has done wholesome deeds
Has gone from this world to the beyond....

....

225. They who are gentle sages,
Constantly restrained in the body,
Go to the Unshakeable Abode,
Whither having gone, they do not grieve.[4]

These passages teach the adherents of Buddhism to view the material world as a mere "bubble" which has no reality when compared to the spiritual "refuge" of "heaven." Buddhism must convince its devotees that this world is "a mirage" because the perceptible evidence of the material world testifies that abandoning material reality leads to disaster, not release "from all misery." Buddhism must promise its adherents that they can fly "from this world to the beyond" on the wings of their "psychic power" because nothing perceptible by the senses substantiates the reality of "the world of the Gods" which Buddhism offers its devotees in exchange for their worldly estates. Like Christianity, Buddhism cannot substantiate its dogmas by reference to the physical or the perceptible so it purveys the notion of a metaphysically Ideal reality which is more real than the material.

And like Christianity and Buddhism the Jewish religious tradition also proclaims that authentic reality is of the nature of the spiritual, rather than the material. Jewish scholars Ben Zion Bokser and Baruch M. Bokser explain that: "The talmudic rabbis viewed reality not as material existence, but as the meaning that undergirds and suffuses the material. The Psalms are permeated by the belief that man can constantly experience manifestations of God in nature, history, and human acts."[5] Abraham Cohen's *Everyman's Talmud* observes that:

> This is the Platonic idea which was adopted by [the Jewish philosopher] Philo, who wrote: 'God having determined to found a mighty state, first of all conceived its form in His mind, according to which form He made a world conceivable only by the intellect, and then completed one visible to the external senses, using the first one as a model.' The Torah reflected the 'mind' of God; and therefore the Rabbis searched its words [not physical reality] for knowledge about the process of Creation and the structure of the Universe.[6]

And the Hindu scriptures, too, denigrate physical reality in fa-

vor of the spiritual in order to substantiate God's "mighty state."
One of the most essential of the Vedic Upanishads, the *Bhagavad-
gītā*, asserts that, "[t]here is another, eternal nature, which is transcendental [beyond or superior to]...matter. It is supreme...."[7] The
introduction to a respected edition of the *Bhagavad-gītā* represents
this core Hindu scripture as averring that:

> [T]his material world is a reflection of the spiritual world, just as
> the reflection of the tree from the [river] bank is seen to be up-
> side down. This material world is like a shadow. In a shadow
> there cannot be any substance, yet we can understand from the
> shadow that there is a substance. In the [material] reflection of
> the spiritual world there is no happiness, but in the spiritual
> world itself there is real happiness.[8]

"In the material world every entity is called fallible," the *Bhagavad-gītā* itself says, "and in the spiritual world every entity is called
infallible."[9] One should therefore believe in the entities one encounter in the world of the unseen, this verse in effect asserts, and
ignore the illusionary particulars of the material.

And the religion of the Muslims, Islam, is no less dismissive of
this world and insistent concerning the reality of the next. Sura
LVII of that primary Islamic scripture which is the Koran proclaims:

> Know that the life of this world is but a game and pastime and
> show and boast among you; and multiplying riches and children
> is like rain, whose vegetation delighteth the infidels—then they
> wither away, and thou seest them all yellow, and they become
> chaff. And the life to come is grievous torment, or else for-
> giveness from God and His approval: but the life of this world is
> naught but a delusive joy.[10]

Islam prepares its followers to give up "riches and children" by convincing them that, "the life of this world" is but a "delusive" show and a hollow "boast." Devotees are warned of "grievous torment" in the spiritual "life to come" if they do not earn God's "approval" by obeying Islamic tenets. Like Christianity, Buddhism, and Hinduism, Islam cannot substantiate its doctrines by referring to the material and the perceptible so it tries to convince its adherents that, "this world is a game and pastime." For when people no longer believe in the reality they can see they are willing to believe in a reality they can't.

SECULAR IDEALISM

But it is not only religious idealists who have sought to replace the delusive world of the physical and the material with God's other-worldly kingdoms. As was mentioned earlier, there is a secular version of Idealism which has also been used to replace the material world with spiritual worlds that are more hospitable to authoritarian dogmas. Because secular Idealism succeeds religious Idealism historically, and also because secular Idealism mimics religious Idealism's theoretical logic, it is reasonable to assume that the earliest secular idealists were inspired by antecedent religious concepts in developing their secular concepts. Secular idealists, in effect, replaced religious Idealism's explicitly theistic gods with gods which were secular.

The first thinkers to replace religion's gods with secular or secularistic "deities" were certain of the early Greek philosophers. These early or proto-secular idealists may have been prompted to secularize traditional religious dogmas by the appearance in Greece of philosophical theories which all but completely rejected traditional religious representations of reality. These new proto-scientific philosophies doubtlessly threatened the traditional religious doctrines which had underpinned the authoritarian political struc-

tures that dominated pre-democratic Greece. The first of these secularizing idealists were in all likelihood attempting to reinforce traditional political arrangements by intellectually piggy-backing on the
rising legitimacy of Greece's nascent observation-and-logic based
pre-scientific philosophies.

Anaximander, Heraclitus, Parmenides, and Philolaus, were some
of the early Greek metaphysical philosophers who may be named as
having had prominent roles in the development of the new, secularistic Idealism. These philosophers were usually members of the
aristocratic elites who controlled the autocratic politics of the early
Greek city-states.[11] Because we associate Greece with democracy it
can be easy to forget that throughout most of their history the ancient Greek states were politically authoritarian, not democratic, as
we may habitually think. The upper-crust intellectuals who had the
time and money to develop the ideas which dominated public
thinking also had significant reasons to want to protect the authoritarian status quo.

But in contrast to the reactionary intellectual elements strug-
gling to retard Greek cultural development the more enlightened
Greek metaphysicians such as Thales, Anaximenes, Empedocles,
and Democritus advanced metaphysical doctrines which had mini-
mal idealist content. These observation-based, proto-scientific philosophies helped to loosen the grip of authoritarian theologies on
Greek politics—and in one city-state in particular, Athens, that grip
was nearly broken. But Athenian liberal democracy was never as
completely institutionalized in law and process as it was later in the
republics of the modern West, and the condition of the city's democratic institutions was always tenuous. Athens' political and philosophical regressives considered how philosophy could be used to
topple the wobbly Greek Camelot.

The most significant of the Athenian philosophic regressives
were two secular idealist philosophers whom the citizens of con-

temporary Western societies have been educated to reflexively revere, but whose ideas are in fact ultimately anti-Western. These two philosophers were Socrates and his aristocratic young student Plato.[12] Before we discuss the metaphysical ideas of Socrates and Plato it should be noted that, because Socrates did not write anything down, we only know his ideas through Plato and through another of Socrates' presumed acquaintances, Xenophon. However, since Socrates' admirers base their interpretation of his ideas on these sources it is reasonable for his critics to do the same.

Socratic and Platonic Idealism mimics religious Idealism in portraying the material world as a kind of shadow of the real. The real world, Socrates and Plato said, is a world of supernatural "Forms," or Ideas, which beam their spiritual influence throughout the universe the way the sun beams light upon the earth. The supernatural Forms are what really is, or what is supposed to be, Socrates and Plato said, and in the realm of politics the Forms prescribe the sort of authoritarian political arrangements Socrates and Plato themselves preferred. Let the reader note that "Platonic Idealism" is often referred to as Platonic *Realism*, because Plato had said that his supernatural Ideas were actual, or "real" things.

The Socratic/Platonic form of Idealism represented an interim step between the completely religious Idealism of theology and the increasingly secular forms of metaphysical Idealism which evolved later. Although the Idealism of Socrates and Plato does not emphasize the significance of God or of deities in its representation of reality it nevertheless presents the world as a manifestation of Forms that are spiritual or "ideal" in nature. After Socrates and Plato a long series of intellectual steps made by a long line of philosophers moved Idealism in the direction of complete theoretical secularization. Ironically, one of the most significant of those steps was taken by a Christian theologian, George Berkeley, Bishop of Cloyne.

Bishop Berkeley wanted to overthrow the idea of physical matter in order to protect the tenets of religion. To accomplish this he said that what human beings think of as matter is really just the human mind's awareness of its own sensations and perceptions, not real things which have an independent existence of their own. But although Berkeley's idea that the world was just a creation of human mental functioning further secularized the idealist notion that the material world is an illusion and the mental world is real, it is not entirely secular because Berkeley also said that human perception is possible only because God is thinking about the things which we perceive before we ourselves perceive them.

The final steps toward the total secularization of Idealism began to be made about thirty years after Berkeley's death with the publication of a metaphysical and epistemological tract entitled *The Critique of Pure Reason* by a late eighteenth century Prussian philosopher named Immanuel Kant. Kant was an employee of the Prussian state educational system[13] and his chief purpose as a philosopher seems to have been that of buttressing the power of that system's principal political and financial patron, the Hohenzollern dynasty of hereditary autocrats who ruled Prussia and Germany from about AD 1500 until the end of World War One. By arguing that what we apprehend as the material world is really just the by-product of the functioning of human mental processes Kant undermined the fact-based premises of political Liberalism while at the same time providing grounds for the faith-based dogmas which kept his Hohenzollern employers in power. What distinguished Kant's almost completely secular Idealism from Berkeley's was its assertion that the world we are aware of is the creation of mental processes that are exclusively human, with little or no assistance from God.

SUBJECTIVE IDEALISM

Kant's Idealism evolved into what is known generically as *Subjective Idealism* because it transferred from God to human "subjects," or selves, the power to create the universe. This type of Idealism had a profound influence on many of the philosophers who were later responsible for the development of the twentieth century's authoritarian political ideologies. Fascism, Nazism, and an early version of Marxism[14] all used this idealist argument as a metaphysical foundation—and perhaps because the founding "philosopher of Fascism" was the ardent Italian idealist Giovanni Gentile the idealist content of Fascism is particularly explicit. The following passages from *The Doctrine of Fascism* by Gentile and Italian fascist strong-man Benito Mussolini demonstrate Fascism's dependence on the spiritual and its aversion to the material:

> There is no way of exercising a spiritual influence in the world as a human will dominating the will of others, unless one has a conception both of the transient and the specific reality on which that action is to be exercised, and of the permanent and universal reality in which the transient dwells and has its being. To know men one must know man; and to know man one must be acquainted with reality and its laws. There can be no conception of the state which is not fundamentally a conception of life: philosophy or intuition, system of ideas evolving within the framework of logic or concentrated in a vision or a faith, but always, at least potentially, an organic conception of the world.
>
> Thus many of the practical expressions of Fascism – such as party organisation, system of education, discipline – can be understood only when considered in relation to its general attitude toward life. A spiritual attitude. Fascism sees in the world not only those superficial, material aspects in which man appears as an individual, standing by himself, self-centered, subject to natur-

al law which instinctively urges him toward a life of selfish momentary pleasure; it sees not only the individual but the nation and the country; individuals and generations bound together by a moral law, with common traditions and a mission which suppressing the instinct for life closed in a brief circle of pleasure, builds up a higher life, founded on duty, a life free from the limitations of time and space, in which the individual, by self-sacrifice, the renunciation of self-interest, by death itself, can achieve that purely spiritual existence in which his value as a man consists.

The conception is therefore a spiritual one, arising from the general reaction of the century against the flacid [sic] materialistic positivism of the XIXth century.[15]

Gentile and Mussolini invite us into a "purely spiritual existence" that is "free from the limitations of time and space" because "superficial, material" reality offers scant evidence to support the authority of the fascist state. Only by taking us outside reality and into unreal "organic conception[s] of the world" (we will be discussing *organicist* conceptions of the world a bit later on) can Gentile and Mussolini convince us of the fascist state's moral legitimacy. And in these excerpts from Adolf Hitler's infamous political manifesto *Mein Kampf* the importance of such concepts to the construction of the politically unifying dogmas which glued together the Nazi body politic is also made apparent; for Nazism, which is usually categorized as a species of Fascism, is also heavily reliant on the doctrines of metaphysical Idealism for its legitimacy. Hitler wrote:

[F]rom the purely metaphysical infinite world of ideas, a clearly delimited faith forms. Assuredly, this is not the end in itself, but only a means to the end; yet it is the indispensably necessary means....

....

But if a spiritual conception of a general nature is to serve as a foundation...the first presupposition is to obtain...clarity with regard to the nature, essence, and scope of this conception, since only on such a basis can a movement be formed which by the inner homogeneity of its convictions can develop the necessary force for struggle. From general ideas a political program must be stamped, from a general philosophy of life a definite political faith....The abstractly correct spiritual conception, which the theoretician has to proclaim, must be coupled with the practical knowledge of the politician....

This transformation of a general, philosophical, ideal conception of the highest truth into a...tightly organized political community of faith and struggle, unified in spirit and will, is the most significant achievement, since on its...solution alone the possibility of the victory of an idea depends. From the army of...millions of men...*one* [italics Hitler's] man must step forward who with apodictic force will form granite principles from the wavering idea-world of the broad masses and take up the struggle for their sole correctness, until from the shifting waves of a free thought-world there will arise a brazen cliff of solid unity in faith and will.[16]

And Karl Marx too, although he eventually settled on metaphysical Materialism as the basis for his mature philosophy, initially experimented with Idealism for this purpose. Of his search for a metaphysical basis for his new brand of authoritarian ideology Marx wrote in a 1837 letter to his father that:

[N]ew gods had to be found....

Setting out from [metaphysical] idealism—which...I had nourished with that of Kant and Fichte—I hit upon seeking the Idea in the real itself. If formerly the gods had dwelt above the world, they had now become its center.[17]

The new god at the center of Marx's world was "Man." German idealist philosophers such as Kant and Johann Gottlieb Fichte had said that it was man, conceived of either as an individual, or as one single collective being,[18] who psychically created the world in a manner analogous to the spiritual creation of the world traditionally ascribed to God. Kant and his followers asserted that the automatic processes of humanity's perceptual and cognitive faculties mechanistically condition the information we receive from the outside world, thus enveloping us in an artificial reality created by our own minds. Post-Kantian idealists modified this doctrine by saying that this artificial reality was not merely the only reality we are aware of, but was indeed the only reality that is. The influence of this idea on the young Marx may be noted in these unctuously obscurantist yet nevertheless decipherable passages from his *Economic and Philosophic Manuscripts of 1844*:

> Species-life [collective life], both for man and for animals, consists physically in the fact that man, like animals, lives from inorganic nature; and because man is more universal than animals, so too is the area of inorganic nature from which he lives more universal. Just as plants, animals, stones, air, light, etc., theoretically form a part of human consciousness, partly as objects of science and partly as objects of art—his spiritual inorganic nature, his spiritual means of life, which he must first prepare before he can enjoy and digest them—so, too, in practice they form a part of human life and human activity. In a physical sense, man lives only from these natural products, whether in the form of nourishment, heating, clothing, shelter, etc. The universality of man manifests itself in practice in that universality which makes the whole of nature his inorganic body....
>
> The practical creation of an *objective world*, the fashioning of inorganic nature, is proof that man is a conscious species-being [collective being]—*i.e.*, a being which treats the species as its own essential being or itself as a species-being. It is true that animals also produce....But they produce only their own immediate

needs...they produce only themselves, while man reproduces the whole of nature....

It is, therefore, in his fashioning of the objective [world] that man really proves himself to be a species-being. Such production is his active species-life. Through it, nature appears as *his* [italics in original] work and his reality. The object of labor is, therefore, the objectification of the species-life of man: for man produces himself not only intellectually, in his consciousness, but actively and actually, and he can therefore contemplate himself in a world he himself has created.[19]

Robert C. Tucker, formerly Professor of Politics at Princeton University, comments on this secular creation of the world in his *Philosophy and Myth in Karl Marx*:

Marx transfers to generic ["species"] man the creativity that Hegel earlier had transferred from the Christian God to the world-self....

In industry we must see a complex of already materialized productive powers of generic man. The history of industry is 'the open book of human essential powers, human psychology sensuously considered'. It is 'the *exoteric* [italics Tucker's] unfolding of human essential powers', and when it is so understood 'the human essence of nature and the natural essence of man are also understood'. Marx means that industry is essentially a subjective phenomenon in relation to man writ large in the species. Machines, factories, etc., are the materialized faculties of generic man's self-expression in productive activity. They are the physical extensions and enlargements of the hands, ears, eyes and brains of the species.[20]

The idea that industry and nature are the materialized phenomena of the subjective psychology of man considered as a "species-being" is a modern, secular expression of the ancient religious doctrine we identified as Creationism. Historically, Creationism has provided a foundation for the claims of authoritarian states by asserting that some great being—usually God but here Marx's "spe-cies-being,"—has a right to control everything because it creates everything. Marx's argument establishes a premise for the claim that collectives, conceived of as one single living being, own the means of production—"machines, factories, etc.,"—because col-lectives, rather than individuals, create these means of production. His use of metaphysical doctrines which are modeled on religious doctrines is almost laughably ironic from the man who referred to religion as "the *opium* of the people,"[21] [italics Marx's] and Professor Tucker writes:

> The religious essence of Marxism is superficially obscured by Marx's rejection of the traditional religions. This took the form of a repudiation of 'religion' as such and an espousal of 'atheism'. Marx's atheism, however, meant only a negation of the trans-mundane God of traditional Western religion. It did not mean the denial of a supreme being. Indeed...denial of the transmun-dane God was merely a negative way of asserting that 'man' should be regarded as the supreme being....Thus his atheism was a positive religious proposition.[22]

But Marx was tempted to use a "religious proposition" to jus-tify transferring political and property rights from actual individuals to his all-creating "species-being" because the material facts of re-ality offer no confirmation of this being's existence. He felt obliged to base his argument upon assertions for which there was no physi-cal evidence or see them collapse from a lack of logical support. Marx's theory illustrates why even the man who would go on to become the champion of modern Materialism experimented with Idealism in his efforts to substantiate the claims of authoritarian states. And because all arguments which seek to supplant the mate-rial with the Ideal are essentially religious, Marx's theory of the spe-cies-being is, as Professor Tucker observed, a form of religion.

CHAPTER THREE

CREATIONISM

The architects of twentieth century authoritarianism used ancient political dialectics to re-establish age-old institutions of tyranny upon new and superficially secular arguments. But long before the emergence of twentieth century forms of implicitly religious authoritarianism humanity was plagued by forms of tyranny which were explicitly religious. Religious tyranny is called theocracy, which is the rule of human politics by God, rather than by people. But because God, being a spirit, is undetectable by human senses, He traditionally rules through visible human representatives whom He Himself has appointed. In his *Principles of Government and Politics in the Middle Ages* Walter Ullmann contrasts theocracy—the rule of humanity by God—with *democracy*—the rule of people by people. Ullmann wrote:

> This one supreme organ, in whom all power is located and who hands it 'downwards', is God Himself who has appointed a vice-gerent on earth: in actual fact it is the vice-gerent who possesses the sum-total of power, having himself derived it from God.

> Strictly speaking, the idea of [democratic] representation does not arise within this conceptual framework, but only that of delegated or derived power in the shape of the specific divinely conferred office. Just as the idea of [democratic] representation is essential to the ascending theme of government and law, so is the concept of office essential to the descending theme: the office itself is of divine origin, because set up by God Himself. Consequently, since all power is anchored in divinity – 'There is no power but of God' – the descending conception can also be called theocratic.[1]

But where does God get the right to appoint vice-gerents on earth and hand down law to human beings from heaven? In the previous chapter we mentioned the concept of Creationism, the idea that God or some other spiritual entity creates the universe, and the concept of Pantheism, the idea that God is the universe and the universe is God. It is these doctrines, born out of the faith-based make-believe worlds of religious Idealism, that provide the intellectual premises for God's right to rule the human race. Creationism provides a foundation for theocracy by asserting that because God created everything He owns everything; while Pantheism provides this foundation by asserting that God has a right to control everything because God *is* everything. These two doctrines are necessarily idealist in their metaphysical grounds because there is absolutely no evidence in the material universe to support them.

But nevertheless, upon such foundations numberless generations of authoritarian theocrats have asserted a right to control everything on earth; either because God has appointed them His "property managers" here below or because they are that part of God—the theocratic state—that God uses to control His earthly realm. These charlatans have been the representatives of every religion, including Christianity, because all religions use essentially the same arguments to make essentially the same claims. Consider for instance how the father of Protestant Christianity, Martin Luther, used Creationism to establish the rule of God and God's vice-gerents: "...God is the Father, the creator of heaven and earth...," Martin Luther said:

> What do these words mean? The meaning is that I should believe that I am God's creature, that he has given to me body, soul, good eyes, reason, a good wife, children, fields, meadows, pigs, and cows, and besides this, he has given to me the four elements, water, fire, air, and earth. Thus this article teaches that you do not have your life of yourself, not even a hair. I would not even have a pig's ear, if God had not created it for me. Everything that exists is comprehended in that little word "creator."

And "if everything is the gift of God, then you owe it to him to serve him with all these things...," Luther says:

> Note that I am basing [everything] [brackets in original] on the word "creator," that is, I believe that God has given to me body and soul, the five senses, clothing, food, shelter, wife, child, cattle, land. It follows from this that I should serve, obey, praise and thank him....The creation...means that I believe that God has given to me...all that I possess. These things I have not of myself...I cannot either give them to myself or keep them by myself.[2]

But it is not only God whom you should serve and obey, Luther asserts. You must also serve and obey the institution which God has created to rule you here on earth: the government. "[W]e have the clear, definite statement of St. Paul in Romans 13 [:1]," Luther says in his *Secular Authority*, "where he says, 'The powers that be are ordained of God'; and again, 'The power...is the minister of God for thy good, and avenger unto him that doeth evil' [Rom. 13:4]....":

If it is God's work and creation, it is good...as Paul says in 1
Timothy 4 [:4], 'Every creature of God is good....' Among
'every creature of God' you must reckon not simply food and
drink, clothes and shoes, but also government...and administration of justice....as a special service of God....Therefore you
should cherish...the government...or any other handiwork which
God has instituted. As a man can serve God...at a trade...and
must serve Him if necessity demand; just so he can also serve
God in the State and should serve Him there...for the state is
God's servant and workman to punish the evil and protect the
good.[3]

A man should serve "God in the State" not only because the
state is God's minister for good, but also because, being God's
creature, the state is intrinsically and necessarily good. The logic of
Creationism thus establishes the legitimacy of the state but does not
limit the authority of God or God's government to the functions of
protector and punisher. If human beings and human possessions
are God's property because they are God's creations then God and
God's viceroy the state can do anything they want with people and
their possessions, on the grounds that a property owner can do
whatever it wants with its property. So Luther says that "it is the
same to God whether He deprives you of goods and life by a just
lord or by an unjust. You are His creature, and He can do with you
as He will...."[4]

God can do with you as He will because He has created you
and a Creator can do with its creations as it likes. It makes no difference to God whether he deprives you of your life and your
goods by a just lord or an unjust because depriving you of life and
of property is the Creator's prerogative and so can never be unjust.
Any lord can deprive you of any value in the name of an invisible
god because all lords are God's creatures created to rule God's creations here on earth. Although these ideas might seem shocking to

someone who has been educated to think of Martin Luther as an enlightened progressive reformer in fact his reputation as a brutal theocratic reactionary is well established. Jonas Lesser notes in his *Germany: The Symbol and the Deed* that:

> Many historians, says Heer, have spoken of "the catastrophic consequences of Luther. He opened a Gulf between Germany and Western Europe by unclogging German irrationalism." Quite a number of non-Catholic theologians, socialists, and politicians called Luther one of the main inaugurators of National Socialism [Nazism], among them Karl Barth, Reinhold Niebuhr and Dean Inge....Ricarda Huch says that Luther called the rulers of earthly states the lieutenants of God, and that "the German princes eagerly and gladly lapped up the new teachings." Professor Wilhelm Roepke says that Luther's teachings "no doubt had influenced...Germany in a manner which can only be called catastrophic....and his teachings about the evil world resulted in the German non-resistance to the power of the state...and their resigned submissiveness to their rulers."[5]

But Luther's teachings are not unique to Protestantism. His ideas, including his ideas about the political implications of divine creation, have deep roots in Christianity. The Apostle Paul, cited by Luther from Romans, says:

> [W]ho are you, O man, to talk back to God? "Shall what is formed say to him who formed it, 'Why did you make me like this?' " Does not the potter have the right to make out of the same lump of clay some pottery for noble purposes and some for common use? (Rom. 9:20, 21, NIV).

Paul says that "we are God's workmanship, created...to do good works, which God prepared in advance for us to do," (Eph. 2:10, NIV). But if the good work which God has prepared for us in

advance is slavery? Then, "each one should retain the place in life
that the Lord assigned to him," Paul says in 1 Corinthians (1 Cor.
7:17, NIV), adding:

> Keeping God's command is what counts. Each one should re-
> main in the situation which he was in when God called him.
> Were you a slave when you were called? Don't let it trouble you...
> (1 Cor. 7:19-21, NIV).

And if slavery is the place that God assigns to us should we
not obey the earthly masters whom He has created to rule over us,
as if we were serving God, not men? "Slaves, obey your earthly
masters in everything," Paul says in Colossians (Col. 3:22, NIV).
"[A]nd do it...with sincerity of heart and reverence for the Lord....as
working for the Lord, not for men....It is the Lord Christ you are
serving," (Col. 3:22-24, NIV).

You are serving Lord Christ when you obey your earthly masters because all of the stations of life are assigned to us by God, and
hence you are working for God when you slave for men. So don't
let it trouble you that your life is squandered in the station of slavery because slavery is the good work which God prepared for you
in advance and which He has created you to do. God and God's
government on earth have a right to hold you in a position of servitude because the potter has a right to make some pots for noble
and some for common use. These dogmas of Christian Creationism
sanctify any injustice, no matter how grievous, and they laid down
the justificatory foundations of the theocratic serfdoms of medieval
Europe.

But all the major religions, not just Christianity, use the moral
logic of Creationism to transfer political rights from individuals to
God and from God to those who claim to represent God. Islam's
Koran, for instance, asserts God's authority over humanity by having God state:

We have made man out of a life-germ (sperm) uniting with another (ovum). We are going to discipline him, so We have made him hearing, seeing. Surely We have guided him in the path, he is either grateful or ungrateful. Surely for the ungrateful We have prepared chains and shackles and a flaming fire.[6]

And having established God's sovereignty over man via the doctrine of Creationism the Koran then peremptorily hands it back to a man, the Koran's ostensive author, the prophet Mohammed himself, by saying:

I will afflict with My punishment whom I please, and My mercy extendeth over everything in the world; and I will appoint it, in the world to come, for those who fear and give the legal alms, and those who believe on Our signs, who shall follow the apostle, the illiterate prophet, Mohammed....He will command them that which is right, and forbid them that which is evil; and will allow them as lawful the good things among those forbidden in their law, and prohibit them the impure....And those who shall believe in him [Mohammed] and honor him and assist him and follow the light which shall be sent down with him, namely the Koran, these shall be prosperous.[7]

So having authored the Koran himself[8]—"the light which [was] sent down with him"—the "illiterate prophet" Mohammed has it instruct its readers to obey his own commands, on the grounds that the Creator has appointed him the apostle, the messenger, of God's laws over the peoples which He has created. No passage in the literature of the authoritarian tradition illustrates more clearly how Creationism is used for political purposes, and no more self-apparent and brazen ideological power-grab is to be found in the record of human intellectual machination. And the scriptures of the eastern religions, too, employ the doctrine of Creationism to require "unalloyed devotional service"[9] to God and men. Consider this passage from Hinduism's *Bhagavad-gītā*:

> I [Krishna] am the source of everything; from Me the entire creation flows. Knowing this, the wise worship Me with all their hearts....
>
> ....
>
> their lives are surrendered to Me....[10]

And among the things that Krishna requires the people of India to surrender to are the "four divisions of human society"—India's notorious caste system—"created by Me,"[11] Krishna says. At the top of this system[12]—no surprise here—are Hinduism's elite priest-class themselves: the Brahmin, by whom Krishna Himself was ultimately created. And just as the Christian fathers employed the doctrine of Creationism to buttress their assertion that "[t]he authorities [governments] that exist have been established by God," (Rom. 13:1, NIV) so do Hinduism's founders use Creationism to substantiate their assertion that the Hindu caste system is instituted by God. Judaism's Torah also requires submission based on Creationism, admonishing Israel to:

> Beware lest you forget the Lord your God by not keeping His commandments; lest when you have eaten and are satisfied, and have built fine houses and dwell in them, and your herds and your flocks multiply, and your silver and gold have increased, that your heart does not become haughty and you forget the Lord your God. And lest you say in your heart, 'My power and the might of my hand have gotten me this wealth.' But you shall remember the Lord your God, for it is He who gives you power to get wealth....[13]

It is God who "created the heaven and the earth,"[14] the Torah says:

Then God said, "Let the earth put forth grass, seed-bearing plants, and many kinds of fruit trees....Let the waters be filled with living creatures, and let birds fly above the earth....Let the earth bring forth the many kinds of living creatures, cattle...and beast"....And God said, "I will make man....Let him rule over the fish of the sea, and the birds of the air, and over the cattle...."[15]

"God was as a host who set a table with every delicacy and then welcomed the guest to his place,"[16] says Jewish commentary upon the Torah. And in return, the Torah says:

[T]he Lord your God require[s]...you...to walk in all His ways...and to serve the Lord your God...and...to keep...the commandments of the Lord and His statutes, which I [Moses, the author of this passage] command you this day.

For to the Lord your God belongs the heaven and...the earth with all there is on it.[17]

And because the earth and all there is upon it was created by and is owned by God we are indebted to Him for the providence which He provides us, and hence we are obliged to keep the Lord our God's commandments and serve His interests. Such literature established the age-old pattern of the use of the doctrine of Creationism as a premise of moral obligation, and ultimately, of political prerogative. As we earlier noted secular authoritarians like Karl Marx had used secular versions of Creationism to provide premises for the secular theocracies they were working to establish. Marx had employed the idea that the means of production was created by man conceived of as one single social "species-being" to supplant the notion that God "gives you the power to get wealth," and both doctrines provide grounds for the demand that you "serve the Lord your God," whether that God is conceived of as "Jehovah" or as a single collective person.

SECULAR CREATIONISM

But Karl Marx was not the only modern apostle of tyranny to have used the creationist logic of the world's religions to underpin a secular form of authoritarianism. "Right-wing"[18] ideologies such as Fascism also employ Creationism for the same political purpose. In the following passages fascist ideologues Gentile and Mussolini use creationist arguments in the same manner as do Marx and Moses, except that they called their all-creating being "the State." In their *The Doctrine of Fascism* Gentile and Mussolini say that:

> The Fascist conception of the State is all-embracing; outside of it no human or spiritual values can exist, much less have value. Thus understood, Fascism, is totalitarian, and the Fascist State—a synthesis and a unit inclusive of all values—interprets, develops, and potentiates the whole life of a people....
>
> ....
>
> It is not the nation which generates the State....Rather is it the State which creates the nation, conferring volition [i.e., free-will] and therefore real life on a people made aware of their moral unity....
>
> ....
>
> The Fascist State, as a higher and more powerful expression of personality, is a force, but a spiritual one....It is no mechanical device for defining the sphere within which the individual may duly exercise his supposed rights....
>
> ....
>
> The Fascist State is wide awake and has a will of its own.[19]

Gentile and Mussolini describe their "State" as a spiritual rather than a physical force because there is no physical evidence that this state, conceived of as a "personality" with "a will of its own," "creates the nation" and confers actual "life on a people." If it is physical human individuals—and physical individuals acting in groups—who are responsible for the creation of these values, then authority over these values must remain with real individuals, and cannot be peremptorily transferred to the "State" as a spiritual "personality." Like Marx's myth of the "species-being":

> The Fascist conception of life is a religious one, in which man is viewed in his immanent [Mussolini here means organismic] relation to a higher law, endowed with an objective [meaning external to the individual, and specifically, meaning ideal, or quasi-divine] will transcending the individual and raising him to conscious membership of a spiritual society.[20]

And like Moses' spiritual Jehovah the fascists' spiritual State creates all of the wealth upon which the collective life of the nation depends; like Marx's species-being the fascist state is a collective being comprising "the whole life of a people." Because "it is the State which creates the nation" the state lays claim to all of the wealth within the nation. And because the people are a "moral unity" who are merely parts of what Mussolini calls "the State, [as] a living, ethical entity…"[21] the people have no reality as individuals and therefore no rights over self or property. Reiterating part of the passage previously cited Gentile's and Mussolini's *The Doctrine of Fascism* says:

> [I]t is the State which creates the nation, conferring volition and therefore real life on a people made aware of their moral unity….[I]t is the State which, as the expression of a universal ethical will, creates the right to national independence. A nation, as expressed in the State, is a living ethical entity….Therefore the State is [the]…Authority which governs….

. . . .

> The Fascist State lays claim to rule in the economic field no less than in the others [because]…all the political, economic, and spiritual forces of the nation…circulate within the State.[22]

And the German Nazis, too, borrowed the logic of religious Creationism to justify their claim to rule. Although major Nazi Party philosophers like Martin Heidegger, Alfred Rosenberg, and Houston Stewart Chamberlain usually proffered the secular variations of idealist arguments as grounds for their claims of authority Hitler himself and Reichsführer of the SS Heinrich Himmler often cited explicitly religious doctrines to buttress such claims. In passages using arguments which might have been lifted straight out of the Old Testament Hitler and Himmler employed the openly religious version of Creationism to justify their power, asserting that the God who created Germany had given the Nazis the right to rule it.

"A thing like this," Hitler said of the National Socialist movement in a speech to political leaders at the Nuremberg Parteitag on September 7th 1934:

> would never have been created out of nothing if a great command had not lain the foundation of this work. And it was no earthly superior who gave us that command; that was given us by the God Who created our people and Who cannot will that His work should go to ruin…[23]

And Himmler wrote:

> [W]e could not have formed this corps [the SS] sworn to unity if we had not the conviction of and faith in a Lord God Who stands above us, Who has created us and our Fatherland, our people and this earth and Who has sent us our Leader [Hitler].[24]

So God has a right to impose a Hitler on the people of Ger-

many because He has created Germany and therefore, to paraphrase Luther, can deprive its people of goods and life by a lord
just or unjust. This passage illustrates how Creationism has been
used throughout the centuries by authoritarians who have variously
referred to themselves as prophets or Führers or Commissars. But
Creationism in its secular and religious forms is but one of the two
major metaphysical premises of authoritarian claims associated with
and/or derived from the tenets of metaphysical Idealism. The other
metaphysical premise, just as important, is most often referred to as
Monism by modern philosophic scholars, and is known as Pantheism in its explicitly religious manifestation. Monism, as was mentioned earlier, is the idea that everything in the universe is just one
thing and has but one nature, while Pantheism is the idea that this
one thing is God. At this point we will move on from our discussion of Creationism to the discussion of the next body of concepts
which are the focus of our study: the religious and secular variations of ideas which are usually referred to as being monistic.

CHAPTER FOUR

MONISM, PANTHEISM, ORGANICISM, AND THE ORGANIC THEORY OF THE STATE

The metaphysical doctrine known as Monism is important to authoritarian philosophers because its principal tenets, which say that everything in the universe is really one thing and that everything has the same nature, can be used to argue against the existence of individual human beings and therefore against the notion of individual rights. For if all things are really one thing then all of the individuals we see around us are not really individuals at all, and so can have no rights as individuals. Although the word Monism is used to denote both theories which say that the one universal thing is spiritual—an instance of metaphysical Idealism—and that it is physical—in the case of metaphysical Materialism—the term is most often used to denote doctrines which say that the universe is one great supernatural being, such as a pantheistic god. Because another term, the term *Organicism*, can be used to more precisely denote such doctrines, and also because this term can be used to denote both the religious and the secular variations of this idea, this study will frequently employ the term Organicism in place of the words Monism and Pantheism. The technical definition of the term Organicism denotes metaphysical doctrines which describe the universe as in some sense a gigantic living being, with all of its features having the same relationship to this being that the organs of a body have to the whole of which they are part.[1]

Historically, the most common manifestation of Organicism is Pantheism. Pantheism says that the whole universe is the one great spiritual organism which is God—and that God is the whole universe. This concept can be used as an authoritarian metaphysical premise because it turns every human individual, and indeed every value, into mere parts of a single divine individual who is all things. Because God thus becomes the only real individual, He becomes the only possessor of political rights.

In both its older, explicitly religious, and its modern secular variations Pantheism is the metaphysical premise of the most common and most famous of all theories of society and government: the *organic theory of the state*. The organic theory of the state says that as an aspect of the organism which is the whole universe the state too is organismic, and so all of the seeming individuals in a society are merely parts of the state, as the cells in a body are parts of a body. Because individuals are merely parts of the greater individual which is the state they have no rights of their own, this theory says, just as the cells in a body have no rights of their own; and because an organism has a right to control those things which are the parts of itself, the organic theory of the state says that the state has a right to control the individuals which are its parts. In his *Contemporary Radical Ideologies: Totalitarian Thought in the Twentieth Century* A. James Gregor, Professor of Political Science at the University of California, Berkeley, explains the significance of Organicism and the organic theory of the state to authoritarian ideologies:

> [C]lassical Marxism, Leninism, and Fascism all share a common normic model of man, a collectivist or communitarian conception of man that conceives the fulfillment of human personality as a function of social interaction. Man outside society is nothing. What Tom Mboya describes as the basic tenets of socialism—the "dictum that man is a social (political) animal which has no potency and no life outside the society," that "society is an organic thing with individuals playing the role of cells in the organism"—are the basic tenets of Italian Fascism as well....[B]ut they are also at least as old as Plato and receive their full modern expression in the philosophy of Hegel. In Hegel, Marx, and Gentile these theses were elaborately developed....These "socialist" tenets are in fact common to all contemporary radical social and political ideologies. They are fundamental to National Socialism [Nazism] and apartheid as well as to Leninism and fascism.[2]

And here is how the idea that "society is an organic thing with individuals playing the role of cells in an organism" is expressed in Gentile and Mussolini's *The Doctrine of Fascism*:

> Anti-individualistic, the Fascist conception of life stresses the importance of the State and accepts the individual only in so far as his interests coincide with those of the State, which stands for the conscience and the universal will of man as an historic entity....
>
> ....
>
> [T]he State equates itself to the will of man, whose development cannot be checked by obstacles and which, by achieving self-expression, demonstrates its own infinity.
>
> The Fascist State, as a higher and more powerful expression

of personality, is a force, but a spiritual one. It sums up all the manifestations of the moral and intellectual life of man....

....

The key-stone of the Fascist doctrine is its conception of the State, of its essence, its functions, and its aims. For Fascism the State is absolute, individuals and groups relative. Individuals and groups are admissable [sic] in so far as they come within the State.[3]

And further, in Mussolini's *Fascism: Doctrine and Institutions*, a different edition of the same volume:

The Italian Nation is an organism having ends, a life and means superior in power and duration to the single individuals or groups composing it. It is a moral, political, and economic unit which finds its integral realisation in the Fascist State.[4]

And here is how the Italian fascists' "right-wing" brothers-in-arms, the German Nazis under Hitler, expressed the same idea. The following passages are from chief German Nazi party ideologist Alfred Rosenberg's *The Myth of the Twentieth Century*:

Employers and workers are not individualities in themselves but parts of an organic whole, without which they all would not signify anything. For this reason the freedom of action both of the employer and the laborer was necessarily restricted as the interests of the *Volk* demand....

....

Man is nothing in himself. He is a personality only insofar as he is fitted intellectually and spiritually into an organic ancestral succession of thousands of generations. To strengthen and confirm this consciousness and hence cultivate the will...to fight for the whole...are the tasks of the state. Only by following this creed can we educate real citizens.[5]

Rosenberg is concerned to restrict the individual's freedom as the interests of the "Volk" demand because the Nazi conception of Organicism is *racial,* which is what Rosenberg means by this reference to the racial dogma of *Volkism.* German Nazi party philosopher Houston Stewart Chamberlain expressed this organic racialism in this passage from his *Foundations of the Nineteenth Century*:

> The individual members of the nation may have ever so different qualities, the direction of their activities may be utterly divergent, yet together they form a moulded unity, and the power—or let us say rather the importance—of every individual is multiplied a thousandfold by his organic connection with countless others.
>
> I have shown above how Lucian with all his gifts absolutely squandered his life; I have shown Augustine helplessly swaying to and fro like a pendulum between the loftiest thoughts and the crassest and silliest superstition: such men as these, cut off from all racial belongings, mongrels among mongrels, are in a position almost as unnatural as a hapless ant, carried and set down ten miles from its own nest....these men are by their own inner composition barred from all genuine community of life.
>
> The consideration of these facts teaches us that...man cannot fulfil his highest destiny as an isolated individual...but only as a portion of an organic whole, as a member of a specific race.
>
> ....
>
> There is no doubt about it! The raceless and nationless chaos of the late Roman Empire was a pernicious and fatal condition, a sin against nature.[6]

But as Professor Gregor noted in the passage previously cited, the organic conception of society, and the organicist metaphysics that underlie it, are not exclusively the canon of the authoritarian "right." The so-called "left" also makes use of these classical authoritarian doctrines in its philosophical postulations. In this passage from a Soviet-era, government published ideological tract Soviet academic philosophers assert that every aspect of society, from the intellectual to the economic—and even including human beings themselves ("the family")—are aspects of a single social organism. The passage is here condensed because the original is long-winded and oblique, but the meaning is rendered faithfully:

> There are numerous things in society which have too many functions to be referred either to the basis or to the superstructure. Thus, language, the family, machines and the productive forces in general, the natural and technological sciences, the nation, and so on....are social phenomena of a particular kind....these social phenomena are part of...an integral social organism....[7]

An implication of the notion that a nation is an integral social organism is the idea that all of the products of human inventiveness—"the natural and technological sciences"—are really the products of a single organic mind. This idea, an instance of Creationism, can be used to subvert a foundational tenet of capitalist economies: the right of intellectual property. In a later passage in the same tract the notion of an organic consciousness is also referred to. The authors call it "social" and/or "aggregate consciousness":

> The notion of spiritual culture is itself a little vague. For this reason Marxists have replaced it by the more exact notion of social consciousness. In this way, they underline the fact that all products of spiritual culture are the result of the activity of man's consciousness. And since man is not isolated from others but is connected with society at large...his conscious life appears as social consciousness, and the aggregate consciousness of the members of the given society.[8]

This reference to "Marxists" alludes to the fact that Soviet ideology was based directly on Marxism, which is itself metaphysically and politically organicist. In these passages from several of his published works Marx extols the notion that man is, or should be, a single organic being, made up of many individual people. In this excerpt from his essay *On the Jewish Question* Marx refers to organic man using his eccentric term "species-being":

> Human emancipation will only be complete when the real, individual man has absorbed into himself the abstract citizen; when as an individual man, in his everyday life, in his work, and in his relationships, he has become a *species-being*; and when he has recognized and organized his own powers (*forces propres*) as *social* powers so that he no longer separates this social power from himself as *political* power,[9] [italics Marx's].

"Man is a species-being..." Marx says in his essay *Alienated Labour*, "in the sense that he treats himself as the present, living species, as a *universal*...being,"[10] [italics Marx's]. And in the preface to his *Capital* Marx compares human economic activity to the function of cells in a living organism, employing this most hackneyed of organicist abstractions:

> The value-form, whose fully developed shape is the money-form, is very elementary and simple. Nevertheless, the human mind has for more than 2,000 years sought in vain to get to the bottom of it, whilst on the other hand, to the successful analysis of much more composite and complex forms, there has been at least an approximation. Why? Because the body, as an organic whole, is more easy of study than are the cells of that body. In the analysis of economic forms, moreover, neither microscopes nor chemical reagents are of use. The force of abstraction must replace both. But in bourgeois society the commodity form of the product of labour—or value-form of the commodity—is the economic cell-form.[11]

And in *Capital* itself Marx compares individual laborers to the organs in a single body:

> The isolated group of labourers to whom any particular detail function is assigned is made up of homogenous elements and is one of the constituent parts of the total mechanism. In many manufactures, however, the group itself is an organized body of labour, the total mechanism being a repetition or multiplication of these elementary organisms....These...detail workers are so many special organs of a single working organism that acts only as a whole, and therefore can operate only by the direct cooperation of the whole five. The whole body is paralysed if but one of its members be wanting.[12]

And if only the whole can act, then only the whole, and none of the "special organs"—individuals—deserves a paycheck.

RELIGIOUS ORGANICISM: PANTHEISM

But the idea that society, and ultimately the whole universe, is one gigantic organism, did not originate with the modern secular authoritarians. Modern secular organicists were inspired to represent the universe and society in this manner by their ancient theocratic forebears. All of the major religions, and probably every religion that has ever been forgotten by time, has featured elements of this idea as a major premise of God's authority over man, and ultimately of man's authority over man. This idea, as it is manifested in religion, is known as Pantheism, and here is how its social and political implications were represented by the late Divine Grace A.C. Bhaktivedanta Swami Prabhupāda, a well-known and widely respected proponent of Hinduism:

> Because we do not know that there is complete arrangement in nature for our maintenance, we make efforts to utilize the re-

sources of nature to create a so-called complete life of sense enjoyment. Because the living entity cannot enjoy the life of the senses without being dovetailed to the complete whole, the misleading life of sense enjoyment is considered illusion. The hand of a body is a complete unit only as long as it is attached to the complete body. When the hand is severed from the body, it may appear like a hand, but it actually has none of the potencies of a hand. Similarly, living beings are parts and parcels of the complete whole, and if they are severed from the complete whole, the illusory representation of completeness cannot fully satisfy them.

The completeness of human life can only be realized when one engages in the service of the complete whole. All services in this world—whether social, political, communal, international or even interplanetary—will remain incomplete until they are dovetailed with the complete whole. When everything is dovetailed with the complete whole, the attached parts and parcels also become complete in themselves.[13]

And the complete whole with which all the social and political services in this world must be dovetailed is the Hindu god Krishna himself, who says that "all living beings are but part of Me...are in Me, and are Mine."[14] As the first Mantra of Hinduism's *Śrī Īśopaniṣad* states, "[e]verything animate or inanimate that is within the universe is controlled and owned by the Lord," so, "[o]ne should therefore accept only those things necessary for himself, which are set aside as his quota, and one should not accept other things, knowing well to whom they belong."[15] All things belong to Lord Krishna because everything is and/or was created by Lord Krishna, according to the Vedic scriptures. Writing in his *Man's Religions* John Noss, former Emeritus Professor of Philosophy at Franklin and Marshall College, interpreted Hindu doctrine as representing that:

According to the monistic view, the evil of man's situation lies in this: he persists in thinking himself a real and separate self, when such is not the fact; for since Brahman-Atman is the sole real being, in whose unity there exists no duality, man is in reality Brahman-Atman and not another.[16]

"The conclusion that, if all is Brahma [Hinduism's god of creation] or some phase of Brahma, there is no true individuality," Noss said:

[M]ade the vigorous soul...feel weak and faint; it overbore and crushed him with a sense of the unreality of all his previous thought about himself; it persuaded him...of the ultimate wrongness of the struggle of the ego, away...from Brahma, toward self-fulfillment....[17]

And if the struggle for self-fulfillment is ultimately wrong, then what is the justification for the fight for individual liberty which makes the individual's "pursuit of happiness" politically possible? "[T]he priestly class...the brahmins searched the Vedas for proof texts which were to repress Indian society for many generations,"[18] said University of Mississippi Professor of Philosophy Quinter Marcellus Lyon in his *The Great Religions*. For such priests, there is no stronger "proof" of their right to repress society than Pantheism.

But although Pantheism and pantheistic arguments play a more prominent role in Eastern religions like Hinduism than in the Western religions, nevertheless, these arguments are an important aspect of the Christian and Jewish theological tradition as well. Especially because Christian theology provided the ideological underpinning for that form of Western theocratic tyranny which was European medieval feudalism we need to consider the role that pantheistic arguments played in the development of Christian theological doctrines. And because Judaism has been influential in many of the same historical eras and political arenas as Christianity, the role of pantheistic arguments in Judaism should also be examined. Consider these passages from the theologically mainstream Talmud as well as from the less orthodox Kabbalah. "The essence of serving God and of all the *mitsvot*," says the Kabbalah:

> [I]s to...understand that all your physical and mental powers and your essential being depend on the divine elements within. You are simply a channel for the divine attributes....You have no independent self and are contained in the Creator. This is the meaning of the verse: "Moses hid his face, for he was in awe." Through his experience of awe, Moses attained the hiding of his face, that is, he perceived no independent self. Everything is part of the divinity.[19]

The typical way that religions represent the pantheistic omnipresence of God is *organismically*: God is portrayed as a great living organism with everything in the universe functioning as parts of His body. Here is how this is represented in the Kabbalah:

> Know and understand that there is no similarity in substance and structure between God and us—except for the intention of the forms of our organs and limbs, which are fashioned as symbols of hidden, supernal realities....God...created in the human body various organs and limbs...as symbols of the divine structure.[20]

And the Talmud says:

> To assist the comprehension of the place of the incorporeal God in the Universe, an analogy is drawn from the incorporeal part of the human being—the soul. 'As the Holy One, blessed be He, fills the whole world, so also the soul fills the whole body....As

the Holy One, blessed be He, dwells in the inmost part of the universe, so also the soul dwells in the inmost part of the body.'[21]

And if everything in the universe is a part of God's body then it can be established that individuals must obey God, or obey that part of God's body which is society and the state. The Talmud states that "[m]an....is a unit in the body of humanity, and that fact creates many duties for him with respect to his relationship with his fellow-men. His life is not his own to do with as he pleases."[22] But what of Christianity? Does Christianity have pantheistic elements as well? Christian theocrats have always been wary of Pantheism, for if God is everything then human beings cannot be condemned for rebelling against His government. So Christian theology has developed dualistically, with the realm of the spiritual and the heavenly being that of God and the realm of the earthly and the material being the abode of the devil—or dismissed as irrelevant. Yet Pantheism has been enormously attractive to Christian theologians, as it has been to Hebrew, because like Creationism it allows them to assert authority over all things, and to make unlimited claims on the proceeds of human productivity. So sprinkled throughout the Christian scriptures, especially in the New Testament, are little pantheistical passages which can be cited to buttress theocratic claims on property and power. "He is before all things," the Bible says of Christ:

[A]nd in him all things hold together. And he is the head of the body, the church...so that in everything he might have the supremacy. For God was pleased to have all his fullness dwell in him, and through him to reconcile to himself all things, whether things on earth or things in heaven... (Col. 1:17-20, NIV).

And because all things on earth and heaven hold together in

Christ there are no human individuals, so, "there is no Greek or Jew, circumcised or uncircumcised, barbarian, Scythian, slave or free, but Christ is all, and is in all," (Col. 3:11, NIV). And because Christ is all, "we are all members of one body," (Eph. 4:25, NIV) and therefore don't have the right to do with our own lives as we wish, because, "[t]he body is a unit [so]....[t]he eye cannot say to the hand, 'I don't need you!' And the head cannot say to the feet, 'I don't need you!..' " (I Cor. 12:12, 21, NIV). And just as a body has a head to give orders and feet to take them, so in the body of Christ:

> [M]embers do not have all the same function, so in Christ we who...form one body....have different gifts, according to the grace given us. If a man's gift is....serving, let him serve...if it is leadership, let him govern... (Romans 12:4-8, NIV).

And you can guess what gift the Christian theocrats who governed feudal Europe thought was their gift.

But while Pantheism and Creationism, in either their religious or secular forms, are the immediate premises that idealist philosophers use to undergird authoritarian claims on political power, metaphysical Idealism is, as we noted earlier, but one of three major metaphysical philosophies that authoritarian intellectuals use to buttress authoritarian claims. Before we consider the other two, Materialism and Heracliteanism, we should review the historical development of idealist metaphysics in order to firmly fix its relationship to authoritarianism in our minds.

As we have seen, there are explicitly religious, exclusively secular, as well as semi-secular versions of the metaphysics of Idealism. Explicitly religious Idealism dates to prehistoric times, but secular and semi-secular versions of Idealism seem to have developed during those periods when humanity has rebelled against religion. One such period was the fifth century B.C. Greek Enlightenment when Greek religion was so weakened by Greek scientific philosophy that it was in danger of being demoted to the status of mere mythology.

Counterattacking against the politically liberalizing effects of this weakening of religion were two primarily idealist Greek philosophers, Socrates and Plato, who are popularly thought of today as political liberals. But Socrates and Plato were in fact allied with the forces of the reactionary Athenian aristocrats who sought to preserve their economic and political privileges against the encroachments of Athenian democracy.[23] Socrates' and Plato's philosophy, as it is expressed in the Platonic *Dialogues*, propounded a semi-secular version of Idealism that deemphasized the idea of God while preserving the supernaturalistic metaphysics of Idealism. This was the first instance in history of a significantly secularist form of metaphysical Idealism being developed as a systematic aspect of an explicitly authoritarian political ideology.

Socratic/Platonic Idealism had a corrosive effect on Greco-Roman culture, eroding its confidence in material reality and preparing the way for the next stage of Idealism's historical career. This stage was the resurgence of the most virulent mode of Idealism, religion, in the form of Christianity. Christian Idealism, explicitly theistic and creationist, and subliminally pantheistic, provided a perfect underpinning for the reinvigoration of theocracy in the classical world. Theocracy was fully reestablished when Christianity was institutionalized as the official religion of Rome in AD 380, and was even more thoroughly reentrenched when Rome fell and Europe collapsed into medieval Christian feudalism.

It may be said that Christian theocracy remained entrenched for fourteen hundred years until being militarily vanquished in 1781 when Washington defeated the armies of British imperialism at Yorktown. But even during the darkest centuries of the dark ages of medieval Christian rule the light that was Greek scientific philosophy had never been completely snuffed out. Having ironically found refuge in the realms of Islam certain of the most crucial ideas of one of the most enlightened of the Greek philosophers, Aristotle, were rediscovered by Western Europeans when the Crusaders invaded the Muslim dominions. One of these Europeans, a disgruntled Catholic theologian named Thomas Aquinas, used an Aristotelian metaphysical idea known as Moderate Realism to re-legitimize the belief in the reality of the physical world.

And thus weakened by Thomas's revivified Aristotelianism that instrument of Christian theocracy which was the Catholic Church eventually surrendered enough cultural and political influence to permit a renaissance of interest in the physical facts about people and the material universe in which they lived. Science was rediscovered and as an ultimate consequence British philosopher John Locke discovered the political principles of modern Liberalism—a political philosophy that is based directly on observations of the physical facts about humanity and material reality. Lockean Liberalism helped inspire the Founding Fathers of the United States to establish a new nation "conceived in liberty"—a nation that finally drove a spike through the heart of theocratic Christianity by its practical separation of church and state. But in a dark corner of Eastern Europe evil men were not prepared to give up feudalism without a fight.

In the last half of the eighteenth century, as the spirit of liberty was beginning its march across the plains of America and the battlefields of Europe, a member of a reactionary Prussian aristocratic family made a last ditch effort to save its little fiefdom of medievalism. This man was Frederick the Great, King of Prussia and a scion of the autocratic Hohenzollern dynasty that ruled Prussia and Germany for four hundred years until finally being deposed upon losing World War One. Frederick sponsored the efforts of an ambitious intellectual hack named Immanuel Kant to develop a new version of metaphysical Idealism—one which would be secularistic enough in its mien to avoid being recognized and denounced as religious while at the same time retaining the most insidious elements of authoritarian theology. Because of its secularity, this doctrine was amenable to the increasingly scientific outlook of the people of Enlightenment Europe; and because it was not obviously religious, it was less likely to be identified by Europeans as authoritarian in its purpose.

Kant's new Idealism said that it is the consciousness of human beings, rather than the spirit of God, which creates the world we apprehend around us. Human consciousness does this, Kant said, by automatically altering the outside information it receives, thus enveloping us in a world made by our own minds. Because our consciousness automatically alters outside information, we can never really know the actual facts of the universe we live in, Kant asserted. But because our consciousness also creates a universe, we can learn everything we need to know about this universe by simply looking within ourselves.

Kant's philosophy ushered in a new age of faith by encouraging people to look within themselves for knowledge while ignoring the facts of outside reality. Because authoritarian dogma is faith-based rather than fact based, Kant's doctrine provided a new epistemological and metaphysical defense for the new authoritarian dogmas that were soon to be developed by Karl Marx, H. S. Chamberlain, Giovanni Gentile, and others. And because his ideas undermined confidence in the empirical facts about human beings and physical nature, it undermined the philosophies of freedom that are based directly on those facts. So although Kant may have intended merely to provide a doctrinal defense for the political legitimacy of his Hohenzollern employers, he ended up establishing the foundations of twentieth century totalitarianism.

Yet as dangerous as Kant's ideas are they remain popular today because the same ideas that provide a defense for the most egre-

gious forms of authoritarianism can also be used to provide defenses for that milder form of authoritarianism which is the economic redistributionism of the modern welfare state. Because
among the places that welfare states redistribute wealth to are the
myriad state universities and colleges where philosophy itself is usually taught, Kantian and other forms of authoritarian philosophy
are likely to remain deeply entrenched in Western culture for some
time to come. Because the citizens of the liberal West are therefore
likely to remain inundated with these ideas they must be able to
identify them in all their innocent guises, so as not to fall prey to
them. The next one of these ideas we will identify is called Materialism.

CHAPTER FIVE

MATERIALISM

Idealism, as we noted earlier, is by far the most significant and historically consequential of the three basic metaphysical doctrines propounded by authoritarian intellectuals. But the metaphysical doctrine known as Materialism has also been influential in this regard, and also has been widely used as a premise of authoritarian political dogmas. And just as the word Idealism does not have the same meaning in popular usage as it does within the province of technical philosophy so neither does the term Materialism. Before the technical definition of Materialism is discussed perhaps we should consider the comments of the late Antony Flew, formerly Professor of Philosophy at the University of Reading, concerning the definition of this term. In his *A Dictionary of Philosophy* he wrote:

> As most commonly understood in philosophy, the term [Materialism] denotes the doctrine that whatever exists is either matter, or entirely dependent on matter for its existence. The precise meaning and status of this doctrine are, however, far from clear....The range of possible answers...makes materialism in ef-

fect a somewhat ill-defined group of doctrines rather than one specific thesis.[1]

The reason that the definition of Materialism is "far from clear" is that while philosophy dictionaries almost always define this term as in some sense meaning that "whatever exists is either matter, or entirely dependent on matter for its existence," this is almost never what modern philosophic scholars actually mean when they designate a philosophy as "materialist." What they almost always mean is that a philosophy designated as materialist describes *human behavior* as being like the behavior of raw matter: determined by the cause-and-effect mechanics that govern crude matter. The idea that human behavior is determined by cause-and-effect mechanics is an implication of the doctrine of *Determinism*, which says that every event in the universe, including all aspects of human activity, is determined by the mechanistic operation of casual laws. The reason why the term Materialism is used to specify an "ill-defined group of doctrines" is that philosophers and theologians have developed a large number of different ways of describing human behavior as mechanistic.

Authoritarian philosophers and theologians describe human behavior as mechanistic because doing so justifies the imposition of brute force upon human politics. For if human beings are like machines then they can't control themselves, and if they can't control themselves then they must be controlled by the brute force of authoritarian states. The older, religious forms of Materialism have usually said that human beings are mechanistically sinful and evil and therefore must be forcibly restrained by God's appointed magistrates here on earth; while the modern, secular versions of this doctrine typically use the idea that human beings are mechanistically irrational to justify the imposition of "natural law,"—"Social Darwinism"—on political life.

ORIGINAL SIN

Although it may seem odd that religions, which are usually identified as metaphysically idealist, should employ materialist arguments, this inconsistency is in fact a reflection of the dualistic nature of most theologies. Dualism in the realm of metaphysics, recall, is the belief that there are two distinct realities which have two distinct natures: that of the spiritual and that of the material. A principal reason for religion's metaphysical Dualism is that if only one source of causality is acknowledged—that of God—then God can be blamed for human evil. So a second source of causality, that of the material and the physical, must be admitted for God to be innocent of evil and people therefore guilty.

The primary representation of Materialism in the Christian religion is called Original Sin. Before we continue the reader should note that Original Sin is not always identified by philosophic and religious scholars as an instance of Materialism. This philosopher believes, however, that this identification should be made, because the most important implication of the doctrine of Materialism is that of the notion of human mechanicality—which is exactly what the dogma of Original Sin asserts. Bernard Susser, Professor of Political Science at Bar-Ilan University in Israel, notes the similarity between the Christian doctrine of Original Sin and the purely secular philosophy of Thomas Hobbes, one of the great modern apostles of secular Materialism:

> Ideas that had derived originally from religious inspiration were often reformulated in secular and civic terms. To mention a single example, the Christian doctrine that humankind is tainted by original sin became secularized into the view—associated with thinkers like Thomas Hobbes—that human character is naturally selfish and pleasure-centered.[2]

The Christian doctrine of Original Sin says that human beings are born in slavery to sinful physical and material appetites as a result of the Original Sin of Adam. Adam's Original Sin, Christian doctrine says, fixed the chains of appetitive sinfulness upon human nature, mechanically compelling people to all kinds of evil lusts and greeds. Christian theologians have historically used this dogma of sinful human nature as an excuse to fix political chains upon the human race. Let's look at St. Paul's description of his own original sinfulness, and then consider Martin Luther's use of the same doctrine to justify theocratic authoritarianism:

"[S]in entered the world through one man," Paul says of Adam. "Consequently...the result of one trespass was condemnation for all men....For...through the disobedience of...one man the many were made sinners..." (Rom. 5:12, 18, 19, NIV). And because all men are made sinners Paul is unable to obey God's spiritual laws prohibiting what he calls "the sinful passions" (Rom. 7:5, NIV):

> We know that the law is spiritual; but I am unspiritual, sold as a slave to sin. I do not understand what I do. For what I want to do I do not do, but what I hate I do. And if I do what I do not want to do, I agree that the law is good. As it is, it is no longer I myself who do it, but it is sin living in me. I know that nothing good lives in me, that is, in my sinful nature. For I have the desire to do what is good, but I cannot carry it out. For what I do is not the good I want to do; no, the evil I do not want to do—this I keep on doing. Now if I do what I do not want to do, it is no longer I who do it, but it is sin living in me that does it.
>
> So I find this law at work: When I want to do good, evil is right there with me. For in my inner being I delight in God's law; but I see another law at work in the members of my body, waging war against the law of my mind and making me a prisoner of the law of sin at work within my members. What a wretched man I am! Who will rescue me from this body of death? (Rom. 7:14-24, NIV).

Paul is unable to obey God's spiritual laws because of the law of sin at work within his physical members. And because all men are slaves to sin, Christian theocrats say, only a government of God—a theocracy—can govern men. So Martin Luther asserts that:

> Since...no one is by nature Christian or pious, but every one sinful and evil, God places the restraints of the law upon them all, so that they may not dare give rein to their desires and commit...wicked deeds....Even so a wild, savage beast is fastened with chains and bands, so that it cannot bite and tear as is its wont....If it were not so, seeing that the whole world is evil and that among thousands there is scarcely one true Christian, men would devour one another, and no one could preserve wife and child, support himself and serve God; and thus the world would be reduced to chaos.[3]

Men are mad and savage beasts, Luther says, who must be bound and chained by God's government on earth:

> [G]od hath ordained civil laws, yea all laws to punish transgressions. Every law then is given to restrain sin....These do bridle and restrain me that I sin not, as bonds and chains do restrain a lion or a bear, that he tear and devour not every thing that he meeteth....For as a mad or wild beast is bound, lest he destroy not everything that he meeteth: even so the law doth bridle a mad and furious man....
>
> The first use, then, of laws is to bridle the wicked. For the devil reigneth throughout the whole world, and enforceth men to all kinds of wickedness. Therefore God hath ordained magistrates...laws, bonds, and all civil ordinances, that...they may bind the devil's hands, that he rage not in his bondslaves....[4]

SOCIAL DARWINISM

The idea that human beings are the bondslaves of wickedness implies, as Martin Luther indicates, that human beings are like "beasts." For if human behavior is slavish—that is, involuntary—then it is like the instinctive, mechanistic behavior of animals. This idea not only provides a justification for taking political authority away from people and giving it to God and the magistrates He ordains, it also provides a premise for imposing the natural laws that govern relationships between animals on human politics. These laws include the survival-of-the-fittest, evolution-through-extermination laws associated with Charles Darwin.

Charles Darwin's principles of biology and evolution, when they are applied to human political and social life, became known as Social Darwinism. Social Darwinism is the premier representation of metaphysical Materialism found in twentieth century authoritarian ideologies such as Nazism and Marxism. The Nazis and the Marxists promised that if Darwinian principles were applied to human politics the result would be evolutionary progress for both humanity and society. The Nazis said that survival-of-the-fittest contests between races would result in evolutionary progress for humanity, so their form of Social Darwinism was *racist*. The Marxists said that evolution-through-extermination struggles between classes—"class struggle"—would result in evolutionary progress for society, so their form of Social Darwinism was *classist*.

The Nazis and the Marxists believed that different types of people have inherently different moral and intellectual characteristics, so that the key to social evolution is the elimination of human types that have unwanted characteristics and their replacement by types that have desirable characteristics. The Nazis contended that human moral and intellectual traits are determined by race, while the Marxists asserted that they are determined by class (economic background, or profession). Because these traits are inherent, and/or inborn in the person possessing them, the behavior of people cannot be changed by reasoning with them; therefore brute force must be used to facilitate social evolution, just as it facilitates biological evolution.

The Nazis' position that human moral and intellectual attributes were determined by race is expressed in statements like this one, made in Adolf Hitler's notorious testament *Mein Kampf*: "In the blood alone resides the strength as well as the weakness of man," Hitler wrote, using the word "blood" to mean race:

> As long as peoples do not recognize and give heed to the importance of their racial foundation, they are like men who would like to teach poodles the qualities of greyhounds, failing to realize that the speed of the greyhound like the docility of the poodle are not learned, but are qualities inherent in the race. Peoples which renounce the preservation of their racial purity renounce with it the unity of their soul in all its expressions.[5]

And the Marxists expressed their belief that moral and intellectual characteristics were determined by economic class in statements such as this one, excerpted from Marx's *Manifesto of the Communist Party*:

> [Y]our bourgeois notions of freedom, culture, law, etc. Your very ideas are but the outgrowth of the conditions of your bourgeois production and bourgeois property, just as your jurisprudence is but the will of your class made into a law for all, a will whose essential character and direction are determined by the economic conditions of the existence of your class....
>
> ....
>
> Does it require deep intuition to comprehend that man's ideas, views, and conceptions—in one word, man's consciousness—changes with every change in the conditions of

his material existence, in his social relations and in his social life?[6]

Hitler believed that a Darwinian struggle between races would let the stronger race take "possession of this earth," leading to the emergence of a better, "higher" human race. He wrote in *Mein Kampf* that:

> [T]he folkish philosophy finds the importance of mankind in its basic racial elements. In the state it sees...only a means to an end and construes its end as the preservation of the racial existence of man. Thus, it by no means believes in an equality of the races, but...recognizes their higher or lesser value and feels itself obligated...to promote the victory of the better and stronger, and demand the subordination of the inferior and weaker in accordance with the eternal will that dominates this universe. Thus...it serves the basic aristocratic idea of Nature....
>
> And so the folkish philosophy of life corresponds to the inner-most will of Nature, since it restores that free play of forces which must lead to a continuous mutual higher breeding, until at last the best of humanity, having achieved possession of this earth, will have a free path....[I]n the distant future humanity must be faced by problems which only a highest race, become master people and supported by the means...of an entire globe, will be equipped to overcome.[7]

The Nazis' counterparts on the "left," however, the Marxists, believed that a struggle between the *classes* "forms a series of evolutions" leading to a "revolutionary reconstitution of society."[8] "The *Manifesto* being our joint production," Friedrich Engels wrote in the preface to the *Manifesto of the Communist Party*:

> I consider myself bound to state that the fundamental proposition which forms its nucleus belongs to Marx. That proposition

is: That in every historical epoch the prevailing mode of economic production and exchange, and the social organization necessarily following from it, form the basis upon which is built up, and from which alone can be explained, the political and intellectual history of that epoch; that, consequently, the whole history of mankind...has been a history of class struggles, contests between exploiting and exploited, ruling and oppressed classes; that the history of these class struggles forms a series of evolutions in which, nowadays, a stage has been reached where the exploited and oppressed class—the proletariat—cannot attain its emancipation from the sway of the exploiting and ruling class—the bourgeoisie—without at the same time, and once and for all, emancipating society at large from all exploitation, oppression, class distinctions and class struggles.

This proposition, which in my opinion is destined to do for history what Darwin's theory has done for biology, we, both of us, had been gradually approaching for some years....[9]

And Lenin offered this explanation of how Darwin's theory applies to Marxist theory:

The whole theory of Marx is an application of the theory of evolution—in its most consistent, complete, well considered and fruitful form....Marx treats the question of Communism in the same way as a naturalist would treat the question of the evolution of, say, a new biological species....[10]

And the Communists who later ran the Soviet Union spelled out how this theory functioned in practice:

By entertaining a materialist conception of history and applying the yardstick of recurrence to society, Marx and Engels were able to discover the laws of social development and interpret human history not as the result of arbitrary individual action, nor as the result of divine activity, but as an objective natural process developing, like nature, independently of men's intentions.

Marx and Engels conclusively proved that society proceeds from lower to higher forms, through class contradictions and class struggle, to a classless communist society; and that communism was not a utopia but the necessary product of social development. The founders of Marxism not only showed why communism was inevitable but discovered in the working class the force that was to destroy capitalism and build a communist society.[11]

But materialist concepts in the form of Social Darwinism were not only used by the Marxists to justify the destruction of capitalism. The Nazis employed the deterministic implications of Materialism to justify their destruction of the Jews. Explaining that the mechanistic immorality of the Jews made them unfit for life in the human community, Adolf Hitler said that:

> [T]he Jew destroys and must destroy because he completely lacks the conception of an activity which builds up the life of the community. And therefore it is beside the point whether the individual Jew is 'decent' or not. In himself he carries those characteristics which Nature has given him, and he cannot ever rid himself of those characteristics.[12]

"[T]he Jew," Hitler said in *Mein Kampf*:

> lacks those qualities which distinguish the races that are creative and hence culturally blessed....[T]he Jew takes over a foreign culture, imitating or rather ruining it....in reality, he is only...an ape....
>
> No, the Jew possesses no culture-creating force of any sort, since the idealism, without which there is no true higher development of man, is not present in him and never was present. Hence his intellect will never have a constructive effect, but will be destructive....[13]

And because the Jews will always be destructive, Hitler thought, the only way to deal with them is to destroy them as one would destroy pernicious animals. One must exterminate them like insects; one must gas them at Auschwitz.

And not only Hitler on the "right" but also Karl Marx on the "left" used the idea that moral and mental characteristics were inherent in racial types to justify violence against particular groups. Marx describes the Jews, whom he equated with capitalists, as a destructive "historical development" that would necessarily be dissolved by the forces of Marx's "historical materialism." Robert C. Tucker, Professor of Politics at Princeton University, notes in his *Philosophy and Myth in Karl Marx* that "What he [Marx] here called 'Judaism' he later renamed 'capitalism.' "[14]

"What is the worldly cult of the Jew?" Marx asked in his 1843 essay *The Jewish Question*:

> *Bargaining.* What is his worldly god? *Money.*
>
> Very well! Emancipation from *bargaining* and *money*, and thus from practical and real Judaism would be the self-emancipation of our era.
>
> An organization of society that would abolish the pre-conditions of bargaining and thus its possibility would render the Jew impossible. His religious consciousness would dissolve like a dull mist in the actual life-giving air of society....
>
> Thus we perceive in Judaism a general and *contemporary anti-social* element, which has been carried to its present high point by a historical development in which the Jews have contributed to this element, a point at which it must necessarily dissolve itself.
>
> The *emancipation of the Jews*, in the final analysis, is the emancipation of mankind from *Judaism* [italics Marx's].[15]

In addition to using materialist concepts as a premise for racist, classist, and socially Darwinistic ideologies, modern authoritarians have also used these concepts as theologians use the doctrine of Original Sin—to impugn humanity's capacity for self-government. Theologians used the argument that human beings are mechanistically sinful to assert that they must be ruled by God, while the Nazis used the idea that human beings are mechanistically irrational to argue that they must be ruled by Hitler.

"[I]n view of the stupidity of his fellow citizens...." Hitler asked:

> Mustn't our principle of parliamentary majorities lead to the demolition of any idea of leadership?...
>
> ....
>
> There is no principle which, objectively considered, is as false as that of parliamentarianism.
>
> Here we may totally disregard the manner in which our fine representatives of the people are chosen....That only the tiniest fraction of them rise in fulfillment...will at once be apparent to anyone who realizes that the political understanding of the broad masses is far from being highly enough developed to arrive at...political views of their own accord and seek out the suitable personalities.
>
> The thing we designate by the word 'public opinion' rests only in the smallest part on experience or knowledge which the individual has acquired by himself....
>
> Just as a man's denominational orientation is the result of upbringing...the political opinion of the masses represents nothing but the...manipulation of their mind and soul.
>
> By far the greatest share in their political 'education,' which...is most aptly designated by the word 'propaganda,' falls to the account of the press....In Vienna as a very young man I had the best opportunity to become acquainted with...this machine for educating the masses. At first I could not help but be amazed at how short a time it took this great evil power within the state to create a certain opinion even where it meant totally

falsifying profound desires and views which surely existed among the public....[W]hile...at the same time, vital problems fell a prey to public oblivion, or rather were simply filched from the memory and consciousness of the masses.[16]

"This is always the same public," Hitler writes earlier in *Mein Kampf*, "which will never learn anything new, since, aside from lacking the intelligence, it is lacking in the very rudiments of will."[17]

So because Hitler thought people lacking in free will, and because he thought their opinions represented nothing but the automatonic reaction of their minds to the stimuli of their "upbringing" and "propaganda," Hitler viewed the human race as incapable of making intelligent decisions about politics. Yet somehow from this he derived the ironic conclusion that people should allow themselves to be ruled by all-knowing supermen like himself and his fellow Nazis. Hitler's view of human beings as too malleable or too venal to govern themselves politically is typical of metaphysical materialists, whether religious or secular, and has typically been used by them to provide a justification for the rule of brute force in the realm of politics. But the notion that human beings are intellectual and/or moral automatons has other implications for human politics which should also be considered before we move on to the next section concerning metaphysics. For, in addition to the conclusion that people cannot govern themselves, the idea that people are mentally and/or are otherwise mechanistic implies that the products of human inventiveness cannot be attributed to the efforts of intellectually creative individuals. This idea can be used to undermine the right of intellectual property, a moral cornerstone of liberal economics. In the following passages philosophers employed by the now-defunct academic apparatus of the old Soviet Union suggest that because material circumstances determine the functioning of the human brain all of the products of human intellectual accomplishment reflect merely the reaction of human beings to the economic environment of their society.[18] "[S]piritual culture reflects the economic conditions prevailing in society,"[19] these professional Marxists explained:

> Marxism is based on the philosophy of materialism. This means that the question of the relation between mind and matter, between material being and intellectual activity is decided by Marxism in favor of matter, which is considered to be primary, while consciousness is considered to be secondary....This means that...men's economic activity, material production and the relations formed by people in the process of production are at the basis of men's spiritual activity.[20]

And because human spiritual activity is automatically determined by the economic conditions in a society, all of "*the principal forms of human spiritual culture* [italics original]....poems of all kinds, numerous literary productions, music, sculptor's and painter's works, scientific discoveries and inventions...and so on,"[21] are properly attributed to the soulless mechanical clanking of the macro-economic apparatus of material manufacture and exchange, rather than to the intellectual initiative of individual human beings. Marx even went so far as to imply that the manufacturing skills of the lowly factory worker, and even his physical labor, were not attributable to the efforts of the individual worker, because his efforts were driven by some extra-individual mechanism of manufacture. This idea can be used to deny the property rights of any productive individual in a society, not just those who are creative and inventive. "[M]anufacture..," Marx wrote in *Das Capital*:

> unites together handicrafts that were formerly separate. But whatever may have been its particular starting point, its final form is invariably the same—a productive mechanism whose

parts are human beings....[A] labourer who all his life performs one and the same simple operation converts his whole body into the automatic, specialized implement of that operation....[T]he collective labourer who constitutes the living mechanism of manufacture, is made up...of such specialized detail labourers....Manufacture, in fact, produces the skill of the detail labourer by...systematically driving...within the workshop the naturally developed differentiation of trades....[22]

And if the processes of manufacturing themselves produce the skill of the laborer, whose body is but the automatic implement of that process, then shouldn't the credit and the payment for that productivity go to the productive process as an institution, rather than to the mere mechanical parts of the institution who are individual human beings? This view of workers as automatonic parts in the economic institutions of manufacture may help to explain why the economic rights and property of common workers have not been respected in the workers' paradises which have been established upon Marxism—and why the ruling institutions of such societies have been able to convincingly claim those rights and properties for themselves.

But although Materialism as a secular metaphysical concept has been afforded a prominent place within the logical structure of twentieth century authoritarian political ideologies it cannot be said that this doctrine was invented by the Marxists or by the Nazis. Materialism's origins as a secular philosophy are historically traced back to the Greek philosopher Democritus, who believed that all events in the universe occurred as a result of the cause-and-effect movements of the particles or conglomerations of particles which the Greeks had christened atoms. Because he believed that even the processes of human consciousness were determined by such cause-and-effect movements of atoms Democritus believed that human beings as individuals were mentally mechanistic. The logical march toward Marxist Materialism, therefore, may be thought of as beginning with Democritus.

In Western philosophy's post-classical era the overt application to politics of the notion that human beings are mentally mechanistic is primarily attributable to Thomas Hobbes, the seventeenth century British materialist whom we mentioned previously. Like Luther, Hobbes held that human beings were deterministically driven to social destructiveness and like Hitler Hobbes believed that they were mechanistically driven to irrationality. Like both Hitler and Luther, Hobbes believed that innate human destructiveness and irrationality made authoritarian governments unavoidably necessary and democratic governments intrinsically unsustainable.

Materialism, however, as critical as it has been to the support of authoritarian political ideologies, is just one leg of the tripod of metaphysical philosophies upon which all such ideologies rest. The other two authoritarian metaphysical philosophies are Idealism, which we have already considered, and Heracliteanism, which this author has sometimes referred to in his other works as Metaphysical Nihilism or Metaphysical Indeterminism. Heracliteanism as a philosophic concept is named for another Greek philosopher, Heraclitus, who famously said that you can't step into the same river twice because the water in a river is constantly changing. By this Heraclitus meant that nothing has any *identity*—that nothing is anything in particular—because like the water in a river everything is in a constant state of flux. The next section of our study looks into the political implications of this philosophical annulment of the concept of identity.

CHAPTER SIX

HERACLITEANISM

Heracliteanism is the term which refers to the doctrine of the philosopher Heraclitus which says that nothing is anything in particular because everything is in a constant state of flux. In fairness to Heraclitus we should note that the old Ephesian also said that beneath the processes of universal change was an immutable force which he called Logos, meaning reason, which changed all things but itself never changed. This qualification aside, the implication of the doctrine of Heracliteanism is that nothing has any identity because everything is constantly changing. When the term Heracliteanism is used within this exposition what is principally being referred to is this doctrine of anti-identity.

It may be said that Heracliteanism is the direct opposite of the metaphysical doctrine of Materialism. Materialism says that all events are determined by physical, cause-and-effect processes and thus is representative of the doctrine of Determinism. Determinism is the specific name which philosophers have given to the notion that every event in the universe, including every aspect of human behavior, is mechanistically determined in the manner of causal events in states of crude matter. This principle is in turn based on a deeper principle of metaphysics that is known as the Law of Identity.

The Law of Identity says that a thing is what it is and is not something else at the same time. A corollary of the Law of Identity says that what a thing is determines how it will act. Philosophers have given this corollary of the Law of Identity the title of the Law of Causality. It is the Law of Causality that Materialists impose on human beings when they describe human behavior as deterministic.

But for a variety of reasons repudiating the laws of identity and causality can sometimes be convenient for authoritarian philosophers. Repudiating the Law of Identity, for instance, allows authoritarians to repudiate any philosophic doctrine which might be used to provide an intellectual defense of "liberal" rights—the rights upon which doctrines of individual liberty are established. This is because all theories of political rights, and all theories of ethical and political morality, are based on specific theories about human nature and nature generally. If human beings, and reality in general, have no specific nature, then all theories of political and ethical morality, including those upon which liberal societies are based, are invalid.

But most of the authoritarian philosophers who have propounded doctrines that repudiate the Law of Identity, while they are Heracliteans occasionally, are not Heracliteans exclusively. Sometimes they are preponderantly idealists; other times they are predominantly materialists, and most often they employ an eclectic mix of these doctrines hoping that one of them will work as a means to their ends—which means they are philosophical pragmatists. Let us consider some of the specific arguments offered by a variety of authoritarians who have employed the doctrine of anti-identity—Heracliteanism—in order to better learn how to recognize this doctrine wherever it appears.

"Fascism is...opposed to all individualistic abstractions based on eighteenth century materialism....It does not believe in the possibility of 'happiness' on earth as conceived by the economistic literature of the XVIII century, and it therefore rejects the teleological notion that the human family will secure a settlement of all its difficulties," said Benito Mussolini and Giovanni Gentile in their *Fascism: Doctrine and Institutions*:

> This notion runs counter to experience which teaches that life is a continual flux and in process of evolution. In politics Fascism aims at realism; in practice it desires to deal only with those problems which are the spontaneous product of historic conditions and which find or suggest their own solutions. Only by entering in to the process of reality and taking possession of the forces at work within it, can man act on man and on nature.[1]

And in the notes of the same volume they say:

> We do not believe in a single solution, be it economical, political or moral, a linear solution to the problems of life, because....life is not linear....
>
> ....
>
> The concept of freedom is not absolute because nothing is ever absolute in life....The concept of freedom changes with the passing of time.[2]

So because nothing is ever absolute in the continual flux of life's non-linear conditions freedom is not an absolute either, Mussolini and Gentile believe. Therefore the best thing to do is adopt a policy of "realism" as a means of adapting to the spontaneously evolving processes of a reality in which nothing is ever constant.

And what is a realistic policy in a wildly fluctuating universe in which there are no absolutes?

"There are no points of reference nor of comparison," Mussolini and Gentile say:

> From beneath the ruins of liberal, socialist, and democratic doctrines, Fascism extracts those elements that are still vital....it rejects the idea of a doctrine suited to all times and to all people....A doctrine must...be a vital act....Hence the pragmatic strain in Fascism, its will to power...its attitude toward violence, and its value.
>
> The key-stone of the Fascist doctrine is its conception of the State, of its essence, its functions, and its aims. For Fascism the state is absolute, individuals and groups relative.[3]

So there are no points of reference yet somehow the value of the state remains unequivocally absolute, Mussolini and Gentile assert. No doctrine is valid for all time and all people so it's best to adopt a pragmatic attitude toward violence in the pursuit of—in one's "will to"—power. Everything is relative except the key-stones of the state's aims, functions, and essence, Mussolini insists. Democracy and individuals are disposable but the state is absolutely vital.

Mussolini and Gentile oscillate between a Heraclitean universe wherein freedom and individuals are not absolutes and an authoritarian universe wherein the fascist state is unambiguously an absolute. In this they are following their old master, Heraclitus, who was a high-ranking member of the autocratic dynasty that ruled the Ephesus of his day. Heraclitus believed that though:

> All things are in flux; the flux is subject to a unifying measure or rational principle. This principle bound opposites together in a unified tension, which is like that of a lyre, where a stable harmonious sound emerges from the tension of opposing forces....[4]

And so he fulminated that "[i]t is necessary to take what is common as our guide; however, though this logic [Logos, or divine rational principles] is universal, the many live as if each individual had his own private wisdom."[5]

Although it is impossible to ascertain Heraclitus's motives across the centuries which separate our time from his, it is easy to discern a motive for promoting a dualistic metaphysics that demolishes identity while at the same time depicting a universe ruled by universal principles. The motive is to undermine the confidence of one's adversaries in their own beliefs while at the same time providing a premise for the universal certainty of one's own. Oswald Spengler, a pro-Nazi German authoritarian intellectual who wrote his doctoral thesis on Heraclitus, understood clearly the value of demolishing the law of identity and its corollary the law of causality as a precondition of establishing a new certainty:

> Causality is the reasonable, the law-bound, the describable, the badge of our whole waking and reasoning existence. But destiny is the word for an inner certainty that is *not* describable. We bring out that which is in the causal by means of a physical or an epistemological system, through numbers, by reasoned classification; but the idea of destiny can be imparted only by the artist working through media like portraiture, tragedy and music. The one requires us to *distinguish* and in distinguishing to dissect and destroy, whereas the other is *creative* [italics Spengler's] through and through, and thus destiny is related to life and causality to death.[6]

Causality is death to the inner certainty which is beyond the describable and the reasonable, Spengler knows. And so he objects to "[t]he tyranny of the Reason [and]….[i]ts most distinct expression…[in] the cult of exact sciences…of demonstration, of causality." And he foresees that:

> In this very century, I prophesy...a new element of inwardness
> will arise to overthrow the will-to-victory of science. Exact sci-
> ence must presently fall upon its own keen sword....But from
> Skepsis there is a path to "second religiousness," which is the se-
> quel and not the preface of the Culture. Men dispense with
> proof, desire only to believe....[7]

And Spengler did live long enough to see the sieg-heiling mil-
lions who had dispensed with proof believing at the altar of a new
religion. After the philosophic Skepticism which was engendered in
part by Heracliteans like Spengler the German mind was prepared
to believe almost anything, including the gospels of the particular
high-priest whom Spengler supported: Adolf Hitler. But the assault
on the metaphysical premise of reason—identity—did not come
only from the fascists and the Nazis. The "left" too, has made use
of anti-identity doctrines to demolish the premises of Liberalism
and prepare the way for tyranny. In the following excerpts Jean-
Paul Sartre, the Marxist, French existentialist philosopher, shows
how the logic of anti-identity—of Heracliteanism—clears "a path"
for authoritarian conclusions:

> If man, as the existentialist conceives him, is indefinable, it is be-
> cause at first he is nothing. Only afterward will he be something,
> and he himself will have made what he will be. Thus, there is no
> human nature, since there is no God to conceive it. Not only is
> man what he conceives himself to be, but he is also only what he
> wills himself to be....[8]

The idea that man is indefinable because, at first, at the origin
of his existence, he is nothing in particular, is a representation of
the Heraclitean conception of reality: nothing is anything in particular because everything is in an incessant state of change. Sartre
believes that this lack of any fundamental human nature, of any
human *identity*, allows man to become anything that "he wills

himself to be." Although, upon first consideration, the idea that a man can determine for himself "what he will be" may sound like a harmless, Horatio Algerian bromide, Sartre is not in fact talking about some responsible individual's self-determination of the content of his or her own character. Rather, he is expressing the notion of a person's determining the fundamental quality of every aspect of his own and all other human beings' nature. Such a prerogative could be dangerous in the hands of a fascist, or a quasi-Marxist like Sartre, because a fascist or a Marxist might decide to impose upon humanity a nature that is consistent with idealist or materialist metaphysics, and thus with authoritarian politics. And Sartre makes it clear that he is indeed speaking of making exactly such determinations not just for himself, but for "all mankind":

> Man is nothing else but what he makes of himself. Such is the first principle of existentialism. It is also what is called subjectivity....But if existence really does precede essence [i.e., a tree *exists* first, and only afterward receives the essential nature of a tree], man is responsible for what he is. Thus, existentialism's first move is to make every man aware of what he is and to make the full responsibility of his existence rest on him. And when we say that a man is responsible for himself, we do not only mean that he is responsible for his own individuality, but that he is responsible for all men....In fact, in creating the man that we want to be, there is not a single one of our acts which does not at the same time create an image of man as we think he ought to be....[T]he image is valid for everybody and for our whole age. Thus, our responsibility is much greater than we might have supposed, because it involves all mankind.[9]

Sartre is referring to the metaphysical doctrine we identified earlier as Subjective Idealism when he speaks here of "subjectivity." Subjective Idealism is the doctrine which says that reality is created by the consciousness of human "subjects," i.e., people, either individually or collectively. Although there is no specific passage in Sartrean literature which clearly reveals what sort of "nature" he intends to concoct and impose upon an identity-less, nature-less humankind, the fact that Sartre was a quasi-Marxist who fraternized with Communist activists gives us some indication of his thinking concerning this issue. Professor Emeritus of History at Western Michigan University Ernst Breisach cautioned in his *Introduction to Modern Existentialism*, and writing specifically of Sartre's tinkering with human nature, that "[c]ritics have insistently asked again and again whether man is really good and benevolent enough to be entrusted with such a task. What about evil in this world?"[10] In order to understand the political significance of Heracliteanism—the dogma of anti-identity—one should consider that a man such as Sartre felt it necessary to get rid of that specific manifestation of identity which is human nature before he dared attempt to subjectively impose a new human nature upon us.

METAPHYSICS AND POLITICS: SUMMARIZING REMARKS

The discussion of Heracliteanism brings us to the conclusion of the examination of the significance of metaphysical philosophy for authoritarian political philosophy. Before we continue to the next section of this study we should recall some major points that were raised concerning this topic. Firstly, we should remember why metaphysical theory is crucial to political theory: because metaphysical theories provide political theories with their logical foundations.

Metaphysical philosophy, again, is the branch of philosophy that studies the general nature of reality, and also, by implication, the general nature of humanity. Metaphysical theories about reality and human nature provide the philosophical underpinning for both political philosophies of freedom, which in this study are referred to as liberal, or Liberalism, and for political philosophies of authoritarianism, such as Marxism or theocracy. But in addition to their other inherent differences there is a notable distinction which can be made between liberal and authoritarian philosophies that will be the subject of this discussion's next segment: the means by which the tenets of these two opposite philosophical traditions are discovered and confirmed.

The philosophic discipline that studies the means by which knowledge of philosophy or anything else is discovered and confirmed is called epistemology. Epistemology, we noted earlier, is the branch of philosophy that is concerned to discover how we get knowledge and discover also what it is that actually qualifies as knowledge. Because the ideas that constitute the liberal and the authoritarian traditions of philosophy are so different the epistemological methods by which knowledge of the tenets of liberal philosophy are discovered and confirmed cannot conversely discover and confirm the tenets of authoritarian philosophy—and the same may be said of authoritarian philosophy concerning liberal philosophy. Indeed, many tenets of the liberal and the authoritarian traditions of epistemology are so profoundly opposed that they in fact logically annihilate one another.

To understand what sort of epistemological methods could confirm the tenets of authoritarian philosophy one need only consider the nature of the foundational doctrines of authoritarian philosophy. The most significant of these doctrines, metaphysical Idealism, says that reality is spiritual, not material, and implies that reality is the product of some mind. A second foundational authoritarian metaphysical doctrine, Materialism, says that reality is material, not spiritual, and implies that human beings lack free will because they are governed by the cause-and-effect mechanics which govern crude matter. And the third, the one we have just considered, Heracliteanism, says that nothing is anything in particular and that no effect results from any particular cause. The job of authoritarianism's epistemological philosophies—its philosophies of knowledge—is to confirm these three irreconcilably contradicttory doctrines.

But how would one confirm Idealism? If reality is spiritual rather than physical it cannot be perceived by the faculties of sense-perception, such as eyesight, hearing, and touch. And what of the notion that human beings lack free will: can it be confirmed by sense-perception? Even arguing against the idea of free will provides perceptual evidence that its opponents believe in it, or why would they be arguing in the first place? And consider Heracliteanism: do not the eyes and ears and other senses actually affirm the identity of existing things and the certainty of cause-and-effect? Clearly, the faculties of sense-perception are of little use to authoritarians as a means of substantiating their metaphysical doctrines.

And what about logic? Can logic support authoritarian doctrines? A crucial tenet of religious authoritarianism, Creationism, says that God owns everything because God creates everything. But if God creates everything then would it not be logical to hold God responsible for the evil that men do when they are under the influence of the "law of sin,"—Original Sin—which Saint Paul laments in his *Epistles*? Plainly, logic can be dangerous to religious authoritarianism.

And consider the danger of employing the epistemological methods of logic and sense-perception to sustain arguments based on the authoritarian metaphysical doctrine of Organicism. In its pantheistic form Organicism implies that God has a right to control everything because God is everything. But sense-perception reports that individual human beings are distinct entities, not parts of any larger organisms. And logic implies that if human beings are not parts of larger organisms then they have a right to control their own lives—but if they are parts of larger organisms logic asks how they can be justly punished for rebelling against the organism that supposedly is responsible for everything they do. It seems that wherever authoritarian epistemologists look for credible methods of confirming authoritarian dogmas they find only contradiction and frustration.

Because of this authoritarian epistemologists have always looked beyond the realms of sense-perception and logic for methods of and faculties for substantiating their doctrines. And they have attacked that method of combining sense-perception and logic to forge the system of apprehending reality which is properly understood as *reason*. We will now consider the nature of these attacks, and consider also the nature of the methods and faculties of knowledge that authoritarian epistemologists propose as legitimate alternatives to sense-perception and reason.

PART TWO

AUTHORITARIAN
EPISTEMOLOGY

CHAPTER SEVEN

FAITH

Authoritarian epistemological philosophy has two traditions: one which attacks the theories of knowledge which support liberal political theory, and one which defends the theories of knowledge which support authoritarian political theory. The aspect of authoritarian epistemological philosophy which attacks the epistemological supports of liberal political theory attacks sense-perception and also attacks that form of sense-perception-based logic which is known as reason. The aspect of authoritarian epistemological philosophy which supports authoritarian political theory promotes methods of gaining knowledge that it claims are superior to sense-perception and reason.

The reason that the aspect of authoritarian epistemology which attacks the epistemological supports of Liberalism attacks sense-perception and reason is that liberal political theory is based on references to physical entities which can be perceived by the senses and conceptualized by sense-perception-based thinking. And the reason that authoritarian epistemology promotes methods of ac-

quiring knowledge that are "superior" to sense-perception and reason is that authoritarian political theory is *not* based on physical
facts that are discernible by the senses or cognizable by sense-based
thinking. The aspect of authoritarian epistemology which attacks
the epistemological supports of Liberalism is based on arguments
that are elements of an epistemological tradition that is known
technically as *Skepticism*. The aspect of authoritarian epistemology
that supports authoritarian political theory is based on epistemological doctrines that are variations of what is popularly known as
"*faith*."

Because faith and Skepticism are the twin bulwarks of the authoritarian epistemological tradition the section of this study that is
concerned with this tradition is bifurcated into sub-sections that
explore these two subjects. The first section examines faith in its
most significant variations and also examines epistemological strat-
egies that are based on faith; the second section examines Skepticism's arguments and applications. Let us begin these examinations
by defining Skepticism and faith.

When most people hear the word Skepticism they think of the
practice of a rational policy of sober-minded intellectual caution.
But this is not the philosophical meaning of this word. As a technical philosophical term Skepticism generally refers to a group of
epistemological arguments which contend that human faculties of
knowledge—the senses and the mind—are unreliable as means of
learning about reality. The implication of epistemological Skepticism is that no knowledge of reality, and especially of *objective* reality,[1] is possible.

But if no knowledge of reality is possible on what basis can we
discover and confirm the tropes of authoritarian theory? This
question leads us to the political significance of faith. Regarding the
definition of faith, perhaps we should let an indisputable expert on
this subject, the Apostle Paul, enlighten us. On the subject of faith

the *New International Version of the Holy Bible* translates Paul as writing:

> Now faith is being sure of what we hope for and certain of what we do not see....
>
> By faith we understand that the universe was formed at God's command, so that what is seen was not made out of what was visible. (Heb. 11:1, 3)

And the *King James Version* renders the same verses so:

> Now faith is the substance of things hoped for, the evidence of things not seen....
>
> Through faith we understand that the worlds were framed by the word of God, so that things which are seen were not made of things which do appear.

St. Paul says that faith is believing in something because we hope it is so, which means because we prefer it be so, even when there is no perceptible evidence that it is so. *The HarperCollins Dictionary of Philosophy* (sic) includes these definitions of faith: "belief in something despite the evidence against it....belief in something even though there is an absence of evidence for it."[2] To understand the political significance of faith consider what Adolf Hitler thought of faith as a method of acquiring knowledge:

> When the National Socialist Party, filled with fiery faith in a Weltanschauung, [i.e., world-view, or philosophy] began its fight for Germany, in the very nature of such an undertaking it could not be but that faith sent more recruits than abstract knowledge—a knowledge often wise only in its own conceit. With the faith and the ardour of these unspoilt, unperverted men it was possible to change the whole axis of a State—*but not otherwise* [emphasis added].[3]

Hitler thought he could change the whole axis of German politics with his Nazi weltanschauung, but there was a problem with his philosophy: it couldn't be substantiated by empirical (perceptible) evidence, or by reason ("abstract knowledge"). Nazi philosopher Alfred Rosenberg had asserted that "employers and workers are not individualities in themselves but parts of an organic whole,"[4] and Heinrich Himmler had proclaimed that "a Lord God...stands above us, Who has created us and our Fatherland, our people and this earth and who has sent us our Leader."[5] But how were these statements to be verified by reference to, as Paul put it, "what is seen"?

The Nazi weltanschauung was by Hitler's own description "a spiritual conception of a general nature...to serve as a foundation...."[6] But the spiritual cannot be substantiated by reference to, in Paul's words again, "things which do appear." Hence Hitler said that:

> My great wish for the German Labour Front is that it should never lose its faith: "he who has faith in his heart has the strongest force which there is in the world....The German working man will form the support of the State because he is susceptible to this feeling of faith and confidence which does not consider it necessary to test everything with the probe of its own intelligence but devotes itself to an idea and then is content to follow blindfold."[7]

DOGMATISM AND FAITH

Declining to test an idea with the probe of one's own intelligence and yet following it blindly is a representation of an authoritarian epistemological philosophy called *Dogmatism*. Dogmatism is a faith-based theory of knowledge which says that the best way to get knowledge is simply to refer to the tenets of an already established dogma and then believe whatever they have to say. The more technical of two definitions of Dogmatism offered by *The HarperCollins Dictionary of Philosophy* defines Dogmatism as "the rejection of any examination of an idea and the assertion that the idea is true by authority and is beyond questioning."[8] Nazi Reich Minister of Propaganda Dr. Joseph Goebbels, who held a doctorate in philosophy from Heidelberg University, represented Dogmatism by stating: "Hear nothing that we do not wish you to hear. See nothing that we do not wish you to see. Believe nothing that we do not wish you to believe. Think nothing that we do not wish you to think."[9]

But although the promotion of the epistemological method of Dogmatism was a standard practice of the Nazi ideological leadership the Nazis were not the originators of this philosophy. All authoritarian regimes, including the most ancient, encourage the docile, unquestioning acceptance of "party" dogma as a means of ensuring political, moral, and philosophical correctness. New School for Social Research lecturer Henry M. Pachter, in his essay *"National-Socialist and Fascist Propaganda for the Conquest of Power,"* compared the Nazi promotion of epistemological Dogmatism with that of the Catholic Church, which had for fifteen hundred years been the intellectual bulwark of European theocracy and aristocracy. Pachter writes that "Hitler's approach to programmatic ideas is even more startling":

> [H]is twenty-five 'points' [the twenty-five points of the German National Socialist party program] are incoherent and of different relevance, but, once announced, he [Hitler] declared them to be the 'unalterable foundation of the movement....'
>
> ....
>
> He claimed that he had learned this principle from the Catholic Church, which also will not sacrifice one iota of its dogma....[10]

"[T]he program of the new movement was summed up in a

few *guiding principles, twenty-five* in all...," Hitler himself said in his *Mein Kampf* [italics Hitler's]:

> They are in a sense a *political creed*....
>
> Here the following insight must never leave us: Since the so-called *program of the movement* is absolutely correct in its ultimate aims, but...the conviction may well arise that in individual instances certain of the guiding principles ought perhaps to be framed differently....Every attempt to do this, however, usually works out catastrophically. For in this way something which should be unshakeable is submitted to discussion, which, as soon as a single point is deprived of its dogmatic, creedlike formulation...will...lead to endless debates and confusion. In such a case, it always remains to be considered which is better: a new...formulation which causes an argument within the movement, or a form which...represents a solid, unshakeable, inwardly unified organism. Any examination will show that the latter is preferable....
>
> With a doctrine that is really sound in its broad outlines, it is less harmful to retain a formulation, even if it should not entirely correspond to reality, than...to expose what hitherto seemed a granite principle of the movement to general discussion with all its evil consequences....For how shall we fill people with blind faith in the correctness of a doctrine, if we ourselves spread uncertainty and doubt by constant changes in its outward structure?...
>
> Here, too, we can learn by the example of the Catholic Church. Though its doctrinal edifice...comes into collision with exact science and research, it is none the less unwilling to sacrifice so much as one little syllable of its dogmas. It has recognized quite correctly that its power...does not lie in...adaptation to...scientific findings...but rather in rigidly holding to dogmas...for it is only such dogmas which lend to the whole body the character of a faith. And so today it stands more firmly than ever. It can be prophesied that in exactly the same measure in

which appearances evade us, it will gain more and more blind support....

And so, anyone who really...desires the victory of a folkish philosophy must not only recognize that...such a movement will stand firm only if based on unshakable certainty and firmness in its program. It must not run the risk of making concessions...but must retain forever a form that has once been found favorable....any attempt to bring about arguments...splinters the solidity and the fighting force of the movement...as its adherents participate in...discussion....

The National Socialist German Workers' Party obtained with its program of twenty-five theses a foundation which must remain unshakable [italics Hitler's]. The task of the present and future members of our movement must not consist in a critical revision of these theses, but rather in being bound by them.[11]

And binding people to "dogmatic, creedlike" theses is the purpose of those who propound the epistemological method of Dogmatism. Once people accept that the way to make certain that their beliefs are true is to blindly submit themselves to the authority of a dogma they become intellectual zombies, helplessly spell-bound by empirically baseless faiths. But Dogmatism is not the only epistemological philosophy that authoritarians use to bind people to faith-based doctrines. Another such epistemological philosophy is ironically known as *Rationalism.*

RATIONALISM AND FAITH

Rationalism is a term which has two principal epistemological meanings. On the one hand it refers to any philosophy or method of knowledge (such as "reason" and mathematics) that employs logic and/or logical deduction as a means of arriving at truths. On the other hand it refers to an epistemological philosophy which says that *only* logic and/or logical deduction, and *never* the faculties of sense-perception, are useful as a means of discovering knowledge. This latter species of Rationalism can and has been used as an epistemological weapon by authoritarians, despite the fact that logic is intrinsically dangerous to their doctrines.

The intrinsic danger posed by logic to authoritarians stems from its tendency to drag them inexorably from their own premises to conclusions about politics which are destructive to their political purposes. This is exemplified by the logical quandaries presented by the doctrine of Pantheism, which is one of the most significant of authoritarian metaphysical premises. Pantheism provides a premise for the argument that an authoritarian state can do anything it wants by saying that the state is part of God, who can do anything He wants because He is everything. But if God is everything then He is also any rebel movement that seeks to overthrow the state!

Despite such difficulties authoritarians advocate their version of Rationalism because the use of logic without the use of sense-perception can lead people to authoritarian conclusions. This is so because people are powerfully impressed by conclusions that are logically based on premises they have already accepted, and because sense-perception is the primary epistemological faculty that people use to check the premises of their beliefs. If people cannot check the premises of their beliefs against the evidence of sense-perception they can be led logically from false metaphysical theories about the nature of reality to false conclusions about the nature of political morality and political rights. Here Eugen Diesel, a Weimar era German social critic, describes the effect of rationalistic epistemological methods on German intellectual culture in a book published two years before Adolf Hitler came to power:

> Nowhere else in the world does one find so...keen an application of the abstract and logical method, leading often enough into obscure realms of speculation and overriding all common

sense and natural feeling in the process. A clear scheme of judgments or opinions will be surrendered...to some juridical principle....

....

On top of all this we have the peculiarly vague and unactual quality of the German mind, which loves to go on spinning abstractions out of abstractions in endless series....[T]his tendency to give exaggerated importance to man's abstract intellectual powers is typical of Germans....'has destroyed all direct perceptions and dissolved them into mere abstractions,' with the result that the...German spiritual heritage have had a confusing and fateful effect rather than the reverse.[12]

But Rationalism as a theory of knowledge which eschews sense-perception and exalts logical deduction was not a German invention, any more than was the epistemological method of Dogmatism. Its prominence in modern times is usually attributed to several late Renaissance European philosophers who are not usually identified as authoritarians. These philosophers, however— René Descartes, Benedict Spinoza, and Gottfried Wilhelm Leibniz most prominently among them—persistently employed the method of Rationalism to buttress the credibility of classically authoritarian metaphysical and moral arguments. Regarding Descartes, Spinoza, and Leibniz this should not be surprising, as these philosophers were either members or employees of, or were ideologically supported by, the ruthless upper classes who ruled pre-democratic Europe.[13]

Today late-Renaissance Rationalism is often represented as a liberalizing epistemological advance over the faith-based theories of knowledge which had dominated the medieval period. But it is far more likely that the practice of this form of Rationalism was merely an attempt by fundamentally authoritarian philosophers to capitalize on the then growing prestige of the genuinely rational special sciences such as astronomy and anatomy. During the Renaissance Christian theology had been reduced in its political influence by the philosophical implications of the empirical science of Bacon, Galileo, and other intellectual revolutionaries, and this threatened the authoritarian classes who patronized and otherwise supported the Rationalist philosophers. These classes no doubt saw in the Rationalists' pretensions to scientific method—to "reason"—an opportunity to re-accredit old faith-based dogmas under a veneer of scientific respectability.

INTUITION AND FAITH

But the Rationalism of Descartes, Spinoza, and Leibniz was in fact just as "faith-based" as had been the Christian doctrines that had kept the European aristocracies in power for centuries. Descartes had merely changed the name of faith to "intuition" and then logically—"rationally"—deduced from intuited premises metaphysical and moral ideas that were fundamentally medieval in nature. Later authoritarian philosophers followed the so-called "Continental" Rationalists in this sophistical strategy of secularizing faith, and followed them also in secularizing its name. The significance for politics of what Descartes had called intuition is delineated in this passage from the late Brandeis University political scientist Roy C. Macridis's *Contemporary Political Ideologies*:

> Early in the nineteenth century another German philosopher [Arthur Schopenhauer] wrote a book...entitled *The World as Will and Idea*. It began with the ominous phrase, "The world is my idea...." What this means is that rational and scientific discourse is inadequate to provide us with the understanding of the world surrounding us and that "knowledge" is a matter of intuitive communication that alone can provide full "understanding." Knowledge thus becomes entirely subjective....Science, reason,

measurements, observation give us only a relative, partial, and fragmented knowledge; intuition supplies an "absolute" one.... "The spirit has never had more violence done to it than when mere numbers made themselves its master," wrote Adolf Hitler.

But what is the relevance of intuition or instinct to politics? Simply that logic, persuasion, and argument cannot move people and cannot sustain a political system. In politics the counterpart of intuition is the "myth," that is, an idea, a symbol, a slogan that moves people into action because it appeals to their emotions. They become attached to it and they feel for it....

Myths can take a variety of forms—racial supremacy, racial purity, national superiority and strength, the dictatorship of the proletariat, the resurrection of ancient empires, the reassertion of tribal bonds, the emergence of the superman, and so on.[14]

The crucial phrases in this passage are those which observe that in politics intuition serves as a myth-creating process "that moves people into action because it appeals to their emotions;" and which represent the attitude that "[s]cience, reason, measurements, [and] observation give us only a relative...knowledge [while] intuition supplies an 'absolute' one." Professor Macridis notes that intuition is an emotional feeling-based method of acquiring knowledge and also calls attention to Hitler's aversion to methods of knowledge that were based on science, reason, and observation. These reflections communicate the importance to authoritarians of epistemological philosophies which dismiss empirical evidence and which affirm the emotion-inspired dogmas upon which authoritarian states are based. Dr. Macridis's remarks were antecedently seconded by one of the Nazis' own philosophical supporters, Oswald Spengler, who sang the praises of knowledge that was established on feeling-based intuitions and cursed the dogma-killing power of reason and perception ["measurement"] based cognition in his 1922 volume *The Decline of the West*:

> The nature-researcher can be educated, but the man who knows history is born. He seizes and pierces men and facts with one blow, guided by a feeling which cannot be acquired by learning or affected by persuasion....Direction, fixing, ordering, defining by cause and effect, are things that one can do if one likes. These things are work, but the other is creation....Reason, system and comprehension kill as they "cognize." That which is cognized becomes a rigid object, capable of measurement and subdivision. Intuitive vision, on the other hand, vivifies and incorporates the details in a living, inwardly-felt unity.[15]

The Nazis wanted to replace measurable, definable, "rigid objects" of fact with the intuitively grasped, "inwardly-felt" realities which they had created themselves. Hence their preference for feeling-based epistemological philosophies and their distaste for the sense-perception-and-logic-based epistemologies of reason. Like Saint Paul the Nazis desired some method of acquiring knowledge that would allow them to be certain of what they hoped for and sure of what they could not see. Saint Paul had referred to his hope-driven method of achieving certainty as "faith," while the Nazis called their feeling-based method of confirming their faiths "intuitive vision." Because the feeling of hope is in fact just another feeling both Paul and the Nazis were essentially employing the same intuitional methods in order to arrive at knowledge and to substantiate their beliefs. Université de Louvain Professor F. Gregoire, contributing to the *International Council for Philosophy and Humanistic Studies'* analysis of Nazi culture for UNESCO, observed that:

> To provide a basis for the *Weltanschauung*, will National-Socialist

[Nazi] philosophy exalt the scientific knowledge of races or the strictly historical study of the racial factor? Without neglecting the contribution of the sciences and of history, it appeals much more fundamentally to a cognition of a philosophical type. Not, it is true, resembling rational philosophy [Gregoire means reason-based, not Rationalist]—the understanding is incapable of attaining reality—but of an intuitive type. Everything rests on deep intuitions (*Anschauungen*), on vital experiences (*Erlebnisse*) [italics original] of a metaphysical order....Intuition has no need of previous justification.[16]

But why did the Nazis feel they were justified in simply replacing scientific knowledge with intuitions that merely reflected their own inwardly felt hopes and hatreds? The answer goes back to our earlier discussion of a new type of metaphysical philosophy which had been developed by previous generations of German philosophers and which had been inspired in part by the ideas of Descartes and the other "Rationalists." These German philosophers had invented a new, secular version of the philosophy of metaphysical Idealism which said that reality was a manifestation of the consciousness of human beings—including of their thoughts as they were guided by their feelings—rather than of the consciousness of God. Under the influence of these philosophers the Nazis decided that they would be perfectly justified in simply intuiting their feelings about reality in order to understand it.

EPISTEMOLOGICAL SUBJECTIVISM: SECULARIZED FAITH

The new German version of Idealism became known as Subjective Idealism because it said that reality is just a product of the consciousness—the "ideas"—of human selves, or subjects. If this is true then anything an individual subject or a group of subjects thinks is real becomes real in fact. So there was no reason why the Nazis could not mentally create any reality they desired based on their "inwardly-felt" hopes and dreams. And there was no reason why they could not adopt an epistemological philosophy which prescribed the method of intuiting their own thoughts and feelings about reality in order to understand the facts of existence.

In the last two hundred years the idea that the only thing we need to understand in order to grasp the facts of existence is our own conscious states has become the West's dominant epistemological philosophy. Beginning especially with Immanuel Kant,[17] idealist philosophers started popularizing the notion that human faculties of consciousness actually create, rather than merely apprehend, all of the things that human beings are aware of. Kant had said that this creative process occurs because the innate structures of the human perceptual and cognitive faculties filter or process the raw data they receive, thus enveloping people in a sort of artificial universe of their own making. Because this universe is the only universe that mental faculties such as ours permit us to know, idealist philosophers say, it is for us the only universe which exists.

But although Kant's idea that innate structures in the human brain effectively create the universe we know is itself just a figment of Kant's imagination this idea nevertheless legitimized the epistemological philosophy—itself known as Subjectivism—which says that all that we are knowing when we know anything is our own subjective states. This tenet of Subjectivism in turn legitimizes the practice of intuition as a new form of secular faith—and delegitimizes the idea that it is possible to have objective knowledge of an independently existing reality. Because intuition as a means of getting knowledge untethers us from objective reality it also gives us permission to do as the Nazis did: believe anything we feel like believing. Immanuel Kant expressed the implications of this theory by famously stating: "I have therefore found it necessary to deny *knowledge*, in order to make room for *faith*."[18]

Kant himself had developed his new epistemological philosophy in order to provide polemical defenses for the metaphysical and moral arguments that he used to protect his autocratic Hohenzollern paymasters. But his arguments proved just as useful for defending the empirically baseless dogmas of twentieth century totalitarianism. Marxist, fascist, and especially the Nazi and pre-Nazi philosophic intellectuals soon began using Kant's new theory of knowledge to protect the credibility of their own phantasmagorical political ideologies. In the following cited passages one of the most influential and plain-spoken of the German Nazi party philosophers, Houston Stewart Chamberlain, explained the implications of the new Kantian form of faith for the defense and for the development of the dogmas of the Third Reich:

> [T]he human mind in receiving impressions...is not merely passive, but also active, that is, it contributes its own quota, it colours and shapes what it receives from the outside world, it remodels it in its own way and transforms it into something new; in short, the human mind is, from the very outset, creative, and what it perceives as existing outside of itself is partly, and in the special form in which it is perceived, created by itself. Every layman must immediately grasp the one fact: if the human mind in the reception and elaboration of its perceptions is itself creatively active, it follows of necessity that it must find itself again everywhere in nature; this nature, as the mind sees it, is in a certain sense, and without its reality being called in question, its work. Hence Kant too comes to the conclusion: "It sounds at first singular, but is none the less certain, that the understanding does not derive its laws from nature but prescribes them to nature...the supreme legislation of nature lies in ourselves, that is, in our understanding." The realisation of this fact made the relation

between man and nature...clear and comprehensible. It now became manifest why every investigation of nature...leads back in all cases to...questions directed to man's being; this was what had so hopelessly perplexed Descartes and Locke. Experience...can never be purely objective, because it is our own active organisation which first makes experience possible, in that our senses take up only definite impressions...shaped...by themselves, while our understanding also sifts, arranges and unites the impressions according to definite systems....[I]t now becomes clear how justified the Mystics were in claiming to see everywhere in outer nature the inner essence of man....As the mathematician and astronomer Lichtenberg says: "We must never lose sight of the fact that we are always merely observing ourselves when we observe nature..."[19]

And if we are always merely observing ourselves when we observe nature then "[t]here is no answer, no escape....our knowledge of nature is the ever more and more detailed exposition of something unknowable,"[20]—and we are entirely justified in ignoring the "outside" world as nothing other than a figment of our own imaginations. Yet on the other hand, we are also entirely free to embrace any intuitive insight which we might care to indulge as real for there is no reality except that which our own consciousness creates. So Chamberlain exclaims, quoting Goethe in the first sentence cited, that:

"Within thee is a universe as well!"

It was one of the inevitable results of scientific thinking [Chamberlain means Kant's pseudo-scientific, secularized faith] that this inner universe was now for the first time brought into the foreground. For the philosopher, [Kant] by unreservedly including the whole human personality in nature, that is, by learning to regard it as an object of nature, gradually awoke to a realisation of two facts, first, that the mechanism of nature has its origin in his own human understanding, and secondly, that mechanism [i.e., causality, or cause-and-effect] is not a satisfactory principle for the explanation of nature, since man discovers in his own mind a universe which remains altogether outside of all mechanical conceptions....[F]rom the most direct experience of my own life I perceive—in addition to mechanical nature—the existence of an unmechanical nature [meaning a nature which is subjectively created]. For clearness we may call it the ideal world, in contrast to the real; not that it is less real or less actual—on the contrary, it is the surest thing that we possess, the one directly given thing, and in so far the outer world ought really to be called the "ideal" [meaning subjective] one; but the other receives this name because it embodies itself in ideas, not in objects. Now if man perceives such an ideal world—not as dogma but from experience,—if introspection leads to the conclusion that he himself is not merely and not even predominantly a mechanism, if rather he discovers in himself what Kant calls "the spontaneity of freedom," something utterly unmechanical and anti-mechanical, a whole, wide world, which we might in a certain sense call an "unnatural" world, so great a contrast does it present to that mechanical rule of law with which we have become acquainted by exact observation of nature; how could he help projecting this second nature, which is just as manifest and sure as the first, upon that first nature, since science [again, meaning Kantian pseudo-science] has taught him that the latter is intimately connected with his own inner world? When he does that, there grows out of the experienced fact of freedom [here, meaning the freedom to believe whatever one wishes] a new idea of the Divine, and a new conception of a moral order of the world, that is to say, a new religion.[21]

The new religion Chamberlain was intimating—Nazism—was to be intuited subjectively by examining the contents of the subject's "inner world." Freed from objective reality by Kant's theory that actual reality was created by human consciousness, the Nazis would be empowered to create ideal realities which would be the bases of their new, secular faiths. But as seems obvious from Chamberlain's statements the idea that the innate structures of the human mind automatically color and shape reality could not only free human beings from outside reality, but could also imprison them in the worlds those structures impose upon us. For if those structures could force us to think along certain lines they could as a consequence force us to live in certain particular realities.

RACIAL AND CLASS SUBJECTIVITY

On first consideration the notion that people could be forced to live in particular ideal realities by the inherent structure of their own consciousness might seem to be just another one of those harmless abstractions that Eugen Diesel complained were leading the German people "into obscure realms of speculation." But this idea has proven to be enormously useful to authoritarians, and, as a consequence, enormously harmful to the rest of the human race. For although Kant himself had postulated that the innate structures in all people's minds were essentially the same, the German philosophers who followed him—Georg W. F. Hegel, Karl Marx, H.S. Chamberlain, etc., did not agree. They said that the different nationalities, classes, and races of people all had innately different mental structures, leading them to inherently conflicting beliefs. Georg Hegel, for instance, who like Kant was employed at a Hohenzollern controlled government university, was a nationalist; he argued that:

> In a free [meaning, presumably, independent] nation, reason...is a...living spirit, where the individual...finds his destiny...i.e. his universal and particular nature...given to him....The wisest men of

antiquity for that reason declared that wisdom and virtue consist in living in accordance with the customs of one's own nation.[22]

And Karl Marx, who was a classist, insisted that:

> [Y]our bourgeois notions of freedom, culture, law, etc. Your very ideas are but the outgrowth of the conditions of your bourgeois production and bourgeois property, just as your jurisprudence is but the will of your class made into a law for all, a will whose essential character and direction are determined by the economic conditions of existence of your class.[23]

And Adolf Hitler, who was a racist, said that:

> Certain ideas are...tied up with certain men. This applies most of all to those ideas whose content originates, not in an exact scientific truth, but in the world of emotion, or, as it is so beautifully and clearly expressed today, reflects an 'inner experience.' All these ideas, which have nothing to do with cold logic as such, but represent only pure expressions of feeling, ethical conceptions, etc., are chained to the existence of men, to whose intellectual imagination and creative power they owe their existence. Precisely in this case the preservation of these definite races and men is the precondition for the existence of these ideas.[24]

The notion that certain ideas, "ethical conceptions, etc.," could not be preserved unless certain races of men were preserved—and the idea that moral and political ideas generally were but the "outgrowth" of national, racial, and class identities—provided a premise for the national, racial, and class struggles that politically profited the rulers who controlled the twentieth century's authoritarian states. Using these concepts great masses of people of a particular national, racial, or class identity could be rallied against the people of a differing identity, and the victims—the Jew, the bourgeois, the alien, etc.—could "justly" be stripped of vast amounts of wealth—and even of their lives. This wealth could then be redistributed to the rulers for their own enjoyment and by the rulers to their supporters in exchange for loyalty and obedience. This was the political and economic purpose which the idea that different types of people have innately different types of ideas was meant to serve.

But Immanuel Kant's argument that innate structures in the human mind determine our beliefs and create our realities was not just useful as a premise for subjectivist faiths and for nationalist, classist, and racist epistemological theories. Kant's statement that he had "found it necessary to deny *knowledge*, in order to make room for *faith*," bespoke the second purpose of his innatist theory of human mental functioning. If innate human mental and perceptual processes essentially created the world men knew then not only were people justified in looking within themselves rather than without for knowledge, but they were also prevented from making credible statements about outside, "objective" (as opposed to subjective) reality as well. As we will now consider, this implication of Kantian theory had dire consequences for the philosophical defenders of free societies.

CHAPTER EIGHT

SKEPTICISM

As opposed to authoritarian societies, free societies are based on philosophic ideas which are in turn established upon the observable facts of reality: "empirical" facts. Empirical facts are truths apprehended by the faculties of sense-perception—the faculties of sight and hearing and touch, etc. Because the philosophies that provide the bases of free (again, referred to in this study as *liberal*) societies are established on the empirical evidence provided by the sense-faculties authoritarian philosophers such as Immanuel Kant have always sought to undermine humanity's confidence in these faculties. And they have sought to undermine humanity's confidence in its ability to logically infer ideas, such as philosophic concepts, from the evidence provided by the sense-faculties.

Systematic philosophical attacks on the reliability of sense-perception, and on the reliability of the intellectual faculties and methods that are used to infer ideas from sense-perception, are a feature of an epistemological philosophy known technically as Skepticism.

Epistemological Skepticism, as was noted earlier, is a doctrine that implies or asserts that no knowledge of reality, and especially of objective reality—reality independent of and/or external to the person experiencing it—is possible. If no knowledge of objective reality is possible then the empirically-based philosophies that provide premises for political freedom are groundless. Once the ideas that provide a basis for freedom are overthrown the door is opened for the faith-based phantasies that provide the premises of authoritarian politics.

To appreciate the difference between the empirically-based doctrines which provide a basis for Liberalism and the faith-and-subjectivity-based doctrines which establish the premises of authoritarianism let us consider again some of the metaphysical doctrines which furnish the grounds for these two political traditions. The metaphysically idealist doctrines which help to provide a basis for authoritarianism say, for instance, that the entire universe is created by some great spirit (Theism, Creationism); that the entire universe is this great spirit (Pantheism, Monism, Organicism); and that the entire universe is therefore spiritual (Idealism). These metaphysical doctrines lead, among other places, to a political philosophy which says that individual human beings don't have individual rights because they are not individuals, and that individual human beings don't have a right to the things they create because they do not in fact create anything.

But the empirically-based metaphysical concepts that liberal (free) societies are based on say that everything which exists is created either by the observable, physical (material) forces of nature or by human beings themselves. This idea leads to the political conclusion that no one can be denied access to natural resources by their ostensive owner, God, and that people have a right to the values they create when they turn natural resources into finished goods. Further, the empirically-based metaphysical philosophies that underpin Liberalism lead to the conclusion that people have an *individual* right to the ownership of finished goods because a person's metaphysical status as an individual is a fact *observably*. The Nazi philosopher Chamberlain was so hostile to the epistemology of empirical observation—of sense-perception—that he equated it (here quoting Ernest Renan) with Judaism:

> "The Israelite religion has and knows no secrets, no mysteries." Renan, too...admits that "the Semitic faith (monotheism) is in reality the product of a human race whose religious needs are very few. It signifies a minimum of religion." An important and true remark which has only failed to have effect because Renan did not show...how far and for what...reasons the Semite, who is famed for the glow of his faith, yet possesses a minimum of true religion. The explanation is easy for us...there cannot and must not be any miracle, anything unreachable, any "path into the untrodden, and the not-to-be-trodden," nothing which the hand cannot grasp and the moment...cannot possess. Even such a great mind as the second Isaiah looks upon religious faith as something which is based on empiric foundation and which can be tested, as it were, by a legal process, "Let the people bring forth their witnesses that they may be justified...." The Jewish teacher Philippson...tells in detail how the Jew "believes solely what he has seen with his eyes," a "blind faith" being unknown to him; and in a long note he quotes all the passages in the Bible where "faith in God" is mentioned, and asserts that this expression occurs without exception only where "visible proofs have gone before." It is always, therefore, a question of outward experience, not of inner; the conceptions are always thoroughly concrete, material...as soon as a man has a feeling of a mystery...he is a heretic....But if we wish to appreciate the influence of Semiticism upon religion, it will not suffice to speak of understanding and non-understanding, of feeling and non-feeling of the mystery; we must remember also the creative influence of the

imagination....Imagination is the handmaid of religion...her forms signify more than what the eye alone can see in them, her words proclaim more than the ear alone can hear. She...raises before us the mystery of mysteries and convinces our eyes that its veil cannot be raised.[1]

Chamberlain's assault on the eyes and the ears and the other senses is derived of Kant, whom he calls the "*rocher de bronze* [immovable rock] of our new philosophy."[2] Kant had said that objects of perception were fundamentally unknowable because the perception of objects is filtered through the mechanism of the senses, which completely distort the pure and virgin data they receive from the outside world. Kant said that:

> [W]e must assume "that everything which can be given to our senses (to the external senses in space, to the internal one in time) is intuited by us as it appears to us, not as it is in itself"....
>
> ....
>
> and that all objects in space are mere appearances, i.e., not things in themselves but representations of our sensuous intuition....And as we have just shown that the senses never and in no manner enable us to know things in themselves, but only their appearances, which are mere representations of the sensibility, we conclude that 'all bodies, together with the space in which they are, must be considered nothing but mere representations in us, and exist nowhere but in our thoughts'....that things as objects of our senses existing outside us are given, but we know nothing of what they may be in themselves, knowing only their appearances, i.e., the representations which they cause in us by affecting our senses....
>
> ....
>
> For sensuous perception represents things not at all as they are, but only the mode in which they affect our senses, and consequently by sensuous perception appearances only and not

things themselves are given to the understanding for reflexion....

....

And we indeed, rightly considering objects of sense as mere appearances, confess thereby that they are based upon a thing in itself, though we know not this thing...but only know its appearances, viz., the way in which our senses are affected by this unknown something.[3]

This denial of knowledge acquired through the senses allowed Kant to "make room" for the new authoritarian faiths which Chamberlain said, writing specifically of the political effect of Kant's influence, were "heading us toward a revolution, against which all previous political revolutions shrink into insignificant episodes...."[4] But as significant as his influence was the strategy of denying the veracity of the senses in order to make room for authoritarian dogma does not begin with moderns like Immanuel Kant or with Nazis like Houston Stewart Chamberlain. Skeptic attacks on the senses as a feature of Western political thought appear hundreds of years before Christ in the ideas of some of the most prominent of the Greek philosophers. Preeminently, the Athenians sages Socrates and Plato were the first Western thinkers to employ Skepticism as a systematic aspect of an explicitly authoritarian epistemological philosophy.

But before we discuss Socrates' and Plato's contributions to authoritarian epistemological concepts we should remind ourselves again of some common misunderstandings about these two towering figures of Greek philosophy. For when unaware members of the contemporary Western public think of Socrates and Plato they usually think of the founding fathers of an intellectual tradition that culminates politically in the institutionalization of liberal democracy and the establishment of liberal republics such as the United States of America. Socrates in particular is popularly thought of as a sort of wise and kindly old sage whose sculpted visage makes him look a little like a benevolent philosophic Santa Claus. But Socrates is not at all the sort of goodhearted intellectual patriarch in whose grandfatherly lap a responsible parent can safely place a vulnerable young mind.

Socrates and Plato wanted to establish a society wherein, to quote Professor of Politics Thomas G. West in his *Four Texts on Socrates*, "the citizen has a duty to obey as limitless as a son's duty to his father or a slave's to his master."[5] Or, as Socrates himself asked rhetorically in Plato's *Crito*, "since you were brought into the world and nurtured and educated by us [the state, or country], can you deny in the first place that you are our child and slave...?"[6] Plato, and Socrates as he is represented by Plato, delineated a political philosophy that in the words of one of the twentieth century's eminent students of political authoritarianism, Karl R. Popper, was "purely totalitarian and anti-humanitarian."[7] In order to provide a metaphysical premise for their politics these two wily old Greeks proposed the existence of an ideal authoritarian "alternative reality" that was apprehensible by the mind while being invisible to the senses.

This Socratic/Platonic alternative reality was intended to be grasped by the mind as an assortment of divine "Forms" or ideas, which constituted what Socrates and Plato insisted was the real or actual world. Because the use of the senses would reveal this world of Forms to in fact be a devious sham Socrates and Plato wanted to discourage the use of the sense-faculties as a means of acquiring knowledge. To accomplish this they concocted what is certainly the most famous epistemological allegory in the history of Western thought, the Allegory of the Cave in Plato's dialogue *The Republic*. In the Cave people who rely on the senses for knowledge are portrayed as epistemologically chained in a dark cave of illusions.

SKEPTICISM AND RELIGION

But of course it is in fact the dark world of authoritarian dogma that is the real cave of illusions, not the world perceived by the senses. The world revealed by the senses is in reality the actual, sunlit world where the truths about political morality and political rights are both physically and metaphorically visible. These truths were feared by philosophers like Socrates, Plato, Kant, and Chamberlain because they testified against the baseless dogmas which these philosophers purveyed in order to rationalize authoritarian interests. And long before the Greeks invented secular philosophy they were feared by the overtly religious theologians who wrote the Bible, the Koran, the *Bhagavad-gītā*, and the other major scriptures of the religious tradition. Regarding explicitly religious authoritarian theories the late Vanderbilt University political scientist Professor Avery Leiserson commented in J. C. Wahlke and A. N. Dragnich's *Government and Politics: An Introduction to Political Science* that "[t]he parallel assumptions of the oligarchic-authoritarian political system are, first, that political authority emanates from some source above the people—a supernatural being, an idealized conception of a desirable social order...."[8] And John Noss wrote of the Eastern religions' disparagement of the physical world revealed by the senses that:

> If we are to trust the testimony of their religions, the peoples of India...are not easily satisfied with what this world offers in material fare; the physical world is always of secondary or tertiary importance to them; there are realities—those of life, mind, and spirit—that matter far more....To most of the leading minds of India...the world of Nature not only presents real difficulties to the fulfillment of the higher potentialities of life, mind, and spirit; it must be given the value of an evil construct or else of a deceptive "appearance." The motive of much Hindu, Jaina, and

Buddhist thought in India has been *escape,* as the Jains view it, from…gross matter, or escape as the Hindus and Buddhists think, from the misleading appearances and experiences of the physical world, into mental and spiritual realms that have an unshakeable reality….[9]

This observation speaks to the ethical and specifically the ascetic aspects of Hinduism, Buddhism, and Jainism (and we will be discussing the relationship between ethics, asceticism, and author-itarian politics a bit later on) as well as to these theologies' meta-physical and epistemological characters. But beneath the ethical implications of Eastern metaphysical Idealism lie political motives that are much less ascetic morally and far more sordid materially. The following purport of the *Invocation* to the Hindu *Śrī Īśopaniṣad* by the late Divine Grace A.C. Bhaktivedanta Swami Prabhupāda, repeated here from the earlier section on metaphysics, makes plain the connection between authoritarian political motives and the ascetics' hostility to the physical world revealed by the senses. "Be-cause we do not know that there is a complete arrangement in nature for our maintenance," His Grace wrote:

we make efforts to utilize the resources of nature to create a so-called complete life of sense enjoyment. Because the living entity cannot enjoy the life of the senses without being dovetailed to the complete whole, the misleading life of sense enjoyment is considered illusion. The hand of a body is a complete unit only as long as it is attached to the complete body. When the hand is severed from the body, it may appear like a hand, but it actually has none of the potencies of a hand. Similarly, living beings are parts and parcels of the complete whole, and if they are severed from the complete whole, the illusory representation of com-pleteness cannot fully satisfy them.

The completeness of human life can only be realized when one engages in the service of the complete whole. All services in this world—whether social, political, communal, international or even interplanetary—will remain incomplete until they are dovetailed with the complete whole. When everything is dovetailed with the complete whole, the attached parts and parcels also become complete in themselves.[10]

Swami Prabhupāda's commentary illustrates the importance of rendering the real world of the senses an "illusion" in order to establish that all "living beings are parts...of the complete whole,"—a fundamental purpose of pantheistic theories of reality and organismic theories of politics. Once this is established it is possible to justify dovetailing "[a]ll the services in this world—whether social, political [or] communal" with the interests of "the complete whole," rather than with the interests of the individual person. Hence religions that have a history of successful authoritarian machination, as Hinduism and Buddhism do, have consistently assaulted the veracity of sense-perception in order to blind people to the falseness of and so prepare them to accept their credos. As the *Bhagavad-gītā* says: "[w]hen a sensible man ceases to see different identities, which are due to different material bodies, he attains to the Brahman conception,"[11]—a passage which Swami Prabhupāda purports as meaning that:

When one can see that the various bodies of the living entities arise due to the different desires of the individual soul and do not actually belong to the soul itself, one actually sees. In the material conception of life, we find someone a demigod, someone a human being, a dog, a cat, etc. This is material vision, not actual vision. This material differentiation is due to a material conception of life. After the destruction of the material body, the spirit soul is one. The spirit soul, due to contact with material nature, gets different types of bodies. When one can see this, he attains spiritual union; thus being freed from differentiations like man, animal, big, low, etc., one becomes beautified in his consciousness and able to develop Kṛṣṇa consciousness....[12]

And impugning both the senses and the mind as distorted by physical and material appetites and lusts (and at the same time impugning the senses as inciting lust), the *Bhagavad-gītā* says:

> As a fire is covered by smoke, as a mirror is covered by dust, or as the embryo is covered by the womb, similarly, the living entity is covered by different degrees of this lust.
>
> Thus, a man's pure consciousness is covered by his eternal enemy in the form of lust, which is never satisfied and which burns like fire.
>
> The senses, the mind and the intelligence are the sitting places of this lust, which veils the real knowledge of the living entity and bewilders him.
>
> Therefore, O Aruna, best of the Bharatas, in the very beginning curb the great symbol of sin [lust] by regulating the senses, and slay this destroyer of knowledge and self-realization.[13]

And helping to bring the connection between Hinduism's assaults upon the senses and its idealist, organicist metaphysics into focus, Professor Noss writes:

> The human soul, according to [Hindu philosopher Adi] Sankara, can apprehend only the deceptive appearance of things when he relies on his senses for knowledge. The sensible world in which his everyday experience takes place is the subjective spatio-temporal frame of reference through which his ignorance...self-deceivingly perceives the Real. The notion that the objects of sense-experience are "realities" is the work of this ignorance....
>
> Therefore, to believe in the reality of the individual soul, as

is the common experience, is to move in the world of Maya [the Hindu and Buddhist god of illusion], and to have only the lower kind of knowledge; but to know that our separate selves are identical with the one Self, Brahman-Atman, is to apprehend reality and have the higher knowledge.[14]

And Buddhism and Christianity, too, insult or discount the senses, in order to protect the ethical or the metaphysical tenets of their faith-based systems. Buddha purportedly says, in a passage cited by Professor Wm. T. de Bary in his *The Buddhist Tradition*:

The senses are as though illusions and their objects as dreams. For instance a sleeping man might dream that he had made love to a beautiful country girl, and he might remember her when he awoke. What do you think—...does the beautiful girl he dreamed of really exist?

No, Lord.

And would the man be wise to remember the girl of his dreams, or to believe that he had really made love to her?

No, Lord, because she doesn't really exist at all, so how could he have made love to her—though of course he might think he did under the influence of weakness or fatigue.

In just the same way a foolish and ignorant man of the world sees pleasant forms and believes in their existence.[15]

"Perception therefore is no proof of the existence of any entity," Dr. de Bary notes of some of the Buddhist epistemological doctrines, "and all perceptions may be explained as projections of the percipient mind."[16]

And Christianity similarly impugns the senses, saying that the really important things are apprehended by faith, not by sight. Recall that we earlier cited Jesus in Luke (Luke 17:20, 21, NIV) as explaining that: "The kingdom of heaven does not come with your careful observation, nor will people say, 'Here it is,' or 'There it is,' because the kingdom of God is within you." And Paul in 2 Corinthians says that "as long as we are at home in the body we are away from the Lord. We live by faith, not by sight," and disparages "those who take pride in what is seen rather than in what is in the heart" (2 Cor. 5:6, 7, 12, NIV).

But as long as human beings live by faith and not by sight they will have no way to refute the faith-based dogmas that provided the foundations of the Christian theocracies that dominated medieval Europe for over a thousand years—and they will have no way to prove the validity of the philosophies which provide the foundations of free societies. So the purveyors of such dogmas have labored long and arduously to amass and disseminate a body of skeptical arguments that can be directed against the faculties of sense-perception. Although many of the skeptical arguments that are directed against the senses were developed by philosophers and theologians whose political opinions are not obviously authoritarian—in part because many of these thinkers lived so long ago that their political opinions have been largely lost to history—nevertheless, any and all skeptical arguments against the senses are useful to authoritarian intellectuals. This study will therefore catalog the majority of these arguments so that the reader may better recognize them where they appear in explicitly authoritarian literature.

In modern times the most influential skeptical argument directed against the senses is the one which is associated with Hohenzollern Dynasty philosophic flunkey Immanuel Kant. Kant, as was noted earlier, had said that "sensuous perception represents things not at all as they are, but only the mode in which they affect our senses...."[17] In practical terms this means that everything which we think we see, or hear, or touch is really just an hallucinatory illusion caused by the manner in which our minds process raw sense-data, such as waves of light or sound. All "things as objects of our senses existing outside us are given," Kant had said, "but we know nothing of what they may be in themselves, knowing only...the representations which they cause in us by affecting our senses."[18]

This theory of sense-perception—that automatic faculties in our brains cause our senses to misrepresent what they perceive— set off a wave of skeptic euphoria among nineteenth century conservative and authoritarian philosophers. Typical of these philosophers' attitudes toward the senses were those of Friedrich Nietzsche, who was one of the founding fathers of modern Existentialism. Nietzsche considered that one of the most significant of the automatic mechanisms which "dominate" the functioning of the sense-faculties were the human faculties of emotional response which produce the feelings of "fear, love, hatred, and...laziness," etc. Nietzsche said that "it is only late, and then imperfectly, that our senses learn to be subtle, faithful, cautious organs of understanding":

> It is more comfortable for our eye to react to a particular object by producing again an image it has often produced before than by retaining what is new and different in an impression....To hear something new is hard and painful for the ear; we hear the music of foreigners badly. When we hear a foreign language we involuntarily attempt to form the sounds we hear into words which have a more familiar and homely ring....The novel finds our senses...hostile and reluctant; and even in the case of the 'simplest' processes of the senses, the emotions, such as fear, love, hatred, and the passive emotions of laziness, *dominate*....Even when we are involved in the most uncommon experiences we still do the same thing: we fabricate the greater part of the experience and can hardly be compelled *not* [emphasis Nietzsche's] to contemplate some event as its 'inventor'.[19]

The idea that the human faculties of consciousness fabricate and invent the preponderance of the things that we experience has been advanced by a variety of dissimilar and contradictory skeptical arguments. All of these arguments are ultimately based on the three fundamental authoritarian theories of reality we have identified as Idealism, Materialism, and Heracliteanism. Among the most commonly represented of these arguments are those based on the theory of Materialism as it is applied to the functioning of the human faculties of perception and cognition. Metaphysical Materialism, recall, says that everything which exists is made up of physical matter, and obeys the cause-and-effect mechanics that govern crude matter. When this theory is applied to the functioning of perception and cognition it implies that what we are aware of is really just the side-effects of the mechanical operations of the physical processes of our own faculties of consciousness, not actual reality.

The father of the Western tradition of metaphysical Materialism is usually said to be the ancient Greek philosopher Democritus. Democritus had said that all that exists is atoms and atoms in motion. Because we cannot see atoms—just the "phenomenal" (superficial) side-effects of atoms outside us coming into contact with the atoms of which our sense-faculties are made, Democritus, like Kant, believed that everything we perceive is a sort of delusion. One of history's most famous schools of Skepticism, that of Pyrrhonian Skepticism, derives its name from that of a follower of Democritus, Pyrrho of Elis, who was influenced by this idea.

In contrast to skeptical arguments based on metaphysical Materialism are those based on metaphysical Heracliteanism. These arguments are associated with the Greek Sophist philosophers, such as Protagoras and Gorgias, who used them as a basis for their relativist and subjectivist moral theories. Protagoras and Gorgias, following Heraclitus, said that because everything in the universe was in a constant state of flux that real knowledge of the universe was unattainable. Not only is everything we perceive constantly changing, Protagoras and Gorgias asserted, but so are the physical structures of the eyes and the ears and the other senses with which we perceive reality. So reliable perception, they said, is impossible.

And in logical distinction to both the skeptical arguments based on Heracliteanism and Materialism are arguments founded upon the religious variety of metaphysical Idealism. These sorts of arguments, most famously associated with Descartes, propose that what we perceive of as reality is really just an hallucination imposed on us by God, or by some all-powerful, demi-god-like "demon." "[T]here is a God who is all-powerful," wrote Descartes in his *Meditations*:

> How, then, do I know that he has not arranged that there should be neither earth, nor sky, nor any extended thing, nor figure, nor magnitude, nor place, providing at the same time, however, for [the rise in me of the perceptions of all these objects, and] the persuasion that these do not exist other than as I perceive them?[20] [brackets in original].

Or that:

> [S]ome malignant demon, who is at once exceedingly potent and deceitful, has employed all his artifice to deceive me; I will suppose that the sky, the air, the earth, colours, figures, sounds, and all external things, are nothing better than the illusions of dreams, by means of which this being has laid snares for my credulity; I will consider myself as without hands, eyes, flesh, blood, or any of the senses, and as falsely believing that I am possessed of these....[21]

This doctrine, as well as those based on Materialism and Heracliteanism, is among the best-known of modern skeptical arguments. But throughout ancient and modern history a wide variety of such arguments have been established on these or on different combinations of the same fundamental premises. Collectively these arguments are sometimes referred to as the skeptical "modes" or "tropes" and are directed against both the cognitive, or intellectual faculties, as well as against the faculties of sense-perception. A first century B.C. adherent of Pyrrhonian Skepticism, Aenesidemus of Crossus, gathered together many of the ancient "skeptical tropes" that apply specifically to the senses. His compilation of skeptical arguments has come to be known as the Ten "Modes" or "Tropes" and these doctrines continue to impact philosophers in modern times, centuries after they were first advanced.

Many of Aenesidemus's skeptical tropes are based on variables such as *relativity* and *perspective* and are essentially materialist in nature. They are materialist in that they propose that the physical functioning of a being's faculties, or the mechanics of physical nature, lead to the effects which they describe. Arguments which are based on relativity say that because what is perceived by the senses is relative to the particular perceiver that we have no way of knowing whether what we perceive is objectively real or just an illusion. We say that a person is color-blind, for instance, because they cannot see the color red; but how are we to know if there really is a color red? If some people see the color red and others don't, perhaps the person we call "color-blind" is seeing the world as it really is.

Another version of this relativistic argument says that we cannot know what is objectively real because different modes of perception report reality in fundamentally different ways. The eyes of one type of animal do not report the same reality as do the eyes of another, this argument says; and the sense of hearing does not report the same reality as does the sense of touch. The faculties of a sick, or mad, or drunken person do not report the same reality as do the faculties of a person who is healthy, sane, or sober. From the vantage of such premises there are any number of skeptical arguments which can be directed against the veracity of the senses.

Another significant group of relativist arguments against sense-perception pertain to the issue of physical perspective. These arguments say that the variations in a creature's physical relation to the thing being observed—its perspective as it were—so completely distort its perceptions of reality as to render them worthless. We cannot tell how large or small something is, this argument says, because our perception of physical size is completely distorted by the relative size of the observer. To a mouse a cat is the size of an elephant, but to an elephant a cat is the size of a mouse, this hypothesis asserts; so there is really no way of knowing what size a cat is.

And the perception of size is also distorted by an observer's distance from an object, another perspectival argument says. From the perspective of an observer standing near a cathedral, for instance, the cathedral appears mountainous. But someone standing a mile distant from a cathedral may feel that they could hold the cathedral in the palm of their hand. Perspective, this inference avers, makes it impossible for us to know whether cathedrals are actually large or small.

And our ability to determine shape is also distorted by perspective, skeptic theory insists. If three people are looking at the same coin from different angles the person looking at the coin's face will see the coin as round; the person looking at the side of the coin will see a narrow rectangle; and the person looking at the coin obliquely will see the coin as elliptical. Because the same object has different shapes depending on the perspective of the person viewing it, we cannot tell what shape an object really has. These skeptical arguments discredit our sense of sight but variations of perspectival arguments can be used to discredit our other senses.

Another skeptical argument uses the fact that sense-data are affected by the physical mediums they pass through to discredit the accuracy of our perceptions. Light particles and sound waves are distorted as they pass though air and water and other mediums on their way to our faculties of sense. When we look at a mountain range or the skyline of a city what we may really be seeing is simply a mirage caused by the effect that particles of air have on particles of light. So we can have no confidence that the mountains and cities we think we see really exist, this theory maintains.

Yet another argument uses the fact that sounds, sights, and other sensations we perceive can be reproduced by artificial means to undermine the credibility of our sense-faculties. What we think is a bird call or an animal cry may actually be a hunter mimicking an animal's sound; or a thunderclap may actually be a bass drum; or a visual image may be photographic, cinematic, or holographic, rather than real. Because it can be difficult to discern real percepts from artificially recreated percepts, this argument contends, we can never be sure that what we think of as real actually is.

And still another skeptical argument says that we cannot determine whether or not the things we perceive really exist because in the time it takes for sense-data to reach our sense-faculties the thing we believe we are perceiving may have gone out of existence, as a star may cease to exist while the light it generates travels toward us. A variation of this argument says that because we can only observe the things we perceive for limited periods of time that we can never really be sure of the real nature of what we think we are observing. What we are observing may change in some fundamental way before or after we observe it, this thesis holds.

And finally, René Descartes again—who wanted us to restrict our knowledge to what we can learn from intuition and to deductions based on intuited surmises—advises us that we cannot trust our senses because we cannot tell when we are awake and when we are asleep and dreaming. "[T]here exist no certain marks by which the state of waking can ever be distinguished from sleep,"[22] Descartes insists, and then invites us to join him in a state of consciousness that is tantamount to dreaming while awake.

COGNITIVE SKEPTICISM

But it isn't only our sense-faculties from which we get knowledge of reality. Our cognitive, or abstract intellectual faculties, provide us with knowledge of reality as well. Our sense-faculties give us "perceptual" knowledge of reality, but our abstract intellectual faculties give us conceptual knowledge—that is, they give us knowledge in the form of concepts or principles. Because conceptual knowledge can be just as dangerous to authoritarians as perceptual knowledge, skeptical philosophers have always worked to undermine our confidence in both types of knowledge.

Skeptical attacks on conceptual knowledge take two forms. One attacks the reliability of the intellectual faculty which we use to form concepts—the mind, or intellect; and the other assails the validity of the logical methods that we use to form concepts, the methods of *induction* and *deduction*. The principal argument skeptics direct against the reliability of the intellect is the notion that the intellect thinks automatically, and therefore cannot adjust its thoughts to conform to reality. The principal arguments that skeptics direct against logic include this latter argument against the intellect, as well as several other important arguments which will be considered a bit further on.

The skeptical argument against the intellect that says we cannot adjust our thoughts to conform to reality because the mind thinks automatically is associated in modern times with Kant, who said that:

> When I speak of objects in time and in space, it is not of things in themselves, of which I know nothing, but of things in appearance, that is, of...the particular way of cognising objects which is afforded to man. I must not say of what I think in time or in space, that in itself, and independent of these my thoughts, it exists...because space and time, together with the appearances in them, are nothing existing in themselves...but are...only modes of representation....[23]

Kant "reaches the inevitable conclusion that the intellect is forever shut up within the domain of its own forms,"[24] wrote Brandt V. B. Dixon in an introduction to *The Critique of Pure Reason*, the seminal, eighteenth century metaphysical and epistemological tract in which Kant first outlined his theory. These "forms," which Kant referred to as the "categories" of understanding, are innate or inborn ideas installed like computer programs within the human mind which control human thinking and perceiving and thereby seal human beings within an artificial reality of automatic thought. This notion of innate ideas is known to philosophy as *Innatism*, and is associated both with idealist doctrines which say that ideas are placed in the human mind by God, and also with materialist doctrines which say that certain types of ideas evolved in different types of people due to biological (Nazism) or economic (Marxism) forces. In the works of the post-Kantian philosophers who continue to dominate Western philosophy, innatist doctrines have provided the primary premise for skeptical arguments against the reliability of human cognitive faculties.

LOGICAL SKEPTICISM

But arguments against the reliability of human cognitive faculties are but the first of the two-pronged skeptical attacks on the credibility of conceptual knowledge. The second prong is arguments against the reliability of the distinctive methods of human cognition, the methods of logical induction and deduction. Because these methods of logic require that human beings consciously monitor and adjust their thoughts so that they do not contradict either 1), the perceived facts of reality (logical induction), or 2), their own prior thinking (logical deduction), any argument which says that human beings can't freely adjust their thinking necessarily implies the unreliability of logic. Deterministic theories of cognition such as Kant's, therefore, have always provided the first line of attack against the validity of logic.

But beyond deterministic theories of cognition there are also three other avenues of skeptical argument against logic which have been particularly nettlesome for the defenders of logical methods of thinking. These theories say that 1), logical statements cannot be validated by reference to the facts of experience because all of the things that logical statements refer to haven't been experienced yet. 2), that logical statements can't be validated because any validation of such statements would have to refer to deeper premises in logic, leading to infinite regresses of logic which validate nothing. And 3), that because any attempt to validate the methods of logic would first have to assume the truth of those methods, that no logical statement can ever be validated. Because these arguments can seem befuddlingly abstruse when considered in the abstract we will examine them within the context of a general explanation of how logic is actually used to acquire conceptual knowledge.

Logic is the method of acquiring conceptual knowledge that works by creating abstract models of reality and then applying those models to reality in order to deduce new knowledge. The method of acquiring conceptual knowledge by creating abstract models of reality is called *logical induction* while the method of acquiring conceptual knowledge by applying these models *to* reality is called *logical deduction*. Logical induction is correctly employed as a method of acquiring conceptual knowledge by inventing (inferring) concepts (ideas) that are consistent with the facts of reality we directly experience; while logical deduction is correctly employed by applying the concepts we invent to the facts in order to learn something new about them. We use logical induction to gain conceptual knowledge of the facts of reality when, for instance, after reading a thermometer and observing that water is freezing, we formulate a law (concept) of nature which says that *water freezes at thirty-two degrees*. We use logical deduction to gain new knowledge of the facts of reality when, upon observing that the temperature is dropping to thirty-two degrees, we apply our law of nature to this emerging circumstance in order to deduce that water is about to freeze.

But the argument against logic which says that logical statements cannot be validated by reference to the facts we experience because all of the things the statements refer to haven't been experienced yet implies that this deduction would be unreliable. We would first have to experience every possible past, present, and future instance of water freezing as the temperature dropped to thirty-two degrees in order to be certain that it would in fact freeze, this argument says. Of course, such an assumption would seem puzzling unless we first understood that it is established on the theories of reality which we've previously identified as the creationist aspect of Idealism and as Heracliteanism. Creationism, remember, is the doctrine which says that everything that exists or occurs does so by the decree of some all-powerful mind—usually a god or human beings conceived of as having the powers of a god. And Heracliteanism is the metaphysical philosophy which says that everything is constantly changing and that nothing is therefore anything in particular.

Heraclitean theories of reality undermine logical methods of acquiring knowledge by overthrowing the metaphysical constants which must be presumed if logical statements are to be considered true. If everything is constantly changing and nothing is anything in particular then no statement of inductive logic can be valid and no statement of deductive logic is reliable. This is because the statements inductive logic makes about reality, "water freezes at thirty-two degrees," and the conclusions deductive logic derives from those statements: "the temperature has dropped to thirty-two degrees so the lake is going to freeze," are dependent for their validity on water possessing enduring physical properties. If the fundamental properties of water are constantly changing then inductive and deductive logical statements about water are worthless and inductive and deductive logical methods of acquiring knowledge about water are useless.

And if everything which exists or occurs does so at the whim of some god-like mind then we can never logically deduce when water will freeze because we can never be certain of what that mind will decide. God or something like god may completely change the qualities of water whenever they feel like it, rendering all logical statements about water invalid because the entity they refer to no longer possesses the properties the statements suppose. Creationism, then, like Heracliteanism, renders logical thinking invalid by rendering everything logic refers to utterly arbitrary. In a universe where everything occurs arbitrarily logic will tell you absolutely nothing about the universe.

But the circumstances we actually live in are in fact nothing like the arbitrarily mutating universe postulated by old Heraclitus. And there is absolutely no physical evidence that things exist and events occur as the result of the capricious dictates of some all-powerful mind. Because of this the methods of induction and deduction can indeed be validated by a small number of initial observations and don't need to be validated over and over again in every instance of their application. Further, deductive logic can be validated simply by discerning that a conclusion is logically consistent with a valid premise, because a conclusion that is consistent with a valid premise is necessarily true by implication. That is why one can deduce that water will freeze as the temperature drops to thirty-two degrees even before this is confirmed by the testimony of sense-perception.

All of this means that the skeptical objections to logic that were previously listed are false. One does not need to wait until every possible instance of a law of nature has occurred in order to confirm the validity of such a law. Nor do logical inductions and deductions need to be confirmed by an infinite regress of deeper premises in logic because they can be immediately confirmed either by sense experience or by showing that they are consistent with premises which have previously been demonstrated to be true. Nor do the methods of logic need to be presumed true before one can confirm the validity of these methods, because, as we just noted, the validity of logical methods can be confirmed merely by observing empirical facts or by confirming that a deduction is logically consistent with a factual premise. Because of *these* facts, we can logically conclude that the methods of logic are valid.

REASON AND SKEPTICISM

Logic, when it is used in concert with the faculties of sense-perception, is a powerful instrument for gaining knowledge of reality. But when it is isolated from the information provided by the senses, as it is by the so-called Continental Rationalists Descartes, Leibniz, and Spinoza, it can be misused as a device for creating baseless dogmas. In fact, the word "rationalist," when it is employed to describe these philosophers, refers to their abuse of logic in this manner. But there is something profoundly irrational about shutting one's eyes and thinking in order to understand a world which offers so many challenges to our existence.

A far more rational way of thinking was described previously as "the method of acquiring conceptual knowledge...by creating abstract models of reality and then applying those models to reality in order to deduce new knowledge." This is the method of thinking we use when we discover laws of nature and then apply those laws, for instance, to predict that water is going to freeze. Because this method offers tangible reasons for our beliefs—the evidence of direct experience such as that provided by sense-perception—it is much more deservedly referred to as rationalist, and as rational, than is the epistemological philosophy of Descartes. Indeed, because it provides such reasons it is worthy of being denoted *Reason*.

Reason in this elevated sense is the proper appellative for the method of thinking which uses logic to make concepts out of percepts and grasp percepts in terms of concepts. But because this way of thinking strives to be logically consistent with the empirical facts of reality disclosed by the senses it unavoidably contradicts the empirically baseless dogmas which result from the employment of the epistemological methodology of the Continental Rationalists. Doctrines which are logically established on empirically baseless suppositions, rather than upon the facts testified to by the senses, are, as we have learned, the dialectical supports of authoritarian political establishments. These establishments, therefore, are the enemies of reason.

"The 'Hitlerian' revolution can be said to have been a 'revolution against reason',"[25] wrote historian Edmond Vermeil in a postwar analysis of Nazi culture for the *International Council for Philosophy and Humanistic Studies*. And of all the modern manifestations of authoritarianism and totalitarianism—Fascism, Nazism, and Marxism—none was as overtly and openly irrationalist, in the sense of being anti-reason, as was Nazism. Unlike the fascists and the Marxists, who were usually merely surreptitiously or implicitly anti-rational, the Nazis were flagrantly and boastfully irrationalist. "Activism was important," the distinguished student of National Socialism George L. Mosse wrote in his *Nazi Culture*:

> After all, the Nazis conceived of their party as a "movement." This and the irrational foundations of their world view represented strong opposition to intellectualism. Hitler summarized his own view in 1938: "What we suffer from today is an excess of education. Nothing is appreciated except knowledge. The wiseacres, however, are the enemies of action. What we require is instinct and will."[26]

"Book learning was always secondary in the educational system of the Third Reich," Mosse noted in the same volume. "Anti-intellectualism is an integral part of every movement built upon irrational premises."[27] And what was the intellectual result of this irrationalism? Writing in his *Ernst Kaltenbrunner: Ideological Soldier of the Third Reich* historian Peter R. Black related that:

> Observing [SS-Obersturmbannführer] Adolf Eichmann on the stand at his trial in Jerusalem, Hannah Arendt was struck by the fact that "the only notable characteristic" that she could detect "in his past behavior as well as in his behavior during the trial and throughout the pre-trial police examination was something entirely negative: it was not stupidity but *thoughtlessness*" (emphasis original). Albert Speer once wrote that in his decision to join the Nazi Party, his "inclination to be relieved of having to *think*, particularly about unpleasant facts, helped to sway the balance"... [emphasis Black's].[28]

But what prompted the German people to this mass thoughtlessness? The answer is that during the Hitler regime and beginning with the generations that preceded it unreason had become the formal and institutionalized national epistemology of the German culture. Beginning especially with Kant, who had "found it necessary to deny *knowledge,* in order to make room for *faith,*" reason, defined as logic tied to sense-perception, had increasingly been banished from German society—and was more and more depreciated throughout Europe. Hence the increasingly vitriolic denunciation of reason and its epistemological foundations by German intellectuals leading up to the Nazi takeover, and then its open calumniation by the Nazis themselves. Here is Nazi party philosopher H. S. Chamberlain smearing reason by equating it with the Jews—while at the same time attempting to smear the Jews by equating them with reason:

> [T]hat fundamental truth which the Rigveda centuries and centuries before Christ tried thus to express, "The root of existence, the wise find in the heart"....That is religion!—Now this very tendency, this state of mind, this instinct, "to seek the core of nature in the heart," the Jews lack to a startling degree. They are born rationalists. Reason is strong in them....
>
> ....
>
> [T]he feelings are, as we have said, the fountain head of all genuine religion; this...the Jews had well-nigh choked with their formalism and their hard-hearted rationalism....[29]

The "rationalism" which Chamberlain found "hard-hearted" was not the "Continental Rationalism" that isolated logical deduction from sense-percepts—that was the Rationalism of Descartes. Cartesian Rationalism was an epistemology the Nazis were in fact amenable to because it traps people in a land of logical deductions from unexamined premises—something that the Nazis were perfectly happy to do. What the Nazis objected to was the other epistemological method that the word Rationalism is used to denote—the method of reason. That Rationalism the Nazis found hard-hearted because it alienated them from their "feelings."

Reason alienated the Nazis from their feelings because it exposed their hatreds and appetites as unjust and immoral and their passions as prompting them to actions which were quite literally suicidal. Like all criminals the Nazis were hell-bent on a path that would likely lead them to catastrophe—but they wanted to go down that path anyway. Driven by self-destructive desires—their "feelings"—the Nazis wanted what they wanted, and did not want to know what the consequences of their beliefs and behaviors would be. Hard-hearted Rationalism would have forced them to think about those consequences.

The statement by Chamberlain that the religions he admired had their fountainhead in emotional "feelings" reminds us of the fact that all irrational methods of knowledge have their psychological basis in emotions—usually in the form of desires and hatreds. As Germany descended into madness these emotion-based epistemologies were an increasingly prevalent aspect of German culture. Professor of Economics and History at the German University at Halle Dr. Frederick Hertz noted in his *The German Public Mind in the Nineteenth Century* that:

> [G]erman Romanticism [the cultural precursor of Nazism] is often taxed with having stood for a policy of feeling rather than reason, having judged irrational strivings, old traditions and blind prejudices too favourably....
>
> ....
>
> The turning away from the 'reason' of the protagonists of the Enlightenment is also shown in the exaggerated importance attached to feeling, imagination and the passions.[30]

The "turning away from reason" was the principal characteristic of the late eighteenth-to-the-present century cultural movement known as "Romanticism." Romanticism—philosophic and cultural Romanticism as contrasted with esthetic Romanticism—was the first and primary social manifestation of the philosophic ideas of Immanuel Kant. The implication of Kant's epistemological philosophy was that human perceptual and cognitive faculties could not provide people with reliable knowledge about what was actually real—and this implied that faith and other mystical[31] methods of knowledge were legitimate alternatives to sense-perception and reason. The late Dr. John Herman Randall, Jr. noted the connection between Kant, Romanticism, unreason, and faith in this passage from his respected *The Making of the Modern Mind*:

> Kant's book [*Critique of Pure Reason*] stimulated romanticists to a flood of special systems founded on faith. Man, they claimed, is not fundamentally intellectual. Rather human nature is at bottom made up of instincts and feelings; and his instinctive and emotional life should dominate his career and paint for him both his conception of the world and his conception of human life.[32]

But although Kant was essential to a revolt against reason that was at bottom a reaction against the liberalizing influences that were threatening the old aristocracies of Europe, irrationalism, as the dominant epistemological ethos of German culture, had a much deeper root in German history: Luther. Jonas Lesser, identifying Luther as "one of the main inaugurators of National Socialism,"[33] charged him with having opened "a gulf between Germany and Western Europe by unclogging German irrationalism."[34] And W. T. Jones noted of Luther that "reason seemed to him as fallible as the Church. He would always reject it if and when it conflicted with individual, private, and subjective feeling. Hence Luther was fundamentally an antirationalist."[35] Here H. S. Chamberlain praises Kant as a destroyer of humanity's confidence in the mind—and as a liberator from the restrictions of reason—by comparing him favorably with Luther:

> [I]mmanuel Kant, the Luther of philosophy, the destroyer of spurious knowledge, the annihilator of all systems, who had pointed out to us "the limits of our thinking power" and warned us "never to venture with speculative reason beyond the boundary of experience"; but, after assigning to us such strict and definite outward limits, he had thrown open, as no philosopher had done before him, the doors to the inner world of the Limitless and thus revealed to us the home of the free man.[36]

Throwing open the doors to the inner world of the "Limitless" allowed ambitious ideologues like Luther and Kant the unlimited freedom they needed to concoct any dogmas they wished and impose them upon the human race without fear of moral recrimination. No wonder Nazi doctrinaires like Chamberlain thrilled at such freedom! Kant used this limitless freedom to develop a new secular gospel with which to protect his Hohenzollern paymasters, while Luther used it to free himself from the power of the Catholic Church and set himself up as the pope of a new Christianity. Here Luther rails against reason and the restrictions it places on his new faith:

> [W]e, excluding all works, do go to the very head of this beast which is called Reason, which is the fountain and the headspring of all mischiefs. For reason feareth not God, it loveth not God, it trusteth not in God, but proudly contemneth him. It is not moved either with his threatenings or his promises. It is not delighted with his words or works, but it murmureth against him, it is angry with him, judgeth and hateth him: to be short, "it is an enemy to God," Rom. 8 [:7], not giving him his glory. This pestilent beast (reason I say)

being once slain, all outward and gross sins should be nothing.

Wherefore we must first and before all things go about by faith, to kill infidelity, the contempt and the hating of God, murmuring against his judgment, his wrath, and all his words and works; for then do we kill reason, which can be killed by none other means but by faith, which in believing God, giveth unto him his glory, notwithstanding that he speaketh those things which seem both foolish, absurd, and impossible to reason; notwithstanding also, that God setteth forth himself otherwise than reason is able either to judge or to conceive....If reason then be not killed, and all kinds of religion and service of God under heaven that are invented by men to get righteousness before God, be not condemned, the righteousness of faith can take no place.[37]

As these passages indicate the effort to kill reason in Germany had begun long before unreason was institutionalized in that country by the Nazis. Professor of History Henry M. Pachter noted in his article on the Third Reich published by *The International Council for Philosophy and Humanistic Studies* that:

The 'animal protest' against humanist 'culture' had been smouldering in European philosophy for a long time. Irrationalism, vitalism, and existentialism rebelled against the High Court of Reason; years before Fascism and National-Socialism appeared in the political arena, futurism in Italy and the romantic Youth Movement in Germany gave expression to ideas about the new way of life which were brewing....Some saw the allegedly carefree existence of the soldier as a salvation from philistine moralism; but mostly it was the rebellion of the 'open collars' against the 'stuffed shirts', striving to gain recognition for the senses, the instincts, and the emotions. These movements...soon degenerated into a violent attack on all intellectual values.[38]

Aiding in this attack in Germany was a cabal of reactionary social critics and ideologues who railed against classical Liberalism in politics and against reason in epistemology. Identifying three of the most prominent of these as Paul de Lagarde, Julius Langbehn, and Moeller van den Bruck Columbia University Professor Emeritus of History Fritz Stern noted that "they despised the discourse of intellectuals, depreciated reason, and exalted intuition....For decades they were hailed as Germanic critics and prophets....[T]heir thought and their impact on German life demonstrate the existence of a cultural crisis in modern Germany."[39] And of Julius Langbehn George Mosse wrote that he had "substituted a veritable paean in praise of intuition, stressing the irrational, the mystical, and the subjectively intuitive."[40] And Paul de Lagarde is cited by Jean-Jacques Anstett in his article published in the *ICPHS* study as asserting that "the essence of man is not the intellect but the will...."[41] Yet this was the sort of man who was shaping the German intellect as Germany sped toward its cultural "triumph of the will."

But the culmination of the centuries-long assault on German rationality is found in the statements of the Nazis themselves, and in the statements and writings of the Nazi affiliated dogmatists and doctrinaires. When he wasn't leading them in the *Heil Hitler!* salute Nazi existentialist and academician Martin Heidegger was trying to lead his fellow Germans away from the one thing that might have saved them: knowledge. *"Knowledge and German destiny must come to power above all in the adherence to tradition*, and will do so only when teachers and students alike suspend knowledge as their innermost need,"[42] [italics Heidegger's] Heidegger wrote in the pages of *Freiburger Zeitung* while he was Rector of then Nazi controlled Freiberg University. His students, who would soon be driving panzers across Europe, replied:

[O]ur honored Rector, the philosopher Professor Heidegger, by his entry into the National Socialist German Worker's [Nazi] *Party embraced the spiritual world of National Socialism* [italics in original]. Even though, according to the Professor, one cannot always clearly distinguish between appearance and reality, at any rate our future and our work will gradually turn appearance into reality.

Our position is clear: We fight now as always against the cold arrogance of the intellectual man, who thinks he can trample on our enthusiasm and warmth of feeling....[43]

And disparaging the ability to distinguish between appearance and reality—and following Kant ("I have therefore found it necessary to deny *knowledge,* in order to make room for *faith*"), the Nazi philosophizers dismissed even the possibility of knowledge. Rosenberg said:

The thinkers of Hellenic antiquity assumed that sooner or later reason would make possible a complete knowledge of the universe. Late, very late, it then became clear, that it is essentially human to be unable to grasp absolute truth, or even the presupposed meaning of earthly causation. Even if the "absolute truth" were revealed to us, we could neither grasp nor understand this....[44]

And Chamberlain stated, parroting Kant:

[M]an can only arrive at knowledge of himself, his wisdom will ever only be human wisdom; his *Weltanschauung* [world view, or philosophy; italics Chamberlain's], however macrocosmically it extend itself in the delusion of embracing the All, will ever be but the microcosmic image in the brain of an individual man. The first part of this word *Weltanschauung* throws us imperatively back upon our human nature and it limits. Absolute wisdom (as the Greek formula would have it), any absolute knowledge however small, is out of the question; we can only have human knowledge, only what various men at different times have thought that they knew.[45]

And Spengler added:

It is one thing...to pose problems and quite another to believe in solutions of them....Man is astounded by his life and asks questions about it. But even man cannot give an answer to his own questions, he can only *believe* [italics Spengler's] in the correctness of his answer, and in that respect there is no difference between Aristotle and the meanest savage.[46]

And what did the meanest savages believe? "The Nazis went all out for irrationalism," Professor of Political Science Chester C. Maxey said in his *Political Philosophies*:

Most human beings, they declared, even the literate and educated, are stupid and irrational—seldom guided by intelligent self-interest in matters of direct material concern to themselves. They have little capacity for objective thought, and seldom think at all. Instead, they follow emotion and prejudice. They are easily fooled, will believe the most preposterous lies if they are presented in an agreeable garb of passion or sentiment. Obviously, said the Nazi writers, such pathetically irrational creatures cannot govern themselves.[47]

And the Nazi writer Chamberlain said:

The Teuton...is no good critic; he really thinks little in comparison with other Aryans; his gifts impel him to act and to feel. To call the Germans a "nation of thinkers" is a bitter irony....Hence it was that Luther went so far as to call the Germans "blind people"; the rest of the German races are the same in scarcely less degree; for analytical thought belongs to seeing....The Teuton is occupied with other things....[48]

But liberal societies *are* based on analytical thinking, and on the belief that human beings can discover and understand and commonly agree upon rational principles of political morality and political rights. Maxey had observed that "[a]ll of the liberal and rationalist ideologies of the eighteenth and nineteenth centuries had proceeded on the assumption that man, both individually and collectively, is a rational creature, capable of following the light of reason to objective truth."[49] And Université de Louvain Professor F. Gregoire noted in his essay on Nazism in the *ICPHS* study that liberal societies are established on:

> [T]he idea that, by his abstract and reasoning intelligence, man and, in principle, anything in the shape of man, is capable of arriving at one and the same truth—in other words, that there exist universal and eternal verities; and that, in addition, man is fundamentally characterized by intelligence, which, being alike in all men...makes them all beings equal in value and dignity....[50]

"[A] democratic concept...takes a position of unlimited optimism in regard to man's nature," University of Wisconsin Professor Emeritus J. Lucien Radel related in his *Roots of Totalitarianism*:

> Man is considered a rational being capable of *independent* [italics Radel's] use of his powers of reason and judgment and of applying these abilities to sound decision-making in regard to the betterment of his own life. According to the concept of Democracy, this fundamental rationality is the basis for most human relations.[51]

But the "supporters of totalitarian ideas," Radel notes, "believe that man does not, in most cases, act on rational grounds."[52] And indeed, by the time the Nazis came to power the Germans had stopped acting on such grounds. The "violent attack on all intellectual values" noted by Pachter had penetrated deep into German politics, where it took the form of the Nazi Brown Shirts' physically violent attacks on Hitler's opponents. This political violence had been preceded by decades of philosophic violence directed against reason by generations of German philosophers who, following Kant, and usually supported by the Hohenzollerns, had turned the Germans into "blind people." So pervasive had the influence of these philosophers become that when Hitler said that "faith sent more recruits than abstract knowledge" he was virtually quoting Kant, who had "found it necessary to deny *knowledge*, in order to make room for *faith*" [italics Kant's].

But the Nazis were not the only twentieth century totalitarians who had gone "all out for irrationalism." Although the Nazi intellectuals were distinctive in having adopted irrationality as a formal epistemological value, the fascists and the Marxists, too, employed epistemological arguments against reason in their efforts to overthrow Liberalism and legitimize authoritarianism. Fascist ideologues Giovanni Gentile and Benito Mussolini appreciatively cited Ernest Renan in arguing that the "degenerate" masses were fundamentally irrational and that therefore democracy was impractical. "Reason and science are the products of mankind," Mussolini and Gentile quoted Renan as saying:

> [B]ut it is chimerical to seek reason directly for the people and through the people. It is not essential to the existence of reason that all should be familiar with it; and even if all had to be initiated, this could not be achieved through democracy which seems fated to lead to the extinction of all arduous forms of culture and the highest forms of learning....It is much to be feared that the last word of democracy...would be a form of society in which a degenerate mass would have no thought beyond that of enjoying the ignoble pleasures of the vulgar.[53]

And the Marxists, too, although they postured as the proponents of a "scientific" socialism, argued against human rationality.

The Marxists asserted that all theories of morality were just mindless expressions of class interest, for if this were true then the philosophic foundations of liberal society would come crashing down. Marx's statement that "your bourgeois notions of freedom, culture, law, etc....are but the outgrowth of the conditions of your bourgeois production and bourgeois property..." is the quintessential statement of Marxist irrationalism, and specifically of Marxist Materialism, which argues that all human thought is mechanistically determined by financial or material appetites.

"Men fear thought as they fear nothing else on earth," the philosopher Bertrand Russell wrote in his *Why Men Fight*. But it is not all men but rather authoritarians specifically who have ever worked to institutionalize the contempt for and the hatred of thinking. Russell himself flirted with authoritarianism,[54] but was yet able to shake off his own fear of thought adequately enough to pen some of the noblest words ever written in thought's defense. "Thought is subversive and revolutionary..." he wrote:

> [T]hought is merciless to privilege, established institutions, and comfortable habits; thought is anarchic and lawless, indifferent to authority, careless of the well-tried wisdom of the ages. Thought looks into the pit of hell and is not afraid. It sees man, a feeble speck, surrounded by unfathomable depths of silence; yet it bears itself proudly, as unmoved as if it were lord of the universe. Thought is great and swift and free, the light of the world, and the chief glory of man.[55]

And thought, meaning reason, is free—literally: it is a manifestation of free will. And further, thought and respect for thought are the indispensable preconditions for the establishment and the preservation of a free society. That is why men—some men—fear it.

CHAPTER NINE

PRAGMATISM

The discussion of the significance of reason for politics brings our study of the relationship between epistemological philosophy and political philosophy near to its conclusion. But before we move on to the next part of this exposition, which concerns ethics, there is one last issue pertaining to epistemology which we should consider. This is a manifestation of the authoritarian tradition of epistemology in the form of a popular and respectable American school of philosophy which goes by the name of *Pragmatism*. Because the philosophy of Pragmatism has taken deep root in that paramount rampart of Liberalism which is the United States it merits singular scrutiny.

As with so many other philosophical terms such as Materialism, Idealism, and Skepticism, the term Pragmatism has a different connotation for the general public than it does for philosophers. To the typical citizen of the liberal West the term Pragmatism suggests a commendable concern for the practical as opposed to the spuriously or speciously speculative. But to philosophers themselves it refers to a policy of dismissing the theoretical in the interest of practicality—and, conversely, of adopting almost any theory that proves to be "practical" as a means to almost any ends. Before we consider adopting this theory ourselves we should consider how Benito Mussolini and the fascist philosopher Giovanni Gentile employed it in their manifesto *The Doctrine of Fascism*. Dismissing the reliability of the theoretical, Mussolini and Gentile say that Fascism "rejects the idea of a doctrine suited to all times and to all people."

> Granted that the XIXth [19th] century was the century of socialism, liberalism, democracy....Political doctrines pass; nations remain. We are free to believe that this is the century of authority, a century tending to the "right", a Fascist century. If the XIXth century was the century of the individual (liberalism implies individualism) [parentheses Mussolini's] we are free to believe that this is the "collective" century, and therefore the century of the State.[1]

And having dismissed as passé the liberal-democratic political theories that underlie democracy and individual freedom in favor of the freedom to believe in collectivism Mussolini and Gentile adopt a policy of modifying and adjusting fascist theories in any way they deem necessary to fulfill Fascism's "new needs":

> All doctrines aim at directing the activities of men toward a given objective; but these activities in their turn react on the doctrine, modifying it and adjusting it to new needs, or outstripping it. A doctrine must therefore be a vital act and not a verbal display. Hence the pragmatic strain in Fascism, its will to power, its will to live, its attitude toward violence....[2]

The most significant of these phrases for the new student of the philosophy of Pragmatism is the one which says "all doctrines aim at directing the activities of men toward a given objective." For the primary purpose of the pragmatic practice of philosophy is that of directing the activities, altering the behavior, and steering the conduct of human beings. While it is true that all doctrines aim to tutor human actions, rational doctrines do this by first tutoring people in the truth. What is distinctive about Pragmatism is that directing the "activities of men" is its principal purpose—and the fact that it holds that any doctrine which successfully accomplishes this is "true." Here William James, the Harvard philosopher credited by educator Mortimer J. Adler with having fully developed and popularized Pragmatism, explains the practical purpose of his philosophy, and its attitude toward truth:

> Pragmatism is willing to take anything....She will count mystical experiences if they have practical consequences. She will take a God who lives in the very dirt of private fact—if that should seem a likely place to find him.
>
> Her only test of probable truth is what works best in the way of leading us...nothing being omitted. If theological ideas should do this, if the notion of God, in particular, should prove to do it, how could pragmatism possibly deny God's existence? She could see no meaning in treating as "not true" a notion that was pragmatically so successful.[3]

And addressing Pragmatism's purpose as an instrument for "leading us," James cites Charles Sanders Pierce, often noted as the first, although perhaps not the most influential, of the pragmatist philosophers:

> A glance at the history of the idea will show you still better what pragmatism means. The word is derived from the same Greek word πρáγμá [πρᾶξη], meaning action, from which our words "practice" and "practical" come. It was first introduced into philosophy by Mr. Charles Pierce in 1878....Mr. Pierce, after pointing out that our beliefs are really rules for action, said that, to develop a thought's meaning, we need only determine what

conduct it is fitted to produce: that conduct is for us its sole significance.[4]

The sole significance of a pragmatically formulated thought, then, is that of producing conduct. If an idea proves itself successful as a means of inducing the desired conduct it is "true,"—and "truth," as a consequence, is merely a word for an idea that results in the desired behavior. If all of this sounds suspiciously like an intellectual machinator's philosophy of philosophy, it's because that's exactly what it is. But why should we believe that a doctrine can become true just because it "works best in the way of leading us." Here James, alluding to the German philosopher Hermann Lotze, addresses this issue:

> We naïvely assume, he [Lotze] says, a relation between reality and our minds which may be just the opposite of the true one. Reality, we naturally think, stands ready-made and complete, and our intellects supervene with the one simple duty of describing it as it is already. But may not our descriptions...be themselves important additions to reality? And may not previous reality itself be there, far less for the purpose of reappearing unaltered in our knowledge, than for the very purpose of stimulating our minds to such additions as shall enhance the universe's total value....
>
> It is identically our pragmatistic conception. In our cognitive as well as in our active life we are creative. We *add*, both to the subject and to the predicate part of reality. The world stands really malleable, waiting to receive its final touches at our hands....Man *engenders* [italics James'] truth upon it.[5]

"Man *engenders* truth upon" reality, James indicates, by actually creating, or at least by substantially modifying, the world in which we live. This occurs, James says, not so much because human beings materially alter reality by physical means, but because the "relation between reality and our minds" is "just the opposite of" what "we naturally think." In fact, the human consciousness actually creates the world in which we live by enshrouding us in a "reality" generated by our own mental processes, so that anything we think consequently becomes true. "When we talk of reality 'independent' of human thinking," James says:

> then, it seems a thing very hard to find. It reduces to the notion of what is just entering into experience and yet to be named, or else to some imagined aboriginal presence in experience...before any human conception had been applied....We may glimpse it, but we never grasp it; what we grasp is always some substitute for it which previous human thinking has peptonized and cooked for our consumption. If so vulgar an expression were allowed us, we might say that wherever we find it, it has already been *faked* [italics James']. This is what [pragmatist philosopher] Mr. [F.C.S.] Schiller has in mind when he calls independent reality a mere unresisting ὕλη [substance, or matter], which *is* [italics James'] only to be made over by us.

James then adds meretriciously: "Superficially this sounds like Kant's view...."[6]

Which is because it precisely is Kant's view. Kant, whose influence on the pragmatists is well known,[7] had said that because "space is not at all a quality of things in themselves, but a form of our sensuous faculty of representation; and that all objects in space are mere appearances, i.e., not things in themselves but representations of our sensuous intuition," that " 'all bodies, together with the space in which they are, must be considered nothing but mere representations in us, and exist nowhere but in our thoughts.' "[8] Because all things exist nowhere but in our thoughts, any thought which "works best in the way of leading us" can become true merely because we decide to think that it is true. Hence "[i]f theological ideas should do this, if the notion of God, in particular, should prove to do it, how could pragmatism possibly deny God's existence?"

And indeed, how could it? Because Pragmatism will not deny any idea that works best in the way of leading us, James says:

> A pragmatist turns his back resolutely and once for all up-on....abstraction...verbal solutions...fixed principles, closed systems, and pretended absolutes....He turns towards...action and towards power....It means the open air and possibilities...as against dogma, artificiality, and the pretence of finality in truth.
>
> At the same time it does not stand for any special results. It is a method only....
> ....
>
> *Theories thus become instruments, not answers*....Pragmatism unstiff-ens all our theories...and sets each one at work. Being nothing essentially new, it harmonizes with many ancient philosophic tendencies. It agrees with nominalism for instance, in always appealing to particulars; with utilitarianism in emphasizing practical aspects; with positivism in its disdain for verbal solutions...and metaphysical abstractions.
>
> All these, you see, are anti-intellectualist tendencies. Against rationalism as a pretension and a method, pragmatism is fully armed and militant. But, at the outset, at least, it stands for no particular results. It has no dogmas, and no doctrines save its method....
>
> No particular results then...but only an attitude of orientation, is what the pragmatic method means. *The attitude of looking away from first things, principles...and of looking towards...fruits, consequences* [italics James'].... [9]

The pragmatic method means looking away from fixed princi-ples while at the same time being willing to accept any theory that "works" because Pragmatism is, as James coyly acknowledges, based on Kantianism. Kantianism, recall, is at once completely skeptical—it says that real knowledge is beyond our reach—while at the same time advocating blind confidence in faith, because our minds actually create the worlds which we believe in. So following Kant, the pragmatists dismiss fixed principles as inapplicable to a reality that is "faked" by human consciousness, while at once being willing to accept any idea that works as a means to the fruits that the pragmatists pursue. But in a world in which fixed principles are inapplicable, what would these fruits be? James offers some insights:

> ...Messrs. [F.C.S] Schiller and [John] Dewey appear with their pragmatistic account of what truth everywhere signifies. Everywhere, these teachers say, 'truth' in our ideas and beliefs means....nothing but this, *that ideas...become true just in so far as they help us to get into satisfactory relation with other parts of our experience*....Any idea upon which we can ride, so to speak; any idea that will carry us prosperously from any one part of our experience to any other part, linking things satisfactorily...is true for just so much, true in so far forth, true *instrumentally* [italics James']. This is the 'instrumental' view...that truth in our ideas means their power to "work"....
>
> ....
>
> We say this theory solves it on the whole more satisfactorily than that theory; but that means more satisfactorily to ourselves, and individuals will emphasize their points of satisfaction differently. To a certain degree, therefore, everything here is plastic.[10]

So everything is "plastic" and truth is, in essence, what satisfies, James indicates. Yet James protested the charge that the pragmatists were merely "satisfaction" seeking hedonists:

> When Messrs. Schiller and Dewey now explain what people mean by truth, they are accused of denying *its* [italics James'] ex-

istence. These pragmatists destroy all objective standards, critics say, and put foolishness and wisdom on one level. A favorite formula for describing Mr. Schiller's doctrines and mine is that we are persons who think that by saying whatever you find it pleasant to say and calling it truth you fulfil [sic] every pragmatistic requirement.

I leave it to you to judge whether this be not an impudent slander....The unwillingness of some of our critics to read any but the silliest of possible meanings into our statements is as discreditable to their imaginations as anything I know in recent philosophic history. Schiller says that the true is that which "works." Thereupon he is treated as one who limits verification to the lowest material utilities. Dewey says truth is what gives "satisfaction." He is treated as one who believes in calling everything true which, if it were true, would be pleasant.

Our critics certainly need more imagination of realities.[11]

So let us put our imaginations to work and try to guess what real purposes the pragmatists may intend to serve by their philosophizing—purposes which might not be so silly. We have already read James attribute to Pierce the notion that, for pragmatists, the sole significance of a thought is the conduct the thought is fitted to produce. And we have noted his assertion that the test of truth is what works best "in the way of leading us." So given the parallel significance James places on the achievement of satisfaction as a test of truth would we not be justified in imagining that the principal purpose of Pragmatism is that of altering people's conduct in ways which pragmatists find satisfying?

And while we are entertaining this surmise might it not also be prudent to remind ourselves again of James' expressed contempt for abstractions and fixed principles? Pragmatists turn their backs resolutely on abstractions and fixed principles, James says, and turn instead toward action and toward power. But free societies are based on abstractions and principles which define the liberal rights of individual citizens, while authoritarian societies may fairly be described as sustained by behaviors which are for all intents and purposes morally unprincipled. So recalling Mussolini and Gentile's enthusiasm for the use of pragmatic arguments is it not reasonable to speculate that the originators of Pragmatism—Pierce, James, and John Dewey—may also have been, like the Italian fascists, politically authoritarian?

We previously observed that Pragmatism is based on Kantian arguments and observed also the use to which such arguments have been put by the Nazis and the Marxists. But before we allow ourselves to suspect such venerable philosophic scholars as Dewey and James of authoritarian leanings we should review their overtly political statements, in addition to their epistemological and metaphysical positions. As he is considered the most influential of Pragmatism's originators we will focus on William James' statements concerning politics and political philosophy. Consider these passages from James' essay *The Moral Equivalent of War*:

"Militarism is the great preserver of our ideals of hardihood, and human life with no use for hardihood would be contemptible," James says, making his case for the imposition of martial principles of government upon the civilian population of the United States:

> The duty is incumbent on mankind, of keeping military characters in stock...as ends in themselves and as pure pieces of perfection,— so that [Theodore] Roosevelt's weaklings and mollycoddles may not end by making everything else disappear from the face of nature....
>
> ....
>
> [M]ankind was nursed in pain and fear, and...the transition to a "pleasure economy" may be fatal to a being wielding no powers of defense against its disintegrative influences....

....

All the qualities of a man acquire dignity when he knows that the service of the collectivity that owns him needs them....No collectivity is like an army for nourishing such pride....It is obvious that the United States of America as they exist to-day impress a mind...as so much human blubber. Where is the...contempt for life, whether one's own or another's? Where is the savage "yes" and "no," the unconditional duty? Where is the conscription? Where is the blood tax? Where is anything that one feels honored by belonging to?

Having said thus much in preparation, I will now confess my own utopia. I devoutly believe in the reign of peace and in the gradual advent of some sort of a socialistic equilibrium....

All these beliefs of mine put me squarely into the anti-militarist party. But I do not believe that peace either ought to be or will be permanent on this globe, unless the states...preserve some of the old elements of army-discipline. A permanently successful peace-economy cannot be a simple pleasure-economy. In the more or less socialistic future towards which mankind seems to be drifting we must still subject ourselves collectively to... severities....We must make new...hardihoods continue the manliness to which the military mind so faithfully clings. Martial virtues must be the enduring cement;..contempt for softness, surrender of private interest, obedience to command, must still remain the rock upon which states are built—unless...we wish for dangerous reactions against commonwealths fit only for contempt....

The war-party is assuredly right in affirming and reaffirming that the martial virtues...are absolute and permanent human goods....They are its first form, but that is no reason for supposing them to be its last form....[W]ith time and education and suggestion enough....[w]hy should men not some day feel that it is worth a blood-tax to belong to a collectivity?...Why should they not blush with indignant shame if the community that owns them is vile in any way whatsoever?...It is only a question of blowing on the spark till the whole population gets incandescent, and on the ruins of the old morals of military honour, a stable system of morals of civic honour builds itself up. What the whole community believes in grasps the individual as in a vise. The war-function has graspt us so far; but constructive interests may some day seem no less imperative, and impose on the individual a hardly lighter burden.

Let me illustrate my idea more concretely. There is nothing to make one indignant in the mere fact that life is hard, that men should toil and suffer pain....If now—and this is my idea—there were, instead of military conscription a conscription of the whole youthful population to form for a certain number of years a part of the army enlisted against *Nature*...numerous...goods to the commonwealth would follow. The military ideals of hardihood and discipline would be wrought into the growing fibre of the people; no one would remain blind as the luxurious classes now are blind, to man's real relations to the globe he lives on, and to the permanently sour and hard foundations of his higher life. To coal and iron mines, to freight trains, to fishing fleets in December, to dish-washing, clothes-washing, and window-washing, to road-building and tunnel-making, to foundries and stoke-holes...would our gilded youths be drafted off...to get the child-ishness knocked out of them....They would have paid their blood-tax....

....

I spoke of the "moral equivalent" of war. So far, war has been the only force that can discipline a whole community, and until an equivalent discipline is organized, I believe that war must have its way. But I have no serious doubt that the ordinary prides and shames of social man, once developed to a certain intensity, are capable of organizing such a moral equivalent as I have sketched...for preserv-ing manliness....It is but a question of time, of skillful propagan-dism, and of opinion-making men seizing historic opportunities.

The martial type of character can be bred without war....and we should all feel some degree of it imperative if we were conscious of our work as an obligatory service to the state. We should be *owned*, as soldiers are by the army....We could be poor, then, without humiliation....The only thing needed henceforward is to inflame the civic temper as past history has inflamed the military temper. H.G. Wells, as usual, sees the center of the situation....

....

Wells...thinks that the conceptions of order and discipline...unstinted exertion, and universal responsibility, which universal military duty now is teaching European nations, will remain...permanent...when the last ammunition has been used in the fireworks that celebrate the final peace. I believe as he does.[12]

The most disturbing thing about these excerpts is that they were written by an educator who spent most of his career teaching philosophy at Harvard University, where he was in a position to influence future leaders such as Theodore Roosevelt and Franklin Delano Roosevelt. That the political sentiments in these passages are authoritarian in nature is obvious; but because this section of the study pertains to epistemology let us focus on the relationship between James' epistemological philosophy and his fascistic politics. How, for instance, are these passages relevant to James' statements that a pragmatist "turns away from abstraction and...fixed principles,"[13] and turns instead towards "any idea that will carry us prosperously from any part of our experience to any other part, linking things satisfactorily"?

Well, firstly, it is obvious from James' advocacy of "a stable system of morals" based on "martial virtues" and "ideals of hardihood" that he really has no fixed objection to fixed principles of morality after all. What James, like Mussolini, would object to is the fixed principles of political "liberalism" and "individualism" which could philosophically protect the people of the United States from James' martial principles of governance. But at the same time "any idea upon which we can ride" toward the imposition of martial government would, for James, "become true just in so far as they help us to get into satisfactory relation with other parts of our experience." Just so far, then, as it would have helped him satisfy his desire to impose martial systems of government on the American public James would have happily advocated "any idea."

The American public has been pitched the philosophy of Pragmatism on the basis of its representation as a policy of eschewing ideology in favor of practicality. But ideas—ideologies—are the intellectual basis of a free society and practices that are unmoored from liberal ideas will lead away from freedom, not toward it. James illustrates the connection between his Machiavellian epistemological philosophy and his unscrupulous moral philosophy in this passage from his book *Pragmatism: A New Name for Some Old Ways of Thinking*, published in 1907. " 'The *true*,' " James says, "*is only the expedient in the way of our thinking, just as 'the right' is only the expedient in the way of our behaving.* Expedient in almost any fashion [italics James']...."[14]

Expedient in this context refers to usefulness or utility. But usefulness as a measure of the truth of a thought or the right in behavior is meaningful only if the goals of our thoughts and behaviors are defined. In the absence of fixed principles, what would our goals be? James answers:

> [I]n seeking for a universal principle we inevitably are carried onward to the *most* universal principle,—that *the essence of good is simply to satisfy demand* [italics James']. The demand may be for anything under the sun. There is really no more ground for supposing that all our demands can be accounted for by one

universal underlying kind of motive than there is ground for supposing that all physical phenomena are cases of a single law.[15]

Pragmatism, then, is an epistemological philosophy that advocates the abandonment of principle in practice and the practice of promulgating any principle in order to meet any "demand." Because Pragmatism abandons all principles that demand can be "for anything under the sun." If it seems as though Pragmatism would make an ideal epistemological philosophy for an unscrupulous political criminal that is precisely because it would. In *Mein Kampf* Adolf Hitler demonstrates how useful a pragmatist epistemological philosophy can be to a person of evil intent. "[E]very idea, even the best..." Hitler says:

> becomes a danger if it parades as a purpose in itself, being in reality only a means to one. For me and all true National Socialists there is but one doctrine: people and fatherland....Every thought and every idea, every doctrine and all knowledge, must serve this purpose. And everything must be examined from this point of view and used or rejected according to its utility. Then no theory will stiffen into a dead doctrine....[16]

Every idea must demonstrate its utility to people and fatherland or risk being rejected, Hitler asserts. Even the best idea, Hitler says, becomes a danger if it is held to be immutably true in and of itself. Although Hitler may never have read a word of James, it is obvious that he, like Benito Mussolini, shared James' fundamental epistemological philosophy. We saw in the previously cited passages that James shared Hitler's essential political philosophy as well.

PART THREE

AUTHORITARIAN ETHICS

CHAPTER TEN

THE ETHICS OF THE SLAVES AND
THE ETHICS OF THE MASTERS

Now we will move on from the discussion of metaphysics and epistemology to the subject of ethics. By way of an introduction to
this topic we will say that ethics is the branch of philosophy which
is concerned with morality, and concerned also with formulating
codes of conduct which are or ostensibly are moral. If it seems as
though discussions of morality would be out of place in the study
of a subject as apparently immoral as authoritarianism then appearances in this instance are misleading. For authoritarian ideologues
are as concerned with human conduct—and with formulating theories of ethics and morality with which to manipulate it—as they are
with metaphysics and epistemology.

To understand the nature of authoritarian theories of ethics
and morality the first thing one needs to bear in mind is the nature
of authoritarian states. Authoritarian states are organizations of
thieves, and of the bullies and liars who facilitate thievery. Authoritarian ethical and moral theorists are members of the cadres of

liars who facilitate state thievery, and facilitating this thievery is the fundamental purpose of the ethical and moral theories that these lying ideologues concoct.

The second thing one needs to know about authoritarian ethics is that they are bisected into two distinct branches. This is because authoritarian societies themselves are sub-divided into two distinct classes, the oppressors and the oppressed, with distinct traditions of authoritarian ethical theory developed for each. The German existentialist philosopher Friedrich Nietzsche said that moral theories could be sub-divided into two categories, the morality of the slaves and the morality of the masters. While this is not true of moral theory generally it is true of the authoritarian moral theories with which Nietzsche was concerned. So we are going to follow Nietzsche in subtitling our discussion of authoritarian ethical theory The Ethics of the Slaves and The Ethics of the Masters.

THE ETHICS OF THE SLAVES: ASCETICISM, QUIETISM, AND DUTY

The ethics of the slaves are a body of ethical tenets that the oppressors teach to the people they oppress in order to convince them to submit to oppression, or even to oppress themselves. The ethics of the masters, conversely, are a body of ethical tenets that the oppressors teach to themselves, both to school themselves in a life of evil, and then to justify that life. We will consider the ethics of the masters a bit later on in our study, but will begin the survey of authoritarian ethics by examining the ethics of the slaves. These ethics may be roughly divided into three different categories of ethical concepts; those of *Asceticism*, of *Quietism*, and of *duty*.

Asceticism is a body of ethical tenets that encourage people to ignore or repress their desires and appetites. Ascetic ethics teach people to repress their emotional as well as their physical desires but they are especially identified with doctrines that advise people to repress their appetites for physical values such as food and sex, and material values such as clothes and cars and houses. In Western philosophy Asceticism is associated with the Cynic and Stoic schools of Greek philosophy and so the word *Stoicism* is frequently used to refer to ascetic ethics. But Asceticism as a recorded body of moral tenets goes back much further in history than Greek philosophy, and is an important aspect of most of the ancient religions.

Although Asceticism is most often associated with the repression of physical and material desires a particular aspect of the ascetic tradition emphasizes the repression of emotional impulses, action, and intellectual initiative. This aspect of Asceticism is sometimes referred to as Quietism, and encourages psychological placidity and executive as well as intellectual passivism. In the form of Stoic philosophy this quietist ethic of passivism and apathy is manifested in the Christian ascetic ethics that Stoicism famously influenced. But quietist ethics are also an important feature of the ancient eastern religions such as Buddhism and Hinduism.

A further aspect of the authoritarian ethics is the ethics of duty. Not the Western military officer's concept of duty which obligates him or her to fight to protect his own freedom and that of his fellow citizens, but a supernaturalist conception of duty that obligates the individual to serve, obey, and sacrifice his property and life to a supernatural being such as a god. Every major religion gives prominent expression to this supernaturalist conception of duty, but in modern times secular authoritarian ideologies such as Fascism and Socialism have promulgated versions of this concept as well. These modern, secular authoritarian ideologies, however, have substituted a secularized version of this doctrine in place of an explicitly theistic one, so that "Society," or the "State," or "the

Race," are owed duty, obedience, and sacrifice, rather than Jehovah, or Krishna, or Allah.

ASCETICISM, IDEALISM, AND DUALISM

The function of ascetic doctrines in authoritarian states is to teach people to repress the physical and material appetites that the authoritarian state is going to frustrate anyway and to encourage passivity in the face of the moral outrages imposed upon a population by a malicious state. By teaching people that the indulgence of physical appetites is morally debasing and that the pursuit of material values is immoral, authoritarian intellectuals hope to convince the state's victims that they should not care about the physical discomforts and material privations that result from the state's rapacity. And by teaching people that their emotions and thoughts will merely frustrate them or lead them down the primrose path to sin authoritarian ideologues hope to stifle the anger and discourage the critical thinking that might lead large numbers of people to rise up against the state. There are several arguments that the advocates of Asceticism use to convince people to repress both their physical and material appetites, as well as their impulse to act and to think. We will look at these one at a time and address their political purpose.

The most common arguments that ascetic ethical philosophers use to convince people to repress their physical and material appetites are based on idealist metaphysical premises. These premises are the *immaterialist* aspect of Idealism which says that reality is immaterial, or spiritual; the creationist aspect, which says that reality is the product of some mind, historically a god; and the organicist aspect, which says that reality is all part of one great organism—an implication of Immaterialism and Creationism which subsumes both the secular and the explicitly religious variations of Pantheism.

Ascetic doctrines which are based on the immaterialist aspect of Idealism say that because only the immaterial, or spiritual, is real—and because the material is illusionary and unreal—that human beings should ignore or repress their interest in things that are material and physical. This argument has its origins in religious or quasi-religious concepts of morality which equate spiritual reality with God and God with the morally good. A concern for the spiritual world, these concepts say, equates with moral good and with love for and obedience to God, while a concern for the illusionary world of the material equates with evil and rebellion against God. The reader should note that this dichotomization of reality into the spiritual realm of God and the good and the material realm of evil and illusion is an example of metaphysical Dualism.

Idealist metaphysical arguments are used by both religious and secular authoritarian dogmatists as premises for their ascetic ethics. And just as secular idealist metaphysical and epistemological arguments are usually just secularized versions of religious metaphysical Idealism, so secular versions of ascetic ethics are essentially just secularized forms of religious Asceticism. In this passage which we've cited before to illustrate the metaphysical aspects of secular authoritarian philosophy Benito Mussolini demonstrates how secularized idealist metaphysics provide premises for secularized ascetic arguments:

> There is no way of exercising a spiritual influence in the world as a human will dominating the will of others, unless one has a conception both of the transient and the specific reality on which that action is to be exercised, and of the permanent and universal reality in which the transient dwells and has its being....
>
> ....
>
> [M]any of the practical expressions of Fascism...can only be

understood when considered in relation to its general attitude toward life. A spiritual attitude….Fascism sees in the world not only those superficial, material aspects in which man appears as an individual, standing by himself, self-centered, subject to natural law which instinctively urges him toward a life of selfish momentary pleasure; it sees not only the individual but the nation and the country; individuals and generations bound together by a moral law...and a mission which suppressing the instinct for life closed in a brief circle of pleasure, builds up a higher life, founded on duty, a life free from the limitations of time and space, in which the individual, by self-sacrifice, the renunciation of self-interest, by death itself, can achieve that purely spiritual existence in which his value as a man consists….

. . . .

This positive conception of life is obviously an ethical one….Therefore life, conceived of by the Fascist, is serious, austere, religious; all its manifestations are poised in a world sustained by moral forces and subject to spiritual responsibilities. The Fascist disdains an "easy" life….

The Fascist conception of life is a religious one...in which man is viewed in his immanent relation to a higher law, endowed with an objective will transcending the individual and raising him to conscious membership of a spiritual society.[1]

Notice and compare Mussolini's disdain for the life of pleasure with James' reproach of the American "pleasure-economy" in the passages cited in the section on Pragmatism. Asceticism as a doctrine that censures the "'easy' life" in favor of a life of "duty," "self-sacrifice," austerity, and "death itself" is a time-honored aspect of the authoritarian philosopher's and theologian's ideological stock-in-trade. Mussolini's splitting of reality into "superficial, material aspects" in which individuals pursue their grubby personal satisfactions, and an ideal "higher life...in which the individual...by death itself, can achieve that purely spiritual existence" is an historically typical use of metaphysically dualistic premises to provide foundations for ascetic arguments. But as we noted earlier, such modern ascetic arguments are merely secularized versions of certain vastly older religious doctrines. Long before Benito Mussolini came to power in fascist Italy Catholic Italy had been intellectually saturated with ascetic ethics in the form of Christianity. Consider these examples of Idealism-based Christian ascetic statements excerpted from the New Testament:

> Do not love the world or anything in the world. If anyone loves the world, the love of the Father is not in him. For everything in the world—the cravings of sinful man, the lust of his eyes and the boasting of what he has and does—come not from the Father but from the world. The world and its desires pass away, but the man who does the will of God lives forever (1 John 2:15-17, NIV).

The material world and its desires shall pass away, but the world of the Father will last forever, John the Evangelist says in this passage which exhorts the human race to eschew the cravings of the sinful flesh. And in the following passage from Colossians Saint Paul cleaves the universe into the spiritual world above and the material world of earth below, encouraging people to abandon the world of matter and repress the lusts of their physical being:

> [S]et your hearts on things above, where Christ is seated at the right hand of God. Set your minds on things above, not on earthly things....
> Put to death, therefore, whatever belongs to your earthly nature: sexual immorality, impurity, lust, evil desires and greed, which is idolatry. Because of these, the wrath of God is coming (Col. 3:1, 2, 5, 6, NIV).

And Saint James in his Epistle contrasts the earthly world with the spiritual realm of heaven, blaming our pursuit of selfish pleasures on the influence of the former:

> But if you harbor bitter envy and selfish ambition in your hearts, do not boast about it or deny the truth. Such "wisdom" does not come down from heaven but is earthly, unspiritual, of the devil. For where you have envy and selfish ambition, there you will find disorder and every evil practice.
>
> But the wisdom that comes down from heaven is first of all pure....
>
> ....
>
> What causes fights and quarrels among you? Don't they come from your desires that battle within you? You want something but don't get it. You kill and covet, but you cannot have what you want. You quarrel and fight. You do not have, because you do not ask God. When you ask, you do not receive, because you ask with wrong motives, that you may spend what you get on your pleasures.
>
> You adulterous people, don't you know that friendship with the world is hatred toward God? Anyone who chooses to be a friend of the world becomes an enemy of God (James 3:14-17, 4:1-4, NIV).

But centuries before Christian theologians began using idealist, immaterialist, and metaphysically dualistic premises to ground ascetic dogmas the religions that buttressed the despotisms of the Far East, most prominently Hinduism and Buddhism, were using these same doctrines to encourage physical and material self-denial. In these verses from Hinduism's *Bhagavad-gītā* Lord Krishna counsels His followers to avoid the deluding pleasures of the material world in order to attain entrance to His spiritual kingdom:

> 59. The embodied soul may be restricted from sense enjoyment, though the taste for sense objects remains....

....

62. While contemplating the objects of the senses, a person develops attachment for them, and from such attachment lust develops, and from lust anger arises.

63. From anger, delusion arises, and from delusion bewilderment of memory. When memory is bewildered, intelligence is lost, and when intelligence is lost, one falls down again into the material pool....

....

71. A person who has given up all desires for sense gratification, who lives free from desires, who has given up all sense of proprietorship, and is devoid of false ego—he alone can attain real peace.

72. That is the way of the spiritual and godly life, after attaining of which a man is not bewildered. Being so situated, even at the hour of death, one can enter into the kingdom of God.[2]

"There is another, eternal nature, which is transcendental to this manifested and unmanifested matter," Krishna says in chapter 8, verse 20 of the *Bhagavad-gītā*. "It is supreme and is never annihilated. When all in this world is annihilated, that part remains as it is."[3] And in the introduction to his translation of the *Bhagavad-gītā* His Divine Grace A. C. Bhaktivedanta Swami Prabhupāda explained how this metaphysical duality between material nature and "supreme" or "transcendental" nature provides a premise for Hindu ethical Asceticism:

> *Bhagavad-gītā* is meant to deliver one from the nescience of material entanglement....each of us is full of anxieties because of this material entanglement. Our existence is eternal, but somehow we are put into this position which is *asat*. *Asat* means unreal [italics original]....

....

[I]f we properly follow the instructions in *Bhagavad-gītā*, our lives will be purified, and we will reach our ultimate destination. This destination is also explained in *Bhagavad-gītā*:

Beyond this material sky is a spiritual sky. The material sky is temporary....But there is another nature, which is eternal.

....

Bhagavad-gītā gives us the opportunity to leave this material world and go to that eternal existence in the eternal abode of the Lord....This material world is like a shadow. In a shadow there cannot be any substance....In the reflection of the spiritual world there is no happiness, but in the spiritual world itself there is real happiness....Someone wants to become sir, lord, president or king. These designations belong to the body, but we do not....As long as we are attached to such designations, we are associated with the three modes or qualities of material nature. The Lord says that these attachments are due to our lust. We want to be lords over the material nature, and, as long as we want to lord it over material nature, there is no chance of going back to the spiritual kingdom of God. That eternal kingdom, which is not destructible like this material world, can be approached only by one who is not bewildered or attracted by this material nature.[4]

And the Buddhist tradition, also, uses the doctrine of the metaphysical duality between material nature and the spiritual, or ideal, kingdom as a foundation of ascetic ethics. In this passage from the *Dhammapada*, Buddha exhorts his followers:

409. Who, here in this world, does not take what
          is not given,
     Whether long or short, small or great,
     Pleasant or unpleasant,
     That one I call a *brāhmaṇa* [priest, or holy man].

410. In whom are not found longings
     For this world and for the beyond,
     Without longing, released,
     That one I call a *brāhmaṇa*.
     ....

414. Who has passed over this [muddy] path, this fortress,
     Delusion, which is *saṃsāra*,
     Who has passed over it, gone beyond it, a mediator,
     Passionless, without doubts,
     Without grasping, pacified,
     That one I call a *brāhmaṇa*.

415. Who, here, having renounced lusts,
     Would go forth, a homeless one,
     In whom is extinct sensual lust and existence,
     That one I call a *brāhmaṇa*.

416. Who, here, having renounced craving,
     Would go forth, a homeless one,
     In whom is extinct craving and existence,
     That one I call a *brāhmaṇa*.

417. Who, having abandoned the human bond,
     Has transcended the heavenly bond,
     Who is released from all bonds,
     That one I call a *brāhmaṇa*.

418. Who, having abandoned attachment and aversion,
     Who has become cool, free from substrates,
     A hero overcoming the entire world—
     That one I call a *brāhmaṇa* [italics original].[5]

And recall this passage from the Koran, cited earlier to high-

light Islam's metaphysics; it also illustrates how Islam uses ideal/
material duality to discourage attachment to material values:

> Know that the life of this world is but a game and pastime and
> show and boast among you: and multiplying riches and chil-
> dren is like rain, whose vegetation delighteth the infidels—then
> they wither away, and thou seest them all yellow, and they be-
> come chaff....[B]ut the life of this world is naught but a delusive
> joy. Strive together for forgiveness from your Lord and Para-
> dise, whose width is as the width of heaven and earth....[F]or
> God loveth not any presumptuous boasters, who are covet-
> ous....[6]

But abandoning attachment to material goods and the physical
pleasures and comforts they afford is not for everyone, authoritarians believe. It is not for God, or for God's priests, or for the
political enforcers of theocratic states who use religion to justify
their privileges. Traditionally, the priesthood of religion-based
states exhorts the common people to surrender material goods to
God, and then claim that the state, as God's representative on
earth, has a right to redistribute those goods as God commands.
These divine commands, of course, are communicated to the
people and to the agents of the state by those who claim to know
God personally—the priests themselves, who typically claim a share
of the people's sacrifices for their trouble. In the following text
from the *Bhagavad-gītā*, Lord Krishna—God, commands the common man to give up the fruits of his labor—and then his priest, in
this case His Divine Grace A. C. Bhaktivedanta Swami Prabhupāda,
interprets the verse as instructing the people to give these values to
God.

"Abandoning all attachment to the results of his activities,"
Lord Krishna says of His devoted followers, "ever satisfied and independent, he performs no fruitive action, although engaged in all

kinds of undertakings."[7] And Śrīla Prabhupāda interprets this verse as meaning that:

> This freedom from the bondage of actions is possible only in Kṛṣṇa consciousness when one is doing everything for Kṛṣṇa. A Kṛṣṇa conscious person acts out of pure love for the Supreme Personality of Godhead, and therefore he has no attraction for the results of the action. He is not even attached to his personal maintenance, for everything is left to Kṛṣṇa. Nor is he anxious to secure things, nor to protect things that are already in his possession. He does his duty to his best ability and leaves everything to Kṛṣṇa. Such an unattached person is always free from the resultant reactions of good and bad; it is as though he were not doing anything. This is the sign of *akarma*, [italics original] or actions without fruitive reactions.[8]

The *Bhagavad-gītā* pounds away at this notion. In chapter two, text forty-seven of Śrīla Prabhupāda's interpretation Krishna is represented as saying: "You have a right to perform your prescribed duty, but you are not entitled to the fruits of action."[9] And in chapter five, text ten, He says: "One who performs his duty without attachment, surrendering the results unto the Supreme God, is not affected by sinful action...."[10] And in text twelve of the same chapter He says that: "The steadily devoted soul attains unadulterated peace because he offers the results of all activities to Me; whereas a person who is not in harmony with the Divine, who is greedy for the fruits of his labor, becomes entangled."[11]

But it is not only Krishna who benefits from the common man's detachment from the fruits of his labor. Near the end of the *Bhagavad-gītā* some other intended beneficiaries are revealed as well:

> 11. The performance of sacrifice in terms of the directions of the

scriptures, as a matter of duty and with no desire for material results, is said to be in the mode of goodness....

....

13. Any sacrifice performed...without priestly remuneration [payment]...must be considered to be in the mode of darkness.

14. Austerity of the body consists of offering worship to the Supreme Lord, to *brāhmaṇas* [italics original], to the spiritual master, and to superiors....[12]

The *brāhmaṇas*, or Brahmin, of course, are the Hindu priest-class who self-servingly put such words in Krishna's mouth.

ASCETICISM AND SOUL/BODY DUALISM

But splitting the universe into two opposed realms of the metaphysically ideal and the metaphysically material is not the only way in which dualistic metaphysical arguments are used to provide premises for ascetic ethical doctrines. An implication of spiritual/material metaphysical Dualism, one which applies this theory to human beings specifically rather than to the universe in general, is also used to ground these ethics. Such doctrines, referred to as *Soul/Body Dualism* or *Mind/Body Dualism* by some scholars and as the *Mind/Body Dichotomy* by others, split human nature itself into two conflicting spheres of the spiritual and the physical. Ascetic ethical doctrines based on such theories say that in order to be moral human beings must forsake that part of themselves which is physical and cultivate that part which is spiritual. They are to do this, according to these doctrines, by repressing their physical desires and suppressing their material appetites.

One of the classic expressions of Soul/Body Dualism has already been cited in this study in the section on metaphysics. St.

Paul asserts that the laws to which human beings are properly subject are spiritual but that human beings themselves are actually physical. Paul feels that he himself is being split in two by his desire to live by the laws of the spirit—a desire which places his soul at odds with the raging appetites of his body. Here repeated is the anguished cry of a man who is being pulled apart by his own attempt to live by ascetic ethics:

> We know that the law is spiritual; but I am unspiritual, sold as a slave to sin. I do not understand what I do. For what I want to do I do not do, but what I hate I do. And if I do what I do not want to do, I agree that the law is good. As it is, it is no longer I myself who do it, but it is sin living in me. I know that nothing good lives in me, that is, in my sinful nature. For I have the desire to do what is good, but I cannot carry it out. For what I do is not the good I want to do; no, the evil I do not want to do—this I keep on doing. Now if I do what I do not want to do, it is no longer I who do it, but it is sin living in me that does it.
>
> So I find this law at work: When I want to do good, evil is right there with me. For in my inner being I delight in God's law; but I see another law at work in the members of my body, waging war against the law of my mind and making me prisoner of the law of sin at work within my members. What a wretched man I am! Who will rescue me from this body of death? (Rom. 7:14-24, NIV).

Saint Paul says that he will be rescued from his sinful body by the spirit of God that resides within him. Most dualistic soul/body doctrines say that the part of a human being which is physical is controlled by the Satanic forces of the material universe, while the part which is spiritual is controlled by—or even is, the spirit of God. All that people need to do to escape the soul-damning desires of their bodies and lead a blessed life of Asceticism, these doctrines say, is permit themselves to be controlled by the mind of Christ (or whatever god they believe in) that operates within them. Then they can live in peace with themselves, and indeed, as an aspect of God, they can live forever. Saint Paul continues:

> [T]hrough Christ Jesus the law of the Spirit of life set me free from the law of sin and death. For what the law was powerless to do in that it was weakened by the sinful nature, God did by sending his own Son....And so he condemned sin in sinful man, in order that the righteous requirements of the law might be fully met in us, who do not live according to the sinful nature, but according to the Spirit.
>
> Those who live according to the sinful nature have their minds set on what that nature desires; but those who live in accordance with the Spirit have their minds set on what the Spirit desires. The mind of sinful man is death, but the mind controlled by the Spirit is life and peace; the sinful mind is hostile to God. It does not submit to God's law, nor can it do so. Those controlled by the sinful nature cannot please God.
>
> You, however, are controlled not by the sinful nature but by the Spirit, if the Spirit of God lives in you. And if anyone does not have the Spirit of Christ, he does not belong to Christ. But if Christ is in you, your body is dead because of sin, yet your spirit is alive because of righteousness. And if the Spirit of him who raised Jesus from the dead is living in you, he who raised Jesus from the dead will also give life to your mortal bodies through his Spirit, who lives in you.
>
> Therefore, brothers, we have an obligation—but it is not to the sinful nature, to live according to it. For if you live according to the sinful nature, you will die; but if by the Spirit you put to death the misdeeds of the body, you will live... (Rom. 8:2-13, NIV).

And Hinduism also employs Soul/Body Dualism as a premise of ascetic ethics. In these passages from the *Bhagavad-gītā* Krishna assures his soldiers that they may fight in his wars without fear of death, for their souls will live on even after their bodies are slain:

17. That which pervades the entire body is indestructible. No one is able to destroy the imperishable soul.

18. Only the material body of the indestructible, immeasurable, and eternal living entity is subject to destruction; therefore, fight, O descendant of Bharata.

19. He who thinks that the living entity is the slayer, or that the entity is slain, does not understand. One who is in knowledge knows that the self slays not nor is slain.

20. For the soul there is never birth nor death. Nor, having once been, does he ever cease to be. He is unborn, eternal, everexisting, undying and primeval. He is not slain when the body is slain.

....

25. It is said that the soul is invisible, inconceivable, immutable and unchangeable. Knowing this you should not grieve for the body.

....

30. O descendant of Bharata, he [the soul] who dwells in the body is eternal and can never be slain. Therefore you need not grieve for any creature.

31. Considering your specific duty as a *kṣatriya* [member of the soldier caste in the Hindu class system. Italics original] you should know that there is no better engagement for you than fighting on religious principles; and so there is no need for hesitation.

32. O Pārtha, happy are the *kṣatriyas* [italics original] to whom

such fighting opportunities come unsought, opening for them the doors of the heavenly planets.

33. If, however, you do not fight this religious war, then you will certainly incur sin for neglecting your duties and thus lose your reputation as a fighter.

....

37. O son of Kuntī, either you will be killed on the battlefield and attain the heavenly planets, or you will conquer and enjoy the earthly kingdom. Therefore, get up and fight with determination.

38. Do thou fight for the sake of fighting, without considering happiness or distress, loss or gain, victory or defeat—and, by so doing, you shall never incur sin.[13]

"A person who neither rejoices upon achieving something pleasant nor laments upon obtaining something unpleasant...is to be understood as already situated in transcendence,"[14] Krishna later says in the *Bhagavad-gītā*; and Śrīla Prabhupāda interprets this statement as meaning that one should not be:

> ...illusioned by the false identification of the body with the true self. He knows perfectly well that he is not this body, but is the fragmental portion of the Supreme Personality of Godhead. He is therefore not joyful in achieving something, nor does he lament in losing anything related to this body.[15]

And this same idea was given secular expression thousands of years after the *Bhagavad-gītā* was written by Mussolini, who replaced the Supreme Personality of Godhead with what he called "an objective will transcending the individual and raising him to conscious membership of a spiritual society." This will was the societal equivalent of the will of God commanding the individual to forgo the "'easy' life" in order to meet his "spiritual responsibilities" to the spiritual society of which he is a member. Mussolini acknowledges his debt to religion in this excerpt which we've cited in earlier sections to illustrate different facets of the authoritarian philosophical tradition:

> [L]ife, as conceived of by the Fascist, is serious, austere, religious; all its manifestations are poised in a world sustained by moral forces and subject to spiritual responsibilities. The Fascist disdains an "easy" life.
>
> The Fascist conception of life is a religious one, in which man is viewed in his immanent relation to a higher law, endowed with an objective will transcending the individual and raising him to conscious membership of a spiritual society.[16]

But as an ethic of detachment from material values and forbearance of physical pleasures and comforts Asceticism has not only been founded on the ideal/material, heavenly/earthly metaphysical Dualism outlined in the last few pages. Several other types of metaphysical arguments, which like these are related to metaphysical Idealism, have also provided these premises. The Idealism-based creationist and organicist arguments which we mentioned a bit earlier have frequently been employed to ground Asceticism in metaphysical theory. Let us now give some consideration to these arguments.

ASCETICISM, CREATIONISM, AND ORGANICISM

Creationism is the belief that reality is created by some supernatural being, usually a god or something that is described as having the powers of a god. Organicism—in the realm of philosophy—is the belief that the entire universe is one great organism, typically a pantheistic god or something that has the omnipresent qualities of a pantheistic god. In formal philosophy the word Monism is usually used to refer to doctrines that describe the universe in organicist terms, but we are using the word Organicism for this purpose because using this term helps us better understand the relationship between monistic metaphysical theories and the authoritarian theory of politics known as the *organic theory of the state*. Monism, just as a reminder, is the theory that reality is just one thing and has but one nature—an idea that subsumes organicist doctrines such as Pantheism.

Creationism provides premises for ascetic ethical doctrines by grounding the notion that some great being—customarily a god or something that is like a god—owns everything because it creates everything. Beginning from this premise authoritarian ethical philosophers say that human beings have a duty to use material values as their owner, God, wants them to be used—and have no right to luxuriate in these values as they privately choose. Organicist—usually pantheistic—doctrines, by contrast, provide a foundation for ascetic doctrines by proposing that because God (or something that is like God) is all things, that only God has a right to enjoy material things. This idea is used in turn by ascetic ethicists to ground the notion that people must use physical values as God commands, and have no right to use these values for their own enjoyment.

The Hindu religion, in addition to using doctrines which are metaphysically immaterialist and dualistic to provide premises for ascetic ethics, also makes use of creationist and organicist metaphysical doctrines. In his introduction to his widely-distributed translation of the *Bhagavad-gītā* Hindu swami Śrīla Prabhupāda describes how Hindu theology uses both Creationism, as well as that religious form of Organicism which is Pantheism, to ground the ascetic idea that people should not indulge in physical pleasures such as the eating of food. Śrīla Prabhupāda begins by asserting the pantheistic and creationist premises that all things are part of God and that God is the creator of all values, and then goes on to explain how these assumptions lead to ethical conclusions which are ascetic:

> [B]ecause we are only parts, we tend to be affected by the modes of nature. That is the difference between the individual living entities [individual people] and the Supreme Lord. In contamination [in the state of matter], consciousness says, "I am the Lord. I am the enjoyer." Every material being thinks this. Consciousness has two psychic divisions: One says, "I am the creator," and the other says, "I am the enjoyer." Actually, the Lord is the creator and the enjoyer. The entity [the individual person] cooperates like a part in a machine. In a body, for example, there are hands, legs, eyes, etc. But these parts are not the enjoyers. The stomach [God] is the enjoyer. All the parts of the body are engaged in satisfying the stomach. All food should be given to the stomach. You can become healthy throughout your entire body when the parts of the body cooperate with the stomach. Similarly, the Lord is the enjoyer, and we living beings have only to cooperate with Him. If the fingers try to enjoy the food, they are unable. They must give the food to the stomach in order to receive the benefit of it.
>
> The central figure in existence is the Supreme Lord. The entities, by cooperation, can enjoy. If a master is satisfied, his servants are also satisfied, of course. The entities have this tendency [ability] to create and enjoy because the Lord has it, and the entities are His parts and parcels.[17]

Krishna promises his followers that "[t]hose who are free from anger and all material desires...are assured of liberation in the Supreme in the very near future," and adds:

> 27-28.   Shutting out all external sense objects...the

transcendentalist becomes free from desire....One who is always in this state is certainly liberated.

29.   The sages, knowing Me as the ultimate purpose of all sacrifices and austerities, the Supreme Lord of all planets and demigods, and the benefactor and well-wisher of all living entities, attain peace from the pangs of material miseries.[18]

And secular authoritarians also use creationist and organicist metaphysical premises as grounds for their ascetic exhortations. Here Adolf Hitler, who like most Nazi ideologues thought society an organismic aspect of the larger organism which was the whole universe,[19] harangues the German people to sacrifice their happiness and prosperity to the interests of the living social organism of which they are merely parts. Hitler wrote in *Mein Kampf*:

As soon as this sense [of sacrifice] extends beyond the narrow limits of the family, the basis for the formation of larger organisms and finally formal states is created....This self-sacrificing will to give one's personal labor and if necessary one's own life for others is most strongly developed in the Aryan....In him the instinct of self-preservation has reached the noblest form, since he willingly subordinates his own ego to the life of the community....

....

This state of mind, which subordinates the interests of the ego to the conservation of the community, is really the first premise of every human culture. From it alone can arise all the great works of mankind, which bring the founder little reward, but the richest blessings to posterity. Yes, from it alone can we understand how so many are able to bear up faithfully under a scanty life which imposes on them nothing but poverty and frugality, but gives the community the foundations of its existence. Every worker, every peasant, every inventor, official, etc., who works without ever being able to achieve any happiness or prosperity for himself is representative of this noble idea, even if the deeper meaning of his activity remains hidden from him.[20]

And Benito Mussolini, too, employed organicist doctrines in order to provide a metaphysical premise for exhorting people "to bear up faithfully under a scanty life" of "nothing but poverty and frugality." In the passage we cited earlier to demonstrate his use of immaterialist rationales for Asceticism Mussolini also offered what he referred to as "an organic conception of the world" as a grounds for rejecting "a life of selfish momentary pleasure...." Here is that passage from *The Doctrine of Fascism* again, with the segment expressing Mussolini's organismic world-view included:

> There can be no conception of the State which is not fundamentally a conception of life: philosophy or intuition, system of ideas evolving within the framework of logic or concentrated in a vision or a faith, but always, at least potentially, an organic conception of the world.
>
> Thus many of the practical expressions of Fascism...can only be understood when considered in relation to its general attitude toward life. A spiritual attitude. Fascism sees in the world not only those superficial, material aspects in which man appears as an individual...subject to a natural law which instinctively urges him to a life of selfish, momentary pleasure; it sees... individuals and generations bound together...which suppressing the instinct for [a] life...of pleasure, builds up to a higher life, founded on duty....[21]

As this and the other passages cited in this section indicate, there is a logically intimate relationship between the ways in which the immaterialist, the creationist, and the organicist aspects of

Idealism work together in order to provide grounds for ascetic ethics. All immaterialist arguments try to get us to abandon the illusory world of matter and accept a faith-based world in which God creates and ultimately is everything in order to separate us from the property and pleasures we have legitimately earned. For when people abandon the cursed world of matter for the blessed realm of the spirit they are abandoning the world of their legitimate claims on their right to relish the joys of life for an authoritarian world wherein only God and God's representatives have a right to enjoy anything. In that world, as Krishna says, "I am the only enjoyer."[22]

But teaching people to suppress their "instinct" for a "life of pleasure" and submit instead to "a higher life, founded on duty" is not the only purpose of ascetic ethics. A related function of Asceticism is that of rendering people emotionally inert and intellectually impotent before the moral outrages of authoritarian rule. This specialized function of Asceticism, which is frequently referred to as Quietism, aims to quiet people's psychological and intellectual resistance to the atrocities inflicted upon them by authoritarian regimes. It does this by teaching people to turn off their emotional responses and stifle their intellectual judgment.

QUIETISM

All of the better known and more influential instances of Quietism are religious. And like the other aspects of the ascetic ethical canon quietist ethics rely heavily on the dualist, the immaterialist, the creationist, and the organicist tenets of the idealist metaphysical tradition for their premises. The dualistic and immaterialist aspects of ascetic ethics teach people to turn off their emotional responses by encouraging them to withdraw emotionally from the material world and seek happiness instead in the spiritual.

The creationist doctrines support Quietism by teaching people that because God creates and provides all values that human beings must submit passively to God's will and defer placidly to His judgment. And those aspects of Asceticism which are based on Organicism teach people that because God is the only real individual that human individuals, as mere parts of God's body, must cooperate equanimously with each other and with the greater individual who is God.

The quintessential quietist doctrines are those of the Eastern religions and quasi-religions, such as Hinduism and Buddhism. The quietist doctrines of these religions and philosophies had and still have as their primary political purpose the tranquilizing of the desperate emotions of economically and politically (and even sexually) oppressed peoples. As the freedoms of the peoples of Western societies have progressively been eroded these Hindu and Buddhist forms of Quietism have become increasingly popular in the West—and more and more been popularized. Perhaps the reader knows someone who has taken up yoga, or, as it is known in the West, "transcendental meditation," in order to deal with the frustrations of living in an increasingly constricted political, social, and economic environment.

The discipline of yoga is the specific method by which the quietist ethics of Hinduism and Buddhism are practiced. This practice involves meditating upon the pacifying arguments offered to disciples in a psycho-theological effort to nullify the politically destabilizing anger that results from the thwarting of people's aspirations and the denial of their appetites. In this passage from the *Bhagavad-gītā* the Hindu god Krishna suggests that if a person will just release their attachment to the material world and to material values that they will be able to achieve a state of peaceful psychological equanimity. The argument is an example of a quietist tenet based upon metaphysical Dualism in that it opposes the delusional world of the material to a spiritual world "beyond all miseries":

48. Be steadfast in your duty, O Arjuna, abandon all attachment to success or failure. Such evenness of mind is called *yoga*.

49. O Dhanañjaya, rid yourself of all fruitive [productive, or materially profitable] activities by devotional service, and surrender fully to that consciousness. Those who want to enjoy the fruits of their work are misers.

50. A man engaged in devotional service rids himself of both good and bad actions even in this life. Therefore strive for this *yoga*, O Arjuna, which is the art of all work [italics original].

51. The wise, engaged in devotional service, take refuge in the Lord and free themselves from the cycle of birth and death by renouncing the fruits of action in the material world. In this way they can attain that state beyond all miseries.

52. When your intelligence has passed out of the dense forest of delusion, you will become indifferent to all that has been heard and all that is to be heard.[23]

But there is a flip side to the pursuit of *nirvāṇa* beyond that of the achievement of a state of indifference to good and bad, to success and failure, and to the compulsory surrender of the fruits of one's labor. To induce people to enter a state of quietist emotional anesthesia the apostles of yoga promise that if one completely withdraws from the material world one will not only escape from physical and psychological misery but will also enter an inner world of spiritual bliss which follows from the complete immersion of the self into God. Krishna says that:

21. Such a liberated person is not attracted to material sense pleasure, but is always in a trance, enjoying the pleasure within. In this way, the self-realized person enjoys unlimited happiness, for he concentrates on the Supreme.

22. An intelligent person does not take part in the sources of misery, which are due to contact with the material senses. O son of Kunti, such pleasures have a beginning and an end, and so the wise man does not delight in them.

23. Before giving up this present body, if one is able to tolerate the urges of the material senses and check the force of desire and anger, he is a *yogī* and is happy in this world [italics original].

24. One whose happiness is within, who is active within, who rejoices within and is illumined within, is actually the perfect mystic. He is liberated in the Supreme, and ultimately he attains the Supreme.[24]

And in his purport of a later passage concerning yoga Swami Prabhupāda explains that:

> The ultimate goal in practicing *yoga* is now clearly explained. *Yoga* practice is not meant for attaining any kind of material facility. One who seeks an improvement in health or aspires after material perfection is no *yogī*, according to *Bhagavad-gītā* [italics original]. Cessation of material existence does not mean entering into an existence of void, which is only a myth. There is no void anywhere within the creation of the Lord. Rather, the cessation of material existence enables one to enter into the spiritual sky, the abode of the Lord.[25]

But as was mentioned earlier dualistic arguments which malign material existence and extol the spiritual abode of the Lord are not the only metaphysical arguments employed as premises for quietist tenets. Metaphysical premises which are organicist, or, within the religious context of Hinduism, pantheist, also provide foundations for Hinduism's quietist doctrines. They accomplish this by reminding people that as mere cells in the body of a larger, divine or quasi-divine Self they must cooperate placidly with all of the other cells in that body, and submit passively to the greater Oneness of which everyone is part. In this excerpt from the *Śrī Īśopaniṣad* Hinduism's followers are enjoined to bear no animosity toward anything or anyone—a formula for complete political submissiveness—because all things are really part of Krishna:

> He who sees everything in relation to the Supreme Lord, who sees all entities as his parts and parcels and who sees the Supreme Lord within everything, never hates anything nor any being.[26]

One should never hate anything nor any being, this doctrine says, because in a universe where all things are part of the Supreme Lord there is no injustice. There is no injustice in such a universe because all political and economic events occur within the body of the same Self. Therefore one should adopt an attitude of tranquilized impartiality toward all people and all events knowing that there is no basis for complaints about fairness in a reality where all things are just aspects of the same thing. The *Bhagavad-gītā*, which represents Krishna as a quasi-pantheistic god, asserts that:

> 7. For one who has conquered the mind, the Supersoul [God] is already reached, for he has attained tranquility. To such a man happiness and distress, heat and cold, honor and dishonor are all the same.

> 8. A person is said to be established in self-realization and is

called a *yogī* [or mystic] [italics and brackets in original] when
he is fully satisfied by virtue of acquired knowledge and
realization. Such a person is situated in transcendence and is
self-controlled. He sees everything—whether it be pebbles,
stones or gold—as the same.

9. A person is said to be still further advanced when he regards
all—the honest well-wisher, friends and enemies, the envious,
the pious, the sinner and those who are impartial and
indifferent—with an equal mind.[27]

Hinduism, however, is not the only religion which employs
organicist doctrines as premises for quietist ethics. The Judeo-
Christian theological heritage also utilizes these doctrines to
support such mores, and Judaism's mystical Kabbalah clearly
expresses this. Recall this passage which was cited earlier in the
section on metaphysics to illustrate the metaphysical doctrine of
Organicism. Here it is cited again to illustrate a quietist ethic of
humility—which encourages passivity—that is based on organicist
metaphysics.

The essence of serving God and all of the *mitsvot* [i.e. divine
commandments; italics original] is to attain the state of humility,
that is, to understand that all your physical and mental powers
and your essential being depend on the divine elements within.
You are simply a channel for the divine attributes. You attain this
humility through the awe of God's vastness, through realizing
that there is "no place empty of it." Then you come to the state
of Ayin [i.e. nothingness], the state of humility. You have no independent self and are contained in the Creator. This is the
meaning of the verse: "Moses hid his face, for he was in awe."
Through his experience of awe, Moses attained the hiding of his
face, that is, he perceived no independent self. Everything was
part of divinity.[28]

The Kabbalah also interprets Christianity's Golden Rule in an organicist light, agreeing with Hinduism that this premise implies a quietest impartiality. "[Y]ou and your fellow are one and the same," the Kabbalah says. "That is why we are commanded: 'Love thy neighbor as yourself.' You should...never denigrate him or wish for his disgrace."[29]

And indeed there is no religion which surpasses that with which the Golden Rule is most famously associated—New Testament Christianity—in its emphasis on Quietism. Although Christianity is only quasi-pantheistic in its metaphysical emphasis if Christian texts are read carefully the organicist metaphysical premises beneath its quietist exhortations are readily discernible. In his epistle to the Colossians Saint Paul calls on Christians to "forgive whatever grievances" they have because they are "members of one body":

> Bear with each other and forgive whatever grievances you may have against one another. Forgive as the Lord forgave you. And over all these virtues put on love, which binds them all together in perfect unity.
>
> Let the peace of Christ rule in your hearts, since as members of one body you were called to peace (Col. 3:13-5, NIV).

Such an entreaty to peace and to love may seem benevolently intended, but we can not overlook the explicitly authoritarian statements made by Saint Paul which were cited earlier—nor the connections between Christian doctrine, the Catholic Church, and the fifteen hundred year rule of theocratic feudalism and aristocracy in Europe. The next passage which we will cite, from chapter twelve of Paul's epistle to the Romans, renders more obvious the utility of Quietism to those who are intent on encouraging passivism in the face of evil:

Bless those who persecute you; bless and do not curse....
....

Do not repay evil for evil. Be careful to do what is right in the eyes of everybody. If it is possible, as far as it depends on you, live at peace with everyone. Do not take revenge, my friends, but leave room for God's wrath, for it is written: "It is mine to avenge; I will repay," says the Lord. On the contrary:

"If your enemy is hungry, feed him; if he is thirsty give him something to drink" (Rom. 12:14, 17-20, NIV).

But the most explicit statement of Quietism in the Bible is made by Christ himself in The Gospel According To Matthew. In these verses it is made plain that no resistance is permitted against those who do harm to individual human beings. With regard to this passage the philosopher John B. Noss wrote that "the hard rule is laid down that one should not resist with violence evil done to one's own self."[30] Concerning such resistance Christ says:

You have heard that it was said, 'Eye for eye, and tooth for tooth.' But I tell you, Do not resist an evil person. If someone strikes you on the right cheek, turn to him the other also. And if someone wants to sue you and take your tunic, let him have your cloak as well. If someone forces you to go one mile, go with him two miles. Give to the one who asks you, and do not turn away from the one who wants to borrow from you.

You have heard that it was said, 'Love your neighbor and hate your enemy.' But I tell you: Love your enemies and pray for those who persecute you, that you may be sons of your Father in heaven. He causes his sun to rise on the evil and the good, and sends rain on the righteous and the unrighteous (Matt. 5:38-45, NIV).

The idea that God bestows his blessings impartially upon the evil and the good can seem morally incomprehensible unless one continuously bears in mind the metaphysical premise of such moral Egalitarianism. Organicism, which again, within a religious context, is manifested as Pantheism, implies that there is no such thing as evil because all beings are really parts of one being. Paul references this in his letter to the Colossians when he says that "as members of one body you were called to peace." And his statement in Romans that one should "bless those who persecute you" is metaphysically underpinned a few verses earlier where he says that "just as each of us has one body with many members, and these members do not all have the same function, so in Christ we who are many form one body, and each member belongs to all the others" (Rom. 12:4, 5, NIV). Christ's own statement that we should "not resist an evil person" is given explanation in the Gospel According To John where Jesus says that "I am in my Father, and you are in me, and I am in you" (John 14:20, NIV). Why should we resist evil people in a universe where there is only *one person?*

The notion that we should not resist evil—and that we should forgive anyone against whom we have grievances—suggests a further implication of Christian Quietism: the idea that we should not judge. The maxim that human beings should relinquish their prerogative of judgment—and of moral appraisal—is perhaps the most vicious consequence of the quietist logic. Without the ability to make independent judgments about the goodness or evil of the people around us we are intellectually prostrate before the worst people in our midst. The Bible makes no statements which could have better prepared the people of Europe to submit to the tyranny of Christian feudalism than this one: "Brothers, do not slander one another," the Epistle of James says, seeming innocently to advise against malicious calumny, and then:

> Anyone who speaks against his brother or judges him speaks

against the law and judges it. When you judge the law, you are
not keeping it, but sitting in judgment on it. There is only one
Lawgiver and Judge, the one who is able to save and destroy. But
you—who are you to judge your neighbor? (James 4:11, 12,
NIV).

James' remonstrance slyly feints in the direction of a reasonable ethical proscription—to refrain from libelous gossip—and
then segues into a general injunction against making any judgments
about "the law" at all, whether divine, moral, or legal. And of
course James' reproof has a precedent in the most sacred text in the
New Testament—the renowned passages in Matthew wherein
Jesus says "Do not judge, or you too will be judged. For in the
same way you judge others, you will be judged, and with the
measure you use, it will be measured to you" (Matt. 7:1, 2, NIV).
Christ's warning crudely plays upon people's fears of being judged
themselves to intimidate them from morally assessing their peers,
and, by implication, their rulers. This statement is the ultimate expression of Quietism within the Christian creed.

But Christian Quietism has a foundation not only in the organicist doctrines we have discussed thus far, but also in the
metaphysical doctrine of Creationism. Recall the words of Martin
Luther cited earlier where Luther himself cites Saint Paul admonishing men not to "talk back to God" (Rom. 9:20, NIV). Paul
in that passage is himself paraphrasing the Old Testament prophet
Isaiah warning men not to question their "father" and their
"maker" about the "work of [His] hands." Isaiah's warning is an
instance of Quietism in that it encourages people to adopt an
attitude of intellectual passivity. Representing his own words as
those of God Isaiah says:

"Woe to him who quarrels with his Maker, to him who is but a
potsherd among the potsherds on the ground. Does the clay say

to the potter, 'What are you making?' Does your work say, 'He has no hands'?

Woe to him who says to his father, 'What have you begotten?' or to his mother, 'What have you brought to birth?'

This is what the Lord says—the Holy One of Israel, and its Maker: Concerning things to come, do you question me about my children, or give me orders about the work of my hands? It is I who made the earth and created mankind upon it" (Isaiah 45:9-12, NIV).

And this claim by God that His creation of the earth and mankind upon it gives Him the authority to use mankind as a potter uses pots brings us to the next section of our discussion of authoritarian ethics. For if God has a right to use human beings as though they were merely His possessions then human beings conversely have a duty to submit to being thus used. We will now examine this ethic of duty, and other concepts of morality which have similar implications.

CHAPTER ELEVEN

DUTY

The formal name of the study of theories of duty is *deontology*. This term derives from the Greek word *deon*, meaning moral duty or obligation. A duty is a moral and/or legal obligation binding upon a person or group to fulfill a particular responsibility or set of responsibilities. As this segment of our study is a discussion of authoritarian concepts of morality—specifically, of what we have called the "ethics of the slaves"—it is also a discussion of authoritarian deontological concepts.

Authoritarian doctrines of duty are intended to bind people to the fulfillment of obligations and responsibilities which they do not really have. The purpose of this moral bondage is to compel human beings to fulfill demands imposed upon them by authoritarian states. As we noted earlier a traditional way of buttressing false theories of morality is that of postulating false theories of reality—false theories of metaphysics—wherein false theories of morality may be made to seem true. The idea that there is a god who creates all values, for instance, can be used to provide a basis for the argument that people have a moral duty to submit to being used by this god—and, more significantly, by God's human representatives here on earth.

The idea that there is a god who creates all values is an example of the concepts we have identified as Theism and Creationism. As with other aspects of the "ethics of the slaves" authoritarian concepts of duty have usually been established upon such idealist assumptions, including those of Pantheism. But in the West, and especially in modern times, these metaphysical theories have been secularized, with the result that what are fundamentally religious doctrines are frequently represented as philosophic concepts which have little to do with religion. This discussion of authoritarian deontological concepts will consider both the religious and the secular variations of these ideas in order to help readers recognize ancient authoritarian tropes in modern secular guises.

Authoritarian concepts of duty which are based on explicitly religious versions of Creationism say that because God creates the values which human life depends upon that human beings have a moral obligation to serve God and repay Him for His providence. Political and economic structures which are established on these concepts say conversely that people must obey the governmental states which God establishes to administer His creation, and must make sacrifices to repay God for His beneficence. Deontological doctrines which are based on Pantheism typically say that because everyone is a part of God that people have a duty to serve God, just as the organs of a body have a duty to serve the larger self of which they are part. From this follows the notion that human beings must obey that aspect of God which is the state which He creates to control those parts of Himself which are individual human beings.

Human intellectual history is rife with examples of Creationism and Pantheism being used as premises for deontological theories. We have already touched upon some of the issues which pertain to this topic in the section on metaphysics, but we will now discuss these issues again, from a different perspective, emphasizing their ethical rather than their metaphysical import. Because Christianity provided the deontological concepts which buttressed the feudal theocracies from which the liberal West emerged—and against which it rebelled—let us consider the Christian notions of duty first before we move on to discuss other representations of these ethics. As an introduction to the Christian notion of duty please consider these words by philosophic scholar W.T. Jones:

> There can be no doubt...that Christianity, with its concept of an omnipotent Father who ought to be obeyed in all things, introduced a new emphasis into moral philosophy. Since, in the Christian view, God's commands are rules, the notion of right, or conformity to rule, became important. At the same time, Christian thinkers took up the Stoic emphasis on motivation. These two concepts came together in the notion not merely of punctilious conformity to rule but of conformity because the rule issues from the source it issues from. To conform to the rule because we fear punishment is of no account. And to do so because we hope to be rewarded for obedience, or because conformity is a means to happiness, is to "reduce" morality to the Greek type....From the Christian point of view, then, the morally good is a very special—one might even say a very peculiar—one. To act morally, a man must see that the act is right (that is, commanded) [parenthesis Jones'] and must do it because he sees that it is right. Thus a Christian ethics is likely to focus on the concept of duty as the exclusive moral motive.[1]

And Jones remarked of this same issue in another of his works:

...Christianity...emphasizes duty instead of interest. The Christian claims that doing one's duty (obeying God's commands) [parenthesis Jones'] is the good; this, the Christian recognizes, often conflicts not only with the individual's short range, but also with his long-range, interest.[2]

The Christian's duty, then, is obedience to God's commands—even if this does not result in any reward in the short range or in the long. Such a thoroughly self-abnegating concept of "the good" would seem morally ridiculous—Jones uses the word "peculiar"—unless it had some profound foundation in metaphysical theories of reality. Like all the major religions Christianity employs the doctrines of Creationism, Divine Providence as a feature of Creationism, and variations of the doctrine of Pantheism to provide these metaphysical foundations. As a prelude to a broader discussion of authoritarian concepts of duty let us examine the metaphysical premises of Christianity's ethics of obedience and self-sacrifice.

"The first article teaches that God is the Father, the creator of heaven and earth," Martin Luther says in a segment of the passage we cited earlier in the section on metaphysics. Luther is preparing us to accept our duty to serve and obey God by asserting that God created everything upon which human life depends—his representation of Divine Providence. Here we will cite from this same passage again, at greater length, to allow Luther to explain this doctrine himself:

> What is this? What do these words mean? The meaning is that I should believe that I am God's creature, that he has given to me body, soul, good eyes, reason, a good wife, children, fields, meadows, pigs, and cows, and besides this, he has given to me the four elements, water, fire, air, and earth. Thus this article teaches that you do not have your life of yourself, not even a

hair. I would not even have a pig's ear, if God had not created it for me. Everything that exists is comprehended in that little word "creator"....Therefore, everything you have, however small it may be, remember this when you say "creator," even if you set great store by it. Do not let us think that we have created ourselves, as the proud princes do.

At this time I speak only of these things, for the creator, the Father almighty, has still more in store [than I enumerate here] [brackets in original]. I believe that he has given to me my life, my five senses, reason, wife, and children. None of these do I have of myself. God is the "creator," that is, God has given to me everything, body and soul, including every member of the body. But if everything is the gift of God, then you owe it to him to serve him with all these things and praise and thank him, since he has given them and still preserves them....Note that I am basing [everything] [brackets in original] on the word "creator," that is, I believe that God has given to me body and soul, the five senses, clothing, food, shelter, wife, child, cattle, land. It follows from this that I should serve, obey, praise and thank him.[3]

At first glance this doctrine may not seem so severe—so "peculiar," as Jones puts it. For is Luther not merely recommending that we repay God with obedience in return for our partaking of His Providence? But the Christian notion of the relationship between Creator and creature is not one of mutually considerate reciprocity; rather, it is exemplified by Isaiah and Paul's analogy of the relationship between a potter and his pots. God has created "body, soul, including every member of the body," and in return, Isaiah and Paul say, asserts "the right to make out of the same lump of clay some pottery for noble purposes and some for common use...."[4]

It is this idea—that human beings are just so many pots to be used—that forms the basis of the Christian ethic of duty which Jones says is so "peculiar." In his essay *Secular Authority* Luther defends the absolute authority of God's state representatives on earth by asserting that "it is the same to God whether He deprives you of goods and life by a just lord or by an unjust. You are His creature, and He can do with you as He will...."⁵ This is the radical notion of Christian duty which Jones observes "conflicts not only with the individual's short range, but also with his long-range interest."

But this radical doctrine of complete self-abnegation in the service of God is not exclusively peculiar to Luther. Rather, it has deep roots in the thinking of that earliest of medieval theologians, Saint Augustine, as well as in the Old and New Testaments of the Bible. Here Augustine, whose ideas dominated medieval Europe until the revivification of the philosophy of Aristotle by Thomas Aquinas, lays down the foundation of a Christian ethic of duty based on Creationism which would form the basis of feudal notions of morality for the next nine hundred years. "[M]an was made upright," Augustine says in *The City of God*, "that he might not live according to himself, but according to Him that made him—in other words, that he might do His [God's] will and not his own...."⁶ If this was true then the first duty of every human being would be obedience, and Augustine confirms this view a few pages later:

> [B]y the precept He gave, God commended obedience, which is, in a sort, the mother and guardian of all the virtues in the reasonable creature, which was so created that submission is advantageous to it, while the fulfillment of its own will in preference to that of the Creator's is destruction....
>
> ....
>
> Our first parents [Adam and Eve] fell into open disobedience because already they were secretly corrupted; for the evil act had never been done had not an evil will preceded it. And what is the origin of our evil will but pride? For "pride is the beginning

of sin." And what is pride but the craving for undue exaltation? And what is undue exaltation, when the soul abandons Him to whom it ought to cleave as its end, and becomes a kind of end to itself. This happens when it becomes its own satisfaction....But man did not so fall away as to become absolutely nothing; but being turned toward himself, his being became more contracted than it was when he clave to Him Who supremely is. Accordingly, to exist in himself, that is, to be his own satisfaction after abandoning God, is not quite to become a nonentity, but to approximate to that. And therefore the Holy Scriptures designate the proud by another name, "self-pleasers." For it is good to have the heart lifted up, yet not to one's self, for this is proud, but to the Lord, for this is obedient, and can be the act only of the humble.[7]

"[W]e are God's workmanship, created in Jesus Christ to do good works, which God prepared in advance for us to do," Saint Paul says in his letter to the Ephesians (Eph. 2:10, NIV). Our duty, then, as God's creations, is obedience to God's will—not the fulfillment of our own.

DUTY AND ORGANICISM

The doctrine of Creationism is used by all the major religions to provide premises for religious concepts of duty and religious demands for obedience. But as was noted, a second religious premise, that provided by Pantheism, is just as ubiquitous in this regard. Pantheism provides premises for an ethics of duty by asserting that individuals owe service to God for the same reason that a cell in an organism owes service to the body of which it is part. Although most religions are only quasi or semi-pantheistic, yet all of them all employ this organicist argument to provide foundations for their concepts of ethics. In this passage from 1 Corinthians

Saint Paul explains why each one of us, as parts of one body, have a duty to obey the commands of the greater being of which we are members:

> There are different kinds of working, but the same God works all of them in all men.
>
> Now to each one the manifestation of the Spirit is given for the common good. To one there is given through the Spirit the message of wisdom, to another the message of knowledge by means of the same Spirit, to another faith by the same Spirit, to another gifts of healing by that one Spirit, to another miraculous powers, to another prophecy, to another distinguishing between spirits, to another speaking in different kinds of tongues, and to still another the interpretation of tongues.
>
> All these are the work of one and the same Spirit, and he gives them to each one, just as he determines.
>
> The body is a unit, though it is made up of many parts; and though all its parts are many, they form one body. So it is with Christ. For we were all baptized by one Spirit into one body— whether Jews or Greeks, slave or free—and we were all given the one Spirit to drink.
>
> Now the body is not made up of one part but of many. If the foot should say, "Because I am not a hand, I do not belong to the body," it would not for that reason cease to be part of the body. And if the ear should say, "Because I am not an eye, I do not belong to the body," it would not for that reason cease to be part of the body. If the whole body were an eye, where would the sense of hearing be? If the whole body were an ear, where would the sense of smell be? But in fact God has arranged the parts in the body, every one of them, just as he wanted them to be. If they were all one part, where would the body be? As it is, there are many parts, but one body.
>
> The eye cannot say to the hand, "I don't need you!" And the head cannot say to the feet, "I don't need you!..."

....

> Now you are the body of Christ, and each one of you is a
> part of it (1 Cor. 12:6-21, 27, NIV).

And if each one of us is part of the body of God then we must
do the work "he gives...to each...just as he determines,"—just as the
organs in a body must do the work assigned them in the service of
the organism of which they are part. We cannot go off and be an
end in ourselves because, metaphysically, we are not selves, but rather parts of the real Self who is God. And consider how this same
doctrine is manifested in the credos of the Eastern religions. In the
following passages Lord Krishna, as He is translated and interpreted by the Hindu theologian Śrīla Prabhupāda, explains why the
implications of metaphysical Organicism mean that all people owe
duty to Him.

"And when you have learned the truth," the Supreme Lord
Krishna says in the *Bhagavad-gītā*, "you will know that all living beings are but part of Me—and that they are in Me, and are Mine."[8]
In the next chapter Śrīla Prabhupāda elaborates on the idea that
everything is Lord Krishna's:

> Renunciation is complete when it is in the knowledge that ev-
> erything in existence belongs to the Lord and that no one should
> claim proprietorship over anything. One should understand that,
> factually, nothing belongs to anyone. Then where is the question
> of renunciation? One who knows that everything is Kṛṣṇa's
> property is always situated in renunciation. Since everything be-
> longs to Kṛṣṇa, everything should be employed in the service of
> Kṛṣṇa.[9]

Everything should be in the service of Krishna because everything is part of Krishna—and this includes human beings themselves. From this premise is derived the Hindu doctrine of duty,
which Śrīla Prabhupāda describes thus:

The criterion of perfection is to act in Kṛṣṇa consciousness, and not with a view to enjoying the fruits of work. To act in Kṛṣṇa consciousness is the duty of every living entity because we are constitutionally parts and parcels of the Supreme. The parts of the body work for the satisfaction of the whole body. The limbs of the body do not act for self-satisfaction, but for the satisfaction of the complete whole. Similarly, the living entity, acting for the satisfaction of the supreme whole, not for personal satisfaction, is the perfect *sannyāsī*, the perfect *yogī* [italics original]….[A] person acting in Kṛṣṇa consciousness works for the satisfaction of the whole, without self-interest. A Kṛṣṇa conscious person has no desire for self-satisfaction.[10]

And Krishna Himself confirms this vision of duty as selfless sacrifice:

10. One who performs his duty without attachment, surrendering the results unto the Supreme God, is not affected by sinful action, as the lotus leaf is untouched by water.

    ....

12. The steadily devoted soul attains unadulterated peace because he offers the results of all activities to Me; whereas a person who is not in harmony with the Divine, who is greedy for the fruits of his labor, becomes entangled.[11]

And Judaism, too, employs the doctrine of Organicism as a premise for notions of duty. We cite again this passage from the Kabbalah, this time inviting the reader to contemplate its deontological implications—its implications for doctrines of duty:

The essence of serving God and all of the *mitsvot* [divine commandments; italics original] is to attain the state of humility, that is, to understand that all your physical and mental powers and your essential being depend on the divine elements within. You are simply a channel for the divine elements. You attain this humility through the awe of God's vastness, through realizing that there is "no place empty of it." Then you come to the state of Ayin [nothingness], the state of humility. You have no independent self and are contained in the Creator. This is the meaning of the verse: "Moses hid his face, for he was in awe." Through his experience of awe, Moses attained the hiding of his face, that is, he perceived no independent self. Everything was part of divinity.[12]

And if everything is part of the divinity then everything has a duty to serve the divinity. You have no right to serve self-interest—except the legitimate self-interest of the divine Self of which you are part. But as was mentioned earlier authoritarian concepts of duty have both a theological and a philosophical, or secular, aspect. Modern versions of authoritarian doctrines of duty veer in the direction of the secular but are based on metaphysical concepts—Theism, Pantheism, and Creationism—that have their origins in religion. To illustrate the usefulness of the secularized versions of these concepts we remind the reader of this statement by the head of German Nazi Party ideology under Adolf Hitler, Alfred Rosenberg. The passage at once makes reference to a secular version of the organicist doctrine of Pantheism, and at the same time reveals why modern authoritarians need concepts of duty as much as did ancient authoritarians. In his *The Myth of the Twentieth Century* Rosenberg said:

> Employers and workers are not individualities in themselves but parts of an organic whole, without which they all would not signify anything. For this reason the freedom of action both of the employer and the laborer was necessarily restricted as the interests of the *Volk* demand.[13]

The Nazis thought the "Volk," in the words of Adolf Hitler,

"a national organism,"[14] which was "one mighty body corporate,"[15] and which ultimately constituted the whole universe. All things, including every employer and laborer, were duty-bound to serve the interests and meet the demands of this great organism, just as a person's arms and legs are duty-bound to meet the demands of the organic whole which is itself. Although the Nazis seem to have been influenced by the older, religious, and particularly the Hindu versions of this Pantheism-based doctrine,[16] their more immediate source of metaphysical inspiration were the German idealist philosophers who had in turn been inspired by Immanuel Kant.

Kant's metaphysical doctrines were themselves shot through with religious references. But Kant had moved metaphysical philosophy in a secular direction by postulating that it was the human mind itself, rather than the mind of God, which had created the universe. Thus created, the universe is an organism, Kant's philosophy says, and humanity, as an aspect of this organism, is also organismic.[17] Speaking of the "state" as the embodiment of the "body politic" which is humanity conceived of as a single organism, Kant said that "in a whole of this kind" every individual member "of the entire body...should have his position and function in turn defined by the idea of the whole."[18]

The idea that every individual should have his position and function determined by the idea of a "whole" has obvious ethical implications. And upon such concepts Kant's own ethic of duty was in part established. Although Kant was usually cagey about tying his ethics directly to their metaphysical premises, perhaps recognizing that moral doctrines are more vulnerable to rebuttal if their foundations are readily apparent, the passage just cited, and others in which he says such things as "the end [purpose] of creation" is "the observance of the holy duty that His law imposes on us"[19] reveal that Kant was dependent for the grounds of his ethics on classical metaphysical doctrines such as Organicism and

Creationism. We should expect, then, that he would espouse a doctrine of duty similar to the religious deontologies we have considered thus far—in which the individual was portrayed as either hopelessly indebted to a providential God or merely an obedient organ in a vast body politic.

And indeed, that is exactly what Kant did. His doctrine of duty required the individual to completely negate itself in a life of abject obedience and self-annulling sacrifice. The advantage of such a doctrine to authoritarians like the Nazis, who called Kant "the most sublime teacher of duty"[20] is easy to imagine. We will quote from Kant's opus at length in order to illustrate the emphasis which he placed upon this doctrine, and cite the Nazis' own statements concerning duty to show what they learned from their "teacher."

"[I]t is a duty to maintain one's life...," Kant says in the opening pages of his *Critique of Practical Reason*, in which his theory of duty is comprehensively laid out:

> But on this account the often anxious care which most men take for it has no intrinsic worth, and their maxim [motive] has no moral import. They preserve their life *as duty requires*, no doubt, but not *because duty requires*. On the other hand, if adversity and hopeless sorrow have completely taken away the relish for life; if the unfortunate one, strong in mind, indignant at his fate rather than desponding or dejected, wishes for death, and yet preserves his life without loving it—not from inclination or fear, but from duty—then his maxim has a moral worth.
>
> To be beneficent when we can is a duty; and besides this, there are many minds so sympathetically constituted that, without any other motive of vanity or self-interest, they find a pleasure in spreading joy around them, and can take delight in the satisfaction of others so far as it is their own work. But I maintain that in such a case an action of this kind, however proper, however amiable it may be, has nevertheless no true moral

worth, but is on a level with other inclinations, *e.g.* the inclination to honour, which, if it is happily directed to that which is in fact of public utility and accordant with duty, and consequently honourable, deserves praise and encouragement, but not esteem. For the maxim lacks the moral import, namely, that such actions be done *from duty*, not from inclination [italics Kant's]. Put the case that the mind of that philanthropist was clouded by sorrow of his own…extinguishing all sympathy with the lot of others, and that while he still has the power to benefit others in distress, he is not touched by their trouble because he is absorbed by his own; and now suppose that he tears himself out of this dead insensibility, and performs the action without any inclination to it, but simply from duty, then first has his action its genuine moral worth.[21]

But why must an action be performed simply from duty, "without any inclination to it," in order to have genuine moral worth? The political reason is that authoritarians intend to impose duties on their victims which they will have no inclination to obey. The deeper, metaphysical reason is that an organism considers the first virtue of its appendages—its arms and legs and other organs—to lie in their willingness to do exactly what they are told, regardless of their own inclinations. In the next passages Kant explains that an action derives its moral worth from the "maxim" that motivates it—the willingness to act from duty, from obedience, not from a desire to achieve any particular ends. "[A]n action done from duty derives its moral worth," Kant says:

not from the purpose which is to be attained by it, but from the maxim by which it is determined, and therefore does not depend on the realization of the object of the action, but merely on the *principle of volition* [italics Kant's] by which the action has taken place, without regard to any object of desire. It is clear from what precedes that the purposes which we may have in view in our actions...cannot give to actions any unconditional or moral worth. In what, then, can their worth lie, if it is not to consist in the will and in reference to its expected effect? It cannot lie anywhere but in the *principle of the will* [italics Kant's] without regard to the ends which can be attained by the action....and as it must be determined by something, it follows that it must be determined by the formal principle of volition *when an action is done from duty* [emphasis added], in which case every material principle has been withdrawn from it.[22]

In other words, an action is moral when it is done in accordance with the maxim of duty, not when it is motivated by a desire to accomplish any particular purpose. A concern for purpose, after all, is the prerogative of a sovereign self, not of a hand or a foot or some other appendage—their function is but to obey. But who is this sovereign self whose commands we are duty-bound to obey? For Kant it is the state, whose commands are communicated to us by laws. Kant, the professional state-philosopher, wrote:

> *Duty is the necessity of acting from respect for the law*....simply the law of itself, which can be an object of respect, and hence a command. Now an action done from duty must wholly exclude the influence of inclination, and with it every object of the will, so that nothing remains which can determine the will except objectively the *law*, and subjectively *pure respect*...for this practical law, and consequently the maxim that I should follow this law even to the thwarting of all my inclinations.
>
> Thus the moral worth of an action does not lie in the effect expected from it....The pre-eminent good which we call moral can therefore consist in nothing else but *the conception of law* in itself...in so far as this conception, and not the expected effect, determines the will....
>
> But what sort of law can that be, the conception of which

must determine the will, even without paying any regard to the effect expected from it, in order that this will may be called good absolutely and without qualification? As I have deprived the will of every impulse which could arise to it from obedience to any law, there remains nothing but the universal conformity of its actions to law in general, which alone is to serve the will as a principle, *i.e.* I am never to act otherwise than so *that I could also will that my maxim should become a universal law* [italics Kant's]. Here, now, it is the simple conformity to law in general, without assuming any particular law[23] applicable to certain actions, that serves the will as its principle, and must so serve it, if duty is not to be a vain delusion and a chimerical notion.[24]

The moral worth of an action, then, derives from the extent to which it represents an impassive fulfillment of a duty to obey any law, regardless of one's inclinations, and regardless of the law's effect. The usefulness of such a dictum (Kant called such dicta "categorical imperatives") to authoritarian intellectuals makes it easy to understand why they have ever found in Kant's philosophy an ideological touchstone as well as a polemical redoubt. An ethic that teaches people to will-lessly conform to any command as though they were the mechanical appendages of an organic self is the perfect moral code to propagate in an authoritarian autocracy. We will consider more of Kant's statements about ethics in the pages ahead but first let us recur to statements concerning duty made by the Nazis in order to illustrate why they found Kant's deontological philosophy so "sublime."

"Through widespread and entirely new methods of work procurement, the town of Freiburg has led you to employment and food," the Nazi philosopher and academic administrator Martin Heidegger told a group of unemployed German workers in 1934:

And because of that you are favored over the other unemployed men of the town. But this privilege has its duties, too.

And your duty is to take the employment, and perform the tasks, in whatever manner the Führer of our new state demands.[25]

And the phrase "in whatever manner the Führer of our new state demands" is not merely rhetorical hyperbole. It represents state-philosopher Heidegger's expression of an official doctrine of the Nazi state. In a speech to German youth given at the Nuremberg Parteitag of September fourteenth 1935 Hitler had said:

> Nothing is possible if there is not a single will which issues its commands and which the others must always obey, beginning from above and ending only at the lowest point....We are a 'following'...and that means that it is our duty to 'follow', to obey. We must educate our whole people so that wherever one is appointed to command the others recognize their duty to obey him....That is the expression of an authoritarian State...and in the authoritarian State everyone is proud to owe obedience....[26]

And *that* is the reason why Kant seemed so sublime to the Nazis. Reducing morality to a duty to " 'follow,' to obey"—to "duty for duty's sake"—reduced the German people to the heil-Hitlering zombies seen in the newsreels of the nineteen-thirties. Kant's monstrous ethic prepared the Germans to obey any command that was given to them, hence the excuse ubiquitously offered by German war criminals at their post-war trials—"I was only following orders,"—when they were asked why they committed their monstrous acts. As W. T. Jones noted in his *Kant and the Nineteenth Century*, commenting on the previously cited passage from Kant's *Critique of Practical Reason*:

> To act morally, I must obey "nothing but...law in general." That is, the moral motive is "simple conformity to law in general." If

this means, as it would seem, that I must ignore the specific character of the rule and act simply from the notion of following a rule because it is a rule, the result will be to justify all sorts of acts that most people would call immoral. For instance, during World War II Hitler laid down the rule that all Jews should be exterminated. Kant's argument would not justify the acts of Germans who exterminated Jews because they were afraid of disobeying Hitler or because they hated Jews or because they hoped to acquire the property of the Jews.[27] But it *would* [italics Jones'] justify the acts of any Germans who exterminated Jews for the sole reason that they had been ordered to do so.[28]

THE DELEGITIMIZATION OF THE SELF

But the idea that human beings' exclusive moral function is that of doing as they have been ordered to do highlights another facet of the authoritarian ethical tradition which we have often touched upon obliquely but not yet addressed directly: its attitude toward the private, individual self. Demeaning people to the status of mere organic "parts" whose sole ethical duty is that of obedience to some larger organismic Self has the effect of completely annulling the private individual, hence authoritarians' incessant denigration of self-interest and their exaltation of selflessness, self-denial, and self-sacrifice. Because philosophies which denigrate the self are broadly influential even within contemporary liberal culture this tradition of devaluing the self, with its commensurate aggrandizement of the concept of self-sacrifice, requires distinct consideration within a review of the use of ideas as instruments of political domination. However, before we continue, let us review the theoretical premises of these doctrines.

A liberal society such as the United States of America, with its celebration of the right to the "pursuit of happiness" and its legal guarantees of individual liberties, is founded upon the idea of the moral worth of the individual human being. This idea is in turn established on the metaphysical premise that there is such a thing as an individual human being—that the individuals we see around us are real and distinct entities. But the authoritarian doctrines of self-negation and self-sacrifice are, as we have marked, primarily built upon the idea that the self-apparent individuals we perceive around us do not really exist as individuals; and they are built upon the idea that these pseudo-individuals do not produce, and therefore do not deserve to enjoy, the values which they cherish.

In the realm of ethical speculation the doctrines of Organicism and Creationism are the primary metaphysical premises of moral codes which negate and denigrate the self and extol self-sacrifice. Organicism, again, is the idea that all things are parts of one great organism and hence that every seeming individual is really just part of some greater Individual. The idea that individual human beings do not produce values is an implication of both the religious and the secular versions of Creationism, which say that all values are created either by God, or by some other "ideal" entity conceived of as a single God-like organism (Humanity; the State; Nature, etc.). Without such metaphysical premises providing their logical foundations moral doctrines which annul the self and demand self-sacrifice collapse into heaps of unsupported allegations. After all, if there is no all-encompassing Self in whose body individuals merely have the status of selfless appendages then the interests of the distinct selves we see around us are the supreme interests with which moral philosophy may rationally be concerned. And if there is no Creator creating the things that individual selves value then those things are either being produced by individuals themselves or they are the products of the truly selfless mechanisms of nature. In either case these values may legitimately be claimed by and/or utilized by individual human beings.

All of the major authoritarian dogmas, whether religious or

secular, employ organicist and creationist arguments as premises of
moral doctrines which denigrate the private self. Let us now examine a sampling of these doctrines in order to better understand the
relationship between these metaphysical concepts and the ethics of
selflessness and self-sacrifice. Consider this passage from the New
Testament which expresses the logical nexuses between Organicism
and Creationism, the ethics of self-sacrifice, and the denigration of
the self. In these verses which we cited earlier to illustrate the metaphysical aspects of the authoritarian tradition the Apostle Paul
says:

> Therefore, I urge you, brothers, in view of God's mercy, to offer
> you bodies as living sacrifices, holy and pleasing to God—this is
> your spiritual act of worship. Do not conform any longer to the
> pattern of this world....
>
> ....
>
> Do not think of yourself more highly than you ought, but
> rather think of yourself with sober judgment, in accordance with
> the measure of faith God has given you. Just as each of us has
> one body with many members, and these members do not all
> have the same function, so in Christ we who are many form one
> body, and each member belongs to all the others. We have dif-
> ferent gifts, according to the grace given us. If a man's gift is
> prophesying, let him use it....If it is serving, let him serve; if it is
> teaching let him teach...if it is leadership, let him govern...(Rom.
> 12:1-8, NIV).

So if God's Providence has merely provided you with the gifts
of a servant do not think of yourself so highly as to presume to be
qualified to govern, Saint Paul is saying in this passage. You must
sacrifice your own aspirations and interests to the interests of the
otherworldly body of which you are merely a member, and to
whom you "belong." You were created with certain professional

"gifts" to perform certain divinely ordained functions within the larger whole—the body of Christ—of which you are only a part. "Does not the potter have the right to make...some pottery for noble purposes and some for common use?" Saint Paul said in the Epistles. "God has arranged the parts in the body...just as he wanted them to be" (Rom. 9:21 and 1 Cor. 12:18, NIV).

Upon such premises the Christian tyranny which was Medieval Europe was established. Medieval theocrats such as Saint Augustine took such scriptural sanctions and built a feudal "City of God" upon them. "Man was made...that he might not live according to himself," Augustine said in *The City of God*, "but according to Him that made him...."[29] Such subversion of the moral legitimacy of the interests of the individual self prepared feudalism's subjects to submit to a thousand years of political and economic exploitation.

But Christianity was far from the only religion to promulgate such doctrines. Recall again this passage from Judaism's Kabbalah, which employs organicist and creationist doctrines to eradicate the moral worth of the private self:

> You are simply a channel for the divine attributes. You attain this humility through the awe of God's vastness, through realizing that there is "no place empty of it." Then you come to the state of Ayin [nothingness], the state of humility. You have no independent self and are contained in the Creator. This is the meaning of the verse: "Moses hid his face, for he was in awe." Through his experience of awe, Moses attained the hiding of his face, that is, he perceived no independent self. Everything was part of divinity.[30]

And Hinduism's *Bhagavad-gītā* is filled with verses which use such premises to buttress ethical demands for sacrifice and undermine respect for the private self. In Chapter Two, text 47 of the *Bhagavad-gītā* Lord Krishna uses the doctrine of Creationism to underpin divine demands for wealth and labor, declaring: "[you] have a right to perform your prescribed duty, but you are not entitled to the fruits of [your own productive] action. Never consider yourself the cause of action...."[31] God only is responsible for creative actions, Krishna asserts, and is the only being entitled to their fruits. And continuing along this line in Chapter Three, verse 30, the Supreme Lord impugns his follower's egoistic self-interest as an impediment to the willingness to work and sacrifice for God, saying: "therefore, O Arjuna, surrendering all your works unto Me, with mind always intent on Me, and without desire for gain and free from egoism and lethargy...."[32] Hindu scholar and translator Śrīla Prabhupāda interprets this passage as meaning that:

> One has to sacrifice everything for the good will of the Supreme Lord, and at the same time discharge his prescribed duties without claim of proprietorship....Similarly, one has to take it for granted that nothing in the world belongs to the individual person, but everything belongs to the Supreme Personality of Godhead. That is the real purport of Kṛṣṇa's saying "unto Me."[33]

Please note again how Hindu theologians use the doctrine of Organicism to annul the claims of the private self and provide premises for demands for sacrifice. In the *Invocation* of the *Śrī Īśopaniṣad* it is first established that God creates the universe—and *is* the universe—and then it is asserted in Mantra One that God owns and controls the universe. From this follows the demand that individuals submit to restrictions on their consumption and use of values which are here asserted to be God's:

> The Personality of Godhead is perfect and complete, and because He is completely perfect, all emanations from Him, such as this phenomenal world, are perfectly equipped as complete wholes. Whatever is produced of the complete whole is also

complete in itself. Because He is the complete whole, even though so many units emanate from Him....[34]

....

Everything animate or inanimate that is within the universe is controlled and owned by the Lord. One should therefore accept only those things necessary for himself, which are set aside as his quota, and one should not accept other things, knowing well to whom they belong.[35]

Śrīla Prabhupāda wrote, concerning these passages:

The hand of a body is a complete unit only as long as it is attached to the complete body....Similarly, living beings are parts and parcels of the complete whole....

The completeness of human life can only be realized when one engages in the service of the complete whole. All services in the world—whether social, political, communal, international or even interplanetary—will remain incomplete until they are dovetailed with the complete whole.[36]

The implication of this is the annihilation of the individual self and the establishment of a foundation for unlimited demands for service and self-sacrifice.

SECULAR ATTACKS UPON THE SELF

But it is not only religion which employs attacks upon the moral legitimacy of the self. Secular versions of these doctrines have developed during periods when religion was in retreat and science was ascendant. Modern secular authoritarian philosophy culminates in the ideas of Immanuel Kant, so examining Kant's attitude toward the private self will help us understand Adolf Hitler's and Benito Mussolini's. Kant, remember, believed that the state was a "body" in which each "member"—individual human beings—"should have his position and function in turn defined by the idea of the whole." Because the function of a member of a body is simply that it perform those actions which best serve the interests of the whole, within the "whole" which is a state an individual's moral duty is to serve state interest, not self-interest. Consequently, Kant believed that "moral law...entirely excludes the influence of self-love...."[37] "Self-love..." Kant said later in the *Critique of Practical Reason*, "is in fact the source of all evil."[38]

And because he viewed the pursuit of happiness as the ultimate expression of self-love Kant was adamantly opposed to the whole idea of one's own private happiness as a morally legitimate goal. But although Kant had said it is a sin for the individual to pursue its own happiness, he was not in fact entirely averse to the idea of the pursuit of happiness as an ethical end. Kant's philosophy instead makes it a moral duty for the individual to accomplish the happiness of other people, and also says that one's own personal happiness is possible in the afterlife. The reader should carefully note, however, that the former maxim serves authoritarian purposes by ethically requiring one person to accomplish another person's private objectives, and the latter serves them by representing the achievement of happiness as morally legitimate only after one is dead.

Regarding private happiness Kant said that "the principle of *private happiness*...[italics Kant's] is the most objectionable [principle], not merely because it is false...nor yet merely because it contributes nothing to the establishment of morality...but because the springs it provides for morality are such as rather undermine it and destroy its sublimity...."[39] He further stated that the "principles of the pursuit of happiness cannot possibly produce morality...."[40] These fulminations against felicity overthrow the moral legitimacy of a free society by overthrowing the moral legitimacy of what people do with their freedom when they manage to achieve it: pursue happiness. Let us now revisit certain statements made by Hitler and Mussolini in order to see how they used similar ideas about the self, self-interest, and happiness to accomplish ends which were similar to Kant's.

Fascism "does not believe in the possibility of 'happiness' on earth...and it therefore rejects the teleological notion that at some future time the human family will secure a final solution to all its difficulties,"[41] Mussolini had said in *The Doctrine of Fascism*,[42] and added a few pages later:

> [F]ascism rejects the economic interpretation of felicity [i.e. happiness] as something to be secured socialistically, almost automatically, at a given stage of economic evolution when all will be assured a maximum of material comfort. Fascism denies the materialist conception of happiness as a possibility, and abandons it to the economists of the mid-nineteenth century. This means that Fascism denies the equation: well-being equals happiness, which sees in men mere animals, content when they can feed and fatten....
>
> ....
>
> The maxim that society exists only for the well-being and freedom of the individuals composing it does not seem to be in conformity with nature's plans, which care only for the species and seem ready to sacrifice the individual.[43] It is much to be feared that...democracy...would be a form of society in which a degenerate mass would have no thought beyond that of enjoying the ignoble pleasures of the vulgar.[44]

But Mussolini is not merely expressing his contempt for a hedonistic materialism which might breed discontent in an authoritarian society where material pleasures are certainly going to be few. He means to dissuade the individual from pursuing self-interest in any form because such pursuits distract from what Mussolini represents as a "higher life" of "duty" to "the nation and the country." Consider the implications for ethics of these statements, which were cited before in the section on metaphysics. Mussolini is concerned to philosophically suppress any self-interested activity whatsoever, not just activity directed to the accomplishment of materialistic or hedonistic ends:

> Fascism sees in the world not only those superficial, material aspects in which man appears as an individual, standing by himself, self-centered, subject to natural law which instinctively urges him toward a life of selfish momentary pleasure; it sees not only the individual but the nation and the country; individuals and generations bound together by a moral law...suppressing the instinct for life closed in a brief circle of pleasure, build[ing] up to a higher life, founded on duty...in which the individual, by self-sacrifice, the renunciation of self-interest, by death itself, can achieve that purely spiritual existence in which his value as a man consists.[45]

And suppressing self-interest was also an aspect of the German Nazi ideology, which is not surprising given the explicit influence of Kant on the Nazis' intellectual leadership. Here Hitler promulgates an ethics based on the organic theory of the state—a doctrine which is ultimately based upon the metaphysical philosophy of Organicism—in order to do away with self-interest by doing away with the self, which he here refers to as the ego.

> [T]he nation has been put into a new relation both to business and to government. The underlying idea is to do away with egoism and to lead the people into the sacred collective egoism which is the 'nation'....[46]

The "sacred collective egoism" Hitler refers to is an expression of what he elsewhere calls the "organic folkish state,"[47]—the concept of German society as a gigantic, organismic "I" with a racialist and nationalist identity. To this sacred organic "I" Hitler says the individual owes a duty of service and obedience and must sacrifice its own self-interest. Couching his exhortations in altruistic terms Hitler praises what he represents as the "Aryans" superior ability to completely annul themselves in order to protect what he calls the "life" of the German nation. Not long after his words were published this ability would be tested to the limit on the battlefields of World War Two.

"This self-sacrificing will to give one's personal labor and if necessary one's own life for others is most strongly developed in the Aryan," Hitler had said in *Mein Kampf*:

> The Aryan is not the greatest in his mental qualities as such, but in the extent of his willingness to put all of his abilities in the service of the community. In him the instinct of self-preservation[48] has reached the noblest form, since he willingly subordinates his own ego to the life of the community and, if the hour demands, even sacrifices it.
>
> Not in his intellectual gifts lies the source of the Aryan's capacity for creating and building culture. If he had just this alone ...in no case could he organize; for the innermost essence of all organization requires that the individual renounce putting forward his personal opinion and interests and sacrifice both in favor of a larger group....Now, for example, he no longer works directly for himself, but with his activity articulates himself with the community, not only for his own advantage, but for the advantage of all....Otherwise he designates human activity, in so far as it serves the instinct of self-preservation without consideration for his fellow men, as theft, usury, robbery, burglary, etc.
>
> This state of mind, which subordinates the interests of the ego to the conservation of the community, is really the first premise of every human culture. From it alone can arise all the

great works of mankind, which bring the founder little re-ward....Every worker, every peasant, every inventor, official, etc., who works without ever being able to achieve any happiness or prosperity for himself, is a representative of this lofty idea....In giving one's own life for the existence of the community lies the crown of all sense of sacrifice....[I]t means not to be self-suffi-cient but to serve the community.

The basic attitude from which such activity arises, we call—to distinguish it from egoism and selfishness—idealism. By this we understand only the individual's capacity to make sacrifices for the community, for his fellow men.[49]

But the term Hitler should have used to distinguish "egoism and selfishness" from "the individual's capacity to make sacrifices for the community, for his fellow man," isn't "idealism," it's *Altruism*. Although few people would think to identify Adolf Hitler as an altruist the ethical concept which he is advocating—the sacrifice of the private ego to the "collective ego" which is one's fellow human beings conceived of as an organic community, may technically be denoted by that word. The term "altruism" was originally coined by the French authoritarian philosopher Auguste Comte to identify the ethical doctrine which requires the individual to act as though it was merely the selfless arm or leg of the larger body which Comte desig-nated as "Humanity" represented as a single organism. To assist the reader in distinguishing between this ethic and the philosophic layperson's use of the term Altruism to refer to the ethics of charity and kindness we will give brief consideration to the philosophy of Auguste Comte.

ALTRUISM

Auguste Comte, the son of a tax-collector, lived in Europe at the cusp of a new age of Liberalism—of "classical Liberalism," meaning individual liberty and "free-market" economics. But like many people in any period of liberalization Comte was not merely ambivalent toward this new age of freedom, he was profoundly antagonistic toward it. The old feudal-aristocratic order, which had for centuries suppressed individual liberties in Europe, was collapsing, in large part because the credibility of its foundational ideology, Christianity, was being challenged by science. Comte was a member of a reactionary new breed of authoritarian intellectual who, unnerved by the nascent freedoms afforded by the exhilarating era which history has denominated the Enlightenment, scrambled to put together a new type of pseudo-scientific, quasi-secular ideology which could be used to defend authoritarian institutions.

Comte himself, following the lead of the German authoritarian philosophers then being sponsored by the Hohenzollerns, founded a scientificalized, secularistic "religion" which he called "Positivism." The task of this semi-religion, to quote Paul Edward's *The Encyclopedia of Philosophy*, was to:

> provide a new religion and a new clergy, that could once again unify society. Comte's solution was a science on which all could agree. In place of the Catholic priesthood, Comte proposed a scientific-industrial elite that would announce the "invariable laws" to society....and to meet the problems of modern industrial society with the insights about the need for order and shared certainty that were revealed in the theological-feudal period.[50]

Comte, then, wanted to employ theo-scientific arguments to provide a basis for a new semi-religion which would re-impose the principles of theocratic feudalism on the peoples of the incipient industrial age.

Comte's new philosophic formula for feudalism was based on the ancient organismic and creationist metaphysical doctrines which had been secularized and re-popularized by the German idealist philosophers. These philosophers had asserted, recall,[51] that the consciousness of humanity conceived of as a single being thought and/or perceived the entire universe into existence, including all of the material wealth upon which individual human beings depend for their sustenance. Because they are beholden to this god-like world-creator for the use of its wealth, and/or because they were actually part of this great being, individuals owed a duty of obedience and of sacrifice to it, just as the peoples of the pre-scientific, explicitly religious periods owed duty and sacrifice to the gods of religion. Comte called his version of this all-subsuming, all-creating being "Humanity" and established a new religion, "Positivism," devoted to its worship.

And Comte named his new version of the ancient religious ethics of duty and sacrifice "Altruism." Altruism, as a technical term, is an etymological concoction whipped up by Comte from the French word for "other people," *autrui*, and the Latin word for "other," *alter*—and literally means *otherism*. Comte called his new ethic Altruism not because he viewed other people as distinct individuals to whom duty and sacrifice were somehow arbitrarily owed—that would have made no moral sense even to Comte—but because he viewed other people as parts of the great organism of "Humanity" which each part was naturally required to serve. James Hastings' respected *Encyclopædia of Religion and Ethics* describes the development of the term Altruism thus:

> In Comte's view the human race formed one great organism, Humanity, living a continuous life in accordance with its own laws....The individual as such is an abstraction; for every one is a member...of Humanity, which is made up of all the nations of the earth. On these collective elements the thought and life of each individual depend....
>
> ....

> Humanity thus becomes the new center of unity; the Religion of Humanity, a religion capable of uniting all, and 'Live for others' its guiding principle. The term 'altruism,' now in general use, was introduced by Comte.[52]

And this "general use" of the term Altruism is the reason why it is incumbent upon philosophers to engage the public concerning the definition of this word. For in the vernacular of the average citizen this term is commonly used to refer to a benevolent ethics of charity and kindness, not the malicious dogma of authoritarian duty which is the intended denotation of the term. The reason why the citizens of a free society must be able to distinguish between these two usages is so that they can detect when a malevolently intentioned ideologue is trying to sneak an evil idea into innocent minds beneath the cloak of an innocuous popular usage. Indeed, because confusion about the meaning of the term Altruism leaves the public so vulnerable to intellectual molestation this philosopher recommends that a policy be adopted of *never* employing the term Altruism to refer to the ethics of charity.

■   ■   ■   ■

Here we will conclude the section of our study which was devoted to what we termed "the ethics of the slaves" and continue on to the section entitled *The Ethics of the Masters*. By way of an introduction to this topic it may be said that the ethics of the masters, in contrast to the ethics of the slaves, are doctrines which authoritarian philosophers teach to themselves rather than to their subjects. On first consideration it might seem that authoritarians would be unconcerned to adopt and practice any code of ethics, even one intended exclusively for their own use; but it turns out that certain ethical practices actually facilitate the business of being an authoritarian. We will now examine that business and the ethical codes which abet it.

CHAPTER TWELVE

THE ETHICS OF THE MASTERS

The business of an authoritarian is crime. Not the ordinary sort of crime represented by the mugging of pedestrians and the burglarizing of residences, but the more ambitious species of political crime which uses the institution of the state to commit mass acts of political coercion and economic violence upon whole populations. The ethics of the masters facilitates such crime by justifying it to political criminals themselves and also by encouraging it in people who might potentially be inclined to political criminality. This justification and encouragement permits political criminals to commit moral atrocities without suffering the pangs of conscience which might otherwise inhibit their malicious behavior—and it rallies the criminally inclined to defend the ramparts of political evil during those periods of history when authoritarianism is in retreat.

But how would one go about developing a code of ethics which could be used to justify crime to criminals? Well, it turns out that one would develop an ethical code for criminals in exactly the same way one would develop any other code of ethics. One would establish premises in metaphysical theory upon which to build one's moral theory and then use epistemological theory to defend it. So a discussion of the "ethics of the masters," like that of any code of ethics, necessarily involves a discussion of metaphysics and epistemology.

The concepts of metaphysics and epistemology which provide premises and defenses for the ethics of the masters are not unique to that facet of moral philosophy. Generally, they are exactly the same concepts of metaphysical and epistemological philosophy which provide premises and defenses for every aspect of authoritarian ideological argument. The metaphysical doctrines of Idealism, Materialism, and Heracliteanism provide "the masters" with the foundations for their ethical doctrines, while Skepticism, faith, and faith's secular equivalent, epistemological Subjectivism, provide their epistemological substantiations and defenses.

But the fact that the ethics of the masters are based upon concepts which we are already familiar with will not make acquiring a systematic grasp of this aspect of authoritarian thought particularly easy. That is because this body of doctrines is one of the most obscure, most convoluted, and most logically inconsistent of any branch of authoritarian ideology. This obscurity and abstrusity may possibly result because authoritarian intellectuals, in concocting a canon of thought which is very largely intended for their own consumption, may not feel the need to be as clear and coherent as they are when they are trying to convince the rest of us. It may also result because there is in fact no rational way of demonstrating the morality of what authoritarians do.

Because the branch of authoritarian ideology we are calling the ethics of the masters tends to be inconsistent, abstruse, and obscure, we are going to explain it by expositing its basic arguments rather than by exhaustively tracing the roller-coaster logic of any particular exponent of these doctrines. We will, however, provide examples from the oeuvres of several of the "master" ethicists in order to illustrate their thinking, and also to help the reader better identify who these philosophers are. The reader should be prepared, however, for the challenge of attempting to grasp doctrines which are very far from lucidly rational, for the twists and turns of an evil mind's attempts to justify itself results in arguments which are circuitous and contradictory.

THE SOPHISTS

In the Western tradition of philosophic thought the systematic development of what we are terming the ethics of the masters begins with the Greek *Sophist* philosophers, notably Protagoras. Starting from the Heraclitean metaphysical premise that everything in the universe was in a constant state of chaotic flux Protagoras arrived at the conclusion that no knowledge of reality or morality was possible. From this position of epistemological Skepticism Protagoras determined that all theories of morality reflected merely the arbitrary subjective preferences and prejudices of the society or individual holding them—which is the basic tenet of the doctrine of Ethical Subjectivism. Protagoras then concluded that morality was merely a convention which was relative to particular cultures or particular people—a concept which is known as moral *Relativism*.

But having thus done away with any basis for the development of objective standards of morality Protagoras nevertheless believed that the natural laws of self-preservation required human beings to discover some means of securing their existence. Natural law, then, because it was the one basis for ethics which seemed to be more than merely a subjective convention, was an appropriate premise for ethical philosophy, Protagoras came to believe. However, in the absence of objective moral standards some of the Sophists who followed Protagoras, particularly Callicles, Meno, Critias, and Thrasymachus, decided that natural law actually sanctioned the imposition upon human relationships of the laws of nature which govern the brutal struggles between species in the natural environment. These survival-of-the-fittest laws became for them the premise of a socially Darwinistic politics of "might-makes-right."

And taking these implications of the Sophist's *Ethical Naturalism* a bit further, certain later Greek philosophers, and some of the Sophists themselves, decided that it was not merely an ethics of natural law and a politics of might-makes-right which was sanctioned by the absence of objective moral standards. In the absence of such standards they decided it was permissible to live in any manner they preferred. Because they unsurprisingly preferred to pursue pleasure, these philosophers concluded that it was ethical for them to pursue pleasure however they wished, even if it harmed other people. This ethic of the unscrupulous pursuit of pleasure is known as *Cyrenaic Hedonism* after its original philosophic proponent, Aristippus of Cyrene. *Cyrenaic Hedonism* should also be viewed as one of the ethical doctrines of the masters.

But while the ethics of the masters have a foundation and a beginning in ancient philosophies and theologies there have been a number of advances in philosophy which have provided new opportunities to develop these darkest and most malicious of philosophic creeds. The metaphysical philosophy of Materialism, for instance, which in its earlier, religious manifestation as Original Sin had established that an intrinsically evil humanity needed to be ruled by the iron fists of divinely appointed overlords, later led to the idea that humanity's innate irrationality meant that the Darwinian mechanics of evolution-through-extermination were necessary if civilization was to advance. And metaphysical Idealism, which in its religious form had permitted the prophets of God to make unlimited claims on humanity because their God had created

humanity, later, in its secular, or "subjective" form, permitted ordinary human beings to make these same claims on the grounds
that human consciousness actually creates the individual people we
see around us.

Yet despite having been elaborately developed by both ancient
and modern philosophers, the ethics of the masters have only occasionally played a prominent role in the history of philosophy's influence upon culture. This is most likely so because these ideas
incite people to self-assertion and aggression, which is not at all in
the long-term interest of the stable authoritarian regimes which have
historically dominated human politics. Typically, stable authoritarian
regimes have employed the quietist doctrines which are based on
Idealism, such as the ascetic and deontological (duty) aspects of
Christianity and Hinduism, to encourage dutiful submission in their
subjects. Only rarely, such as when these established regimes have
been threatened by rising tides of political Liberalism, have the
ethics of the masters found new life.

One such liberalizing period was that in which the Sophist
movement itself arose—the Camelot-like age of Athenian Liberalism which represented the apex of the Greek Enlightenment.
Another such was the modern Age of Enlightenment inspired by
the ideas of British philosopher John Locke, which culminated in
eighteenth century American and nineteenth century European
movements toward individual and economic liberty. These periods
manifested two of history's greatest eras of revolution against authoritarian institutions and ideas, and during such intervals people
of authoritarian mindset have often found their "backs against the
wall," sometimes literally, but also economically, politically, philosophically, and psychologically.

And finding themselves so threatened authoritarians have felt
the need to rally in resistance to the growing threat of political and
economic progress toward freedom. One way for them to do this is

to philosophically glorify and justify the predatory impulses which are the hallmark of their master psychology. But such philosophic glorifications and justifications may not only be used to brace the soul of the individual political criminal; they can also be blown like a battle-trumpet to inspire the worst people in any society to rise up to defend or to re-establish a tyranny. The greatest of the modern trumpeters of the new ethics of the masters was the German philosopher Friedrich Nietzsche.

NIETZSCHE

It was Friedrich Nietzsche, please recall, who first noted the distinction between the two variants of authoritarian ethics, which he termed the *"masters morality* and *slave morality."*[1] Nietzsche is one of several modern proponents of the ethics of the masters whose writings we will cite to illustrate these doctrines, and is frequently noted as a major influence on the German Nazi ideologues who supported Adolf Hitler. Wilhelm Grenzmann, whose essay *Nietzsche and National-Socialism* was published in the *ICPHS* study of Nazi ideology, noted that "[a] few prominent figures seem to stand out as having contributed more than most to the [Nazi] disaster. One of these—and he takes a very high place—is Friedrich Nietzsche."[2]

But what was it about the philosophy of Nietzsche that the Nazis found so appealing? To discover this we will examine his philosophy, as well as that of two other philosophers who are closely identified with the Nietzschean tradition of thought. One of these is Martin Heidegger, who was a Nazi Party member and an official state philosopher under Adolf Hitler's National Socialist regime; and another is Heidegger's student, Jean-Paul Sartre, who was a founder of the French *existentialist* school of philosophy and who is noted for his Marxist sympathies. Although the casual student of philosophy may be surprised to learn of an association between *Existentialism* and what Nietzsche referred to as the *"master morality,"* [italics Nietzsche's] Nietzsche, Heidegger, and of course Sartre, are all in fact identified by philosophic scholars as existentialists.

And indeed it may be said that "Existentialism" is just the modern name for the philosophic traditions of Ethical Relativism, Ethical Subjectivism, and Ethical Naturalism which go back to the ancient Greek Sophists. Existentialism manifests all of the major arguments associated with this master morality, and in the work of Nietzsche, Heidegger, and Sartre all of the implications of these arguments are fully developed. Idealism, Materialism, and Heracliteanism are used to provide the metaphysical premises of Existentialism, and the epistemological philosophies of Skepticism and Epistemological Subjectivism are employed to undermine the philosophical foundations of Liberalism and defend the ethics and politics of aggression. Consider how Nietzsche attacks the human faculties of knowledge as dysfunctional—an instance of cognitive and perceptual Skepticism—in order to legitimize his version of Subjectivism. Following the Sophists, he utilizes skeptical arguments to undermine our grip on reality as a preparation for drawing us into a subjective world where "anything goes."

"[Do] I have to add," Nietzsche says in his volume *Daybreak*:

> that when we are awake our drives...do nothing but interpret nervous stimuli and, according to their requirements, posit their 'causes'? that there is no *essential* difference between waking and dreaming? that when we compare very different stages of culture we even find that freedom of waking interpretation in the one is in no way inferior to the freedom exercised in the other while dreaming? that our moral judgments and evaluations too are only images and fantasies based on a physiological process unknown to us..? that all our so-called consciousness is a more or less fantastic commentary on an unknown, perhaps unknowable, but felt text?[3]

SKEPTICISM, SUBJECTIVISM, AND MORALITY

In this abstruse and convoluted passage Nietzsche is giving voice to the metaphysically materialist notion that human consciousness is mechanistically driven by "physiological" processes which propel the individual into a phantasmagorical world of waking dreams. There is no relation between a person's thoughts and any aspect of reality, Nietzsche says, and even our moral judgments and evaluations are just so much cognitive gibberish pumped out by our brain's automatic responses to "nervous stimuli" and/or determined by "unknowable" but nevertheless "felt" drives. Our eyes and ears and other senses, too, Nietzsche says—our perceptual faculties—lead us into a world of "images and fantasies" and thoroughly obstruct our efforts to accurately perceive the real world. In the next passage Nietzsche gives expression to tenets of perceptual Skepticism, which he also bases on the doctrine of metaphysical Materialism:

> *In prison.–* My eyes, however strong or weak they may be, can see only a certain distance, and it is within the space encompassed by this distance that I live and move, the line of this horizon constitutes my immediate fate, in things great and small, from which I cannot escape. Around every being there is described a similar concentric circle, which has a mid-point and is peculiar to him. Our ears enclose us within a comparable circle, and so does our sense of touch. Now, it is by these horizons, within which each of us encloses his senses as if behind prison walls, that we *measure* the world, we say that this is near and that far, this is big and that small, this is hard and that soft: this measuring we call sensation – and it is all of it an error! According to the average quantity of experiences and excitations possible to us at any particular point of time one measures one's life as being short or long, poor or

rich, full or empty: and according to the average human life one measures that of all other creatures – all of it an error! If our eyes were a hundredfold sharper, man would appear to us tremendously tall; it is possible, indeed, to imagine organs by virtue of which he would be felt as immeasurable. On the other hand, organs could be so constituted that whole solar systems were viewed contracted and packed together like a single cell: and to beings of an opposite constitution a cell of the human body could present itself, in motion, construction and harmony, as a solar system. The habits of our senses have woven us into lies and deception of sensation: these again are the basis of all our judgments and 'knowledge' – there is absolutely no escape, no backway or bypath into the *real world!* We sit in our net, we spiders, and whatever we may catch in it, we can catch nothing at all except that which allows itself to be caught in precisely *our* net [italics Nietzsche's].[4]

And now that we are completely estranged from the "real world" we are ready to enter the purely subjective world which Nietzsche has prepared for us. This world is the "prison" of "images and fantasies" generated by the "physiological" processes of our own cognitive and sensory faculties. Nietzsche says that these processes are ultimately dominated—steered and driven—by "the emotions…such as fear, love, hatred, and…indolence." These forces create a subjective universe which is a lie, Nietzsche says, but for creatures such as ourselves is the only universe which exists. He explains:

> Our eyes find it easier on a given occasion to produce a picture already often produced, than to seize upon the divergence and novelty of an impression….It is difficult and painful for the ear to listen to anything new….Our senses are also hostile and averse to anything new; and generally, even in the "simplest" processes of sensation, the emotions *dominate*—such as fear, love, hatred,

and the passive emotion of indolence.—As little as a reader nowadays reads all the single words (not to speak of syllables) of a page—he rather takes about five out of every twenty words at random, and "guesses" the probable appropriate sense to them—just as little do we see a tree correctly and completely in respect to its leaves, branches, color, and shape; we find it so much easier to fancy the chance of a tree. Even in the midst of the most remarkable experiences, we still do just the same; we fabricate the greater part of the experience, and can hardly be made to contemplate any event, *except* as "inventors" thereof. All this goes to prove that from our fundamental nature and from remote ages we have been—*accustomed to lying*....one is much more of an artist than one is aware of.—In an animated conversation, I often see the face of the person with whom I am speaking so clearly and sharply defined before me, according to the thought he expresses, or which I believe to be evoked in his mind, that the degree of distinctness far exceeds the *strength* of my visual faculty—the delicacy of the play of the muscles and the expression of the eyes *must* [italics Nietzsche's] therefore be imagined by me. Probably the person put on quite a different expression, or none at all.[5]

EMOTIONS AS PREEMINENT

This passage introduces us to a nuance of Nietzschean Subjectivism which is central to the development of his philosophy: it is primarily the human emotions, Nietzsche says, which determine just what kind of reality the physiological processes of our consciousness will invent. Because each person has different emotions, and therefore creates a different reality, there are no moral constants, no moral constraints, no absolutes of right and wrong. Such a concept might seem harmless enough, even attractive, to someone who has benevolent emotions—but what kind of emotions does Nietzsche have? "Supposing..." Nietzsche says in his *Beyond Good and Evil*:

that someone goes so far as to regard the emotions of hatred, envy, covetousness, and lust for domination as life-conditioning emotions, as something which must fundamentally and essentially be present in the total economy of life, consequently must be heightened further if life is to be heightened further – he suffers from such a judgment as from seasickness. And yet even this hypothesis is far from being the strangest and most painful in this tremendous, still almost unexplored realm of dangerous knowledge – and there are in fact a hundred good reasons why everyone should keep away from it who – *can*! On the other hand: if your ship *has* been driven into these seas, very well! Now clench your teeth! Keep your eyes open! Keep a firm hand on the helm! – We sail straight over morality and *past* it, we flatten, we crush perhaps what is left of our own morality by venturing to voyage thither – but what do *we* [italics Nietzsche's] matter![6]

And now we can plainly see what sort of emotions create Nietzsche's reality: Hatred! Envy! Lust for domination! "Thus I deny morality as I deny alchemy," Nietzsche says. "[T]hat is, I deny their premises....I also deny immorality...."[7] And why should he not? Each person spider-like spins a web of their own morality in spinning their own reality. And the threads from which all morality and reality are spun are the human emotions:

> Supposing that nothing else is "given" as real but our world of desires and passions, that we cannot sink or rise to any other "reality" but just that of our impulses—for thinking is only a relation of these impulses to one another:—are we not permitted to make the attempt and to ask the question whether this which is "given" does not *suffice*...for the understanding even of the so-called mechanical (or "material") world? I do not mean as an illusion, a "semblance," a "representation" (in the Berkeleyan and Schopenhauerian sense) [parenthetical remarks Nietzsche's], but as possessing the same degree of reality as our emotions

themselves—as a more primitive form of the world of emotions, in which everything still lies in a mighty unity, which afterwards branches off and develops itself in organic processes...as a kind of instinctive life in which all organic functions...are still synthetically united with one another—as a *primary form* of life?—In the end, it is not only permitted to make this attempt, it is commanded by the conscience of *logical method*. Not to assume several kinds of causality...one may not repudiate nowadays.... The question is ultimately whether we really recognize the will as *operating*, whether we believe in the causality of the will; if we do so—and fundamentally our belief *in this* is just our belief in causality itself—we *must* make the attempt to posit...the causality of the will as the only causality....in short, the hypothesis must be hazarded, whether will does not operate on will wherever "effects" are recognized—and whether all mechanical action...is not just the power of will, the effect of will. Granted, finally, that we succeeded in explaining our entire instinctive life as the development and ramification of one fundamental form of will —namely the Will to Power, as *my* thesis puts it...one would thus have acquired the right to define *all* active force unequivocally as *Will to Power* [italics Nietzsche's]. The world seen from within, the world defined and designated according to its "intelligible character"—it would simply be "Will to Power," and nothing else.[8]

WILL TO POWER

It is "will to power," then, which is the dominant emotion creating Nietzsche's world. This world is created in accordance with the principles of a species of metaphysical Idealism which is known technically to philosophy as *Voluntarism*. Metaphysical Voluntarism says that it is specifically that aspect of consciousness which is the emotion of will—desire or aversion mixed with the determination to act (whether divine or human) which is and which creates the universe. Apparently by combining some of the nastier of the Greek Sophists' beliefs in the legitimacy of violence with the biological ideas of Charles Darwin Nietzsche arrived at the conclusion that a life conditioned by "hatred, envy, covetousness, and lust for domination" is necessary not only for the individual to survive, but for the human race to evolve into a higher state. Because he believed that the emotion of will which drove him to concoct this doctrine could actually create the world he wanted to live in, Nietzsche insisted that this socially Darwinistic universe actually existed as a matter of fact. In the following passages from his *Beyond Good and Evil* Nietzsche first expresses his contempt for the liberal philosophers he was opposed to, and then gives voice to his belief in the salutary effects of Social Darwinism:

> [T]he *new* philosophers who are appearing....they belong to the *levelers*...as glib-tongued...slaves of the democratic taste and its "modern ideas"...and are ludicrously superficial, especially in their innate partiality for seeing the cause of almost *all* human misery and failure in the old forms in which society has hitherto existed—a notion which...inverts the truth entirely! What they would...attain...is the universal, green-meadow happiness of the herd, together with security, safety, comfort, and alleviation of life for every one; their two most frequently chanted songs and doctrines are called "Equality of Rights" and "Sympathy with all Sufferers"—and suffering itself is looked upon by them as something which must be *done away with* [italics Nietzsche's]. We opposite ones, however, who have opened our eye and conscience to the question how and where the plant "man" has hitherto grown most vigorously, believe that this has always taken place under the opposite conditions, that for this end the dangerousness of his situation had to be increased enormously, his inventive and dissembling power (his "spirit") had to develop into subtlety and daring under long oppression and compulsion, and his Will to Life had to be increased to the unconditioned

Will to Power:—we believe that severity, violence, slavery, danger in the street and in the heart, secrecy, stoicism, tempter's art and develry of every kind,—that everything wicked, terrible, tyrannical, predatory, and serpentine in man, serves as well for the elevation of the human species as its opposite....[9]

And later in the same volume Nietzsche expresses even more graphically his belief that such "develry" elevates man:

To refrain mutually from injury, from violence, from exploitation ....as *the fundamental principle of society*...would immediately disclose what it really is—namely, a Will to the *denial* of life, a principle of dissolution and decay. Here one must...resist all sentimental weakness: life itself is *essentially* appropriation, injury, conquest of the strange and the weak, suppression, severity...incorporation, and at the least, putting it mildest, exploitation....Even the organisation within which...the individuals treat each other as equal—it takes place in every healthy aristocracy—must itself, if it be a living and not a dying organisation, do all that towards other bodies, which the individuals within it refrain from doing to each other: it will have to be the incarnated Will to Power, it will endeavor to grow, to gain ground, attract to itself and gain ascendency—not owing to any morality or immorality, but because it *lives*, and because life *is* precisely Will to Power. On no point, however, is the ordinary consciousness of Europeans more unwilling to be corrected than on this matter: people now rave everywhere...about coming conditions of society in which "the exploiting character" is to be absent:—that sounds to my ears as if they promised to invent a mode of life which should refrain from all organic functions. "Exploitation" does not belong to a depraved, or imperfect and primitive society: it belongs to the *nature* [italics Nietzsche's] of the living being as a primary organic function;[10] it is a consequence of the intrinsic Will to Power, which is precisely the Will to Life.[11]

MIGHT MAKES RIGHT

And the will to power is the will to life because life *is* injury, violence, exploitation, suppression, and the overwhelming of the weaker. This is why "everything wicked, terrible, tyrannical, predatory, and serpentine in man" is not a matter "of any morality or immorality" but simply the psychological qualities appropriate to mankind's essential existential circumstances. If human beings are supposed to live as beasts of prey, like animals in raw nature,[12] then doing so is simply an issue of sustaining life, not a matter of good and evil. So facilitating a life of will to power should be, according to this theory, the purpose of society as a "fundamental principle."

But a society which is based on exploitation of the weaker cannot be a level society. Someone must be the prey if someone else is going to be the predator. So Nietzsche is an advocate of the stratification of society into divisions of master and slave, of "overman" and *untermensch*. Because he identifies with the masters—the nobles and aristocrats—Nietzsche[13] extols their predatory virtues: "[T]he aristocratic man," Nietzsche begins, applauding the ethical Subjectivism of the masters, "conceives the root idea 'good' spontaneously and straight away, that is to say, out of himself, and from that material then creates for himself a concept of 'bad' "!...

> [T]hese men are...not much better than beasts of prey, which have been let loose. They enjoy there [sic] freedom from all social control, they feel that in the wilderness they can give vent with impunity to that tension which is produced by enclosure and imprisonment in the peace of society, they *revert* to the innocence of the beast-of-prey conscience, like jubilant monsters, who perhaps come from a ghostly bout of murder, arson, rape, and torture, with bravado and a moral equanimity, as though merely some wild student's prank had been played....It is impossible not to recognize at the core of all these aristocratic races the

beast of prey; the magnificent *blond brute* [italics Nietzsche's], av-
idly rampant for spoil and victory; this hidden core needed an
outlet from time to time, the beast must get loose again, must return into the wilderness – the Roman, Arabic, German, and Jap-
anese nobility, the Homeric heroes, the Scandinavian Vikings, are
all alike in this need. It is the aristocratic races who have left the
idea "Barbarian" on all the tracks in which they have marched;
nay, a consciousness of this very barbarianism, and even a pride in
it, manifests itself even in their highest civilisation....This audacity
of aristocratic races, mad, absurd, and spasmodic as may be its
expression...their awful joy and intense delight in all destruction,
in all the ecstasies of victory and cruelty,– all these features become crystallised, for those who suffered thereby in the picture of
the "barbarian," of the "evil enemy," perhaps of the "Goth" and
the "Vandal." The profound, icy mistrust which the German pro-
vokes, as soon as he arrives at power,– even at the present time,–
is always still an aftermath of that inextinguishable horror with
which for whole centuries Europe has regarded the wrath of the
blonde Teuton beast....[14]

And Nietzsche thinks that these aristocratic races would provide the proper foundation of a governmental state—a state which
imposes its will by violence and maintains its authority without the
sanction of the governed. A state which fits "a hitherto unchecked
and amorphous [free and independent] population into a fixed
form...by acts of violence and nothing else"..:

> that the oldest "State" appeared consequently as a ghastly tyr-
> anny, a grinding ruthless piece of machinery, which went on
> working, till this raw material of a semi-animal populace was not
> only thoroughly kneaded and elastic, but also *moulded* [italics
> Nietzsche's]. I used the word "State"; my meaning is self-evident,
> namely, a herd of blond beasts of prey, a race of conquerors and
> masters, which with all its warlike organisation and all its organ-

izing power pounces with its terrible claws on a population....Such is the origin of the "State." That fantastic theory that
makes it begin with a contract is, I think, disposed of. He who
can command, he who is a master by "nature"...what has he to
do with contracts?[15]

The "contract" Nietzsche speaks so contemptuously of here is
a fundamental principle of a liberal society known as *the contract
theory of the state*. This theory says that a legitimate government is
established through a voluntary contractual agreement between the
government and those who are governed. Under the terms of such
a contract the people agree to obey the laws of the state so long as
they perceive that these laws are in their best interest. If they come
to believe that the state is no longer acting in their best interest the
people can, according to this theory, rightfully dissolve the contract
and dissolve along with it the government. Modern democratic
republics are all based on this contract theory of the state, which
effectively makes the people the government and the state their
servant.

But Nietzsche implies that this "fantastic theory" is irrelevant
because the conquerors and the masters legitimately rule "by acts of
violence and nothing else." This attitude manifests Nietzsche's belief that rights are merely a reflection of power—of brute force—
and have no meaningful basis in morality. If this belief is true then
those who have no power also have no moral rights—and those
who have all power legitimately possess all rights. In the following
passages Nietzsche gives expression to his version of this idea that
"might makes right."

"That is how rights originate, recognized and guaranteed degrees of power," Nietzsche says in his volume *Daybreak*:

> If power-relationships undergo any material alteration, rights dis-
> appear and new ones are created – as is demonstrated in the

continual disappearance and reformation of rights between nations. If our power is materially diminished, the feeling of those who have hitherto guaranteed our rights changes...they henceforth deny our 'rights'. Likewise, if our power is materially increased, the feeling of those who have hitherto recognized it but whose recognition is no longer needed changes....*If our power appears to be deeply shaken or broken, our rights cease to exist: conversely, if we have grown very much more powerful, the rights of others, as we have previously conceded them, cease to exist for us* [emphasis added].[16]

HEDONISM

And what will Nietzsche's conquerors and masters do with those whose rights have ceased to exist along with their power? At this point in his moral theory Nietzsche the Social Darwinist morphs into Nietzsche the Cyrenaic Hedonist. We have already noted his enthusing about the "aristocratic races...awful joy and intense delight in all destruction, in all the ecstasies of victory and cruelty...." In the following passages Nietzsche shows that he himself personally relishes those sorts of ecstasies. Writing in his *The Genealogy of Morals* Nietzsche states that "the *infliction* [italic's Nietzsche's] of suffering produces the highest degree of happiness...:

> The sight of suffering does one good, the infliction of suffering does one more good – this is a hard maxim, but none the less a fundamental maxim....Without cruelty, no feast:[17] so teaches the oldest and longest history of man – and in punishment too is there so much of the *festive* [italics Nietzsche's].
>
> Entertaining, as I do, these thoughts...it should be shown specifically that, at the time when mankind was not yet ashamed of its cruelty, life in the world was brighter than it is nowadays....[18]

And in his aptly titled *Beyond Good and Evil* he writes that:

In late ages which may be proud of their humaneness there remains so much fear, so much *superstitious* fear of the 'savage cruel beast'....One should open one's eyes and take a new look at cruelty....Almost everything we call 'higher culture' is based on the spiritualization and intensification of *cruelty* [italics Nietzsche's] – this is my proposition....[I]ndeed fundamentally in everything sublime up to the highest and most refined thrills of metaphysics, derives its sweetness solely from the ingredient of cruelty mixed in with it.[19]

SUBJECTIVE IDEALISM AND THE ETHICS OF THE PREDATORS

But Cyrenaic Hedonism, Social Darwinism, Ethical Naturalism, and Moral Relativism are not the only philosophic arguments employed by the proponents of the ethics of the masters. Thus far we have considered primarily arguments which are immediately based on the epistemological philosophies of Skepticism and epistemological Subjectivism.[20] At this point we will look more closely at the doctrine of *metaphysical* Subjectivism. This form of Subjectivism, which is technically referred to as Subjective Idealism, is the proximate theoretical basis for certain later developments of the master morality.

Idealism, recall again, is the metaphysical doctrine which says that everything which exists is the manifestation of some mind, and is mental or spiritual in nature, like an idea. The two principal versions of this doctrine are the explicitly religious—which says that everything which exists is a projection from the mind of God—and the secular, which says that the universe is an emanation from the minds of people. The religious version of Idealism is simply referred to as religion, but the secular version is usually called Subjective Idealism because it says that everything which exists is a manifestation of the mind of a human subject or subjects.

Over the centuries there have been a number of ancient and modern forerunners of the secular or subjective varieties of Idealism. In modern times Descartes was a precursor and Bishop Berkeley a progenitor of the contemporary variations of this doctrine. But it was the German Idealist philosophers, beginning especially with Immanuel Kant, who really got the modern subjective idealist ball rolling. Today, variations of Subjective Idealism all but completely dominate the field of theoretical metaphysics.[21]

Kant had said that " 'all bodies, together with the space in which they are, must be considered nothing but mere representations in us, and exist nowhere but in our thoughts.' "[22] The German Idealists who followed Kant, men such as Johann Gottlieb Fichte and Georg Wilhelm Hegel, took this idea a bit further, saying that everything which existed *was* consciousness, and that consciousness was all that was. Hegel himself asserted that "consciousness is...all reality,"[23] and that "reality is self-consciousness."[24] Using these metaphysical assumptions as a jumping-off point Hegel concocted a perfect philosophic foundation for the doctrines of later megalomaniacs like Nietzsche.

Asserting that everything was a manifestation of the consciousness of a subject Hegel said that the subject was effectively the creator of the universe. What's more, since the entire universe was essentially an aspect of the consciousness of the subject the subject essentially *was* the universe—and the universe was the subject. The former argument effectively established a secular version of Creationism on a secular version of Theism and the latter argument derived a secular version of Pantheism from the metaphysics of Subjective Idealism. "In this way man becomes [the Hindu god] Brahma," Hegel said. "[T]here is no longer any distinction between the finite man and Brahma. In fact in this universality every difference has disappeared."[25]

And the universal subject, the secular Brahma, derives the same universal prerogatives from the premises of Creationism and Pantheism as does any other god. All things in the universe become the property of the universal subject as soon as he thinks the universe into existence. Because he is the Creator, he is the owner, and because he is All, he has a right to control all. "In thinking an object, I make it into thought and deprive it of its sensuous aspect," said Hegel, "I make it into something which is directly and essentially mine...:

> [I]t then ceases to stand over against me and I have taken from it the character of its own which it had in opposition to me. Just as Adam said to Eve: "Thou art flesh of my flesh and bone of my bone," so mind says: "This is mind of my mind and its foreign character has disappeared"....The variegated canvas of the world is before me; I stand over against it; by my theoretical attitude to it I overcome its opposition to me and make its content my own....If I now let these determinations and differences go, i.e. if I posit them in the *so-called external world* [emphasis added], they none the less still remain mine. They are what I have done, what I have made; they bear the trace of my mind.[26]

And this secular maker of the world, who owns all things and before whom all opposition falls, is the new " 'lord and master of the world' [who] takes himself in this way to be the absolute person, comprising...all existence within himself, for whom there exists no higher type of spirit:

> He is a person: but the solitary single person who has taken his stand confronting all. These all constitute and establish the triumphant universality of the one person....But this master and lord of the world, aware of his being the sum and substance of all actual powers, is the titanic self-consciousness, which takes itself to be the living God.

And this "[l]ord of the world becomes really conscious of what he is...by that power of destruction which he exercises against the...the selfhood of his subjects," says Hegel.[27] For like the gods of the theocratic religions of the past he has authority not merely over the physical universe, but over every aspect of the universe, including human politics. Hegel, who like Kant before him was an employee of the Hohenzollern autocracy's state educational apparatus, may have simply been trying to endear himself to his aristocratic masters by contriving a secular replacement for the crumbling theocratic dogmas which had previously sustained the European nobility. But he ended up helping to provide ideas and inspiration to the new breed of sociopathic intellectuals like Nietzsche who would egg on a new type of aspiring lord and master.

Nietzsche had considered that a principal purpose of his philosophizing was that of "the breeding of a new ruling caste for Europe."[28] And for the political demons he was conjuring no idea could have been more tantalizing than the Subjective Idealism which told them that they had created, and that they *were*, everything they were conscious of. As Hegel himself had noted, "Subjectivity is insatiably greedy to concentrate and drown everything in this single spring of the pure ego."[29] Nietzsche expressed this metaphysical version of Subjectivism in his own philosophical opus, and passed it along to the promulgators of the ethics of the masters who learned from him.

"*What is our neighbor?*" Nietzsche asks of the metaphysical nature of his fellow human beings:

> What do we understand to be the boundaries of our neighbor: I mean that with which he as it were engraves and impresses himself into and upon us? We understand nothing of him except the *change in us* of which he is the cause – our knowledge of him is

like hollow space *which has been shaped.* We attribute to him the sensations his actions evoke in us, and thus bestow upon him a false, inverted positivity. According to our knowledge of ourself we make of him a satellite of our own system: and he shines for us or grows dark and we are the ultimate cause in both cases – we nonetheless believe the opposite! World of phantoms in which we live! Inverted, upsidedown, empty world, yet dreamed of as *full* and *upright* [italics Nietzsche's]![30]

SOCIOPATHIC NARCISSISM

In this passage Nietzsche starts out from the skeptic position that our epistemological faculties distort, rather than apprehend, the world around us. He then proceeds logically to the epistemologically subjectivist conclusion that our knowledge of the world is really just the knowledge of the processes of our own consciousness, not the real world. Then he makes the inferential leap to the *metaphysically* subjectivist position that the world we apprehend, and by implication our neighbor as well, is really just a hallucinatory phantom of which we ourselves are the cause. From that position it is just a logical skip and a jump to the political premise that our neighbor is just a "satellite" of ourselves—in fact, *is* ourselves.

And if our neighbor is just an aspect of ourselves then we have every right to do whatever we want to our neighbor, and indeed, to the whole human race. To a political predator this particular implication of Subjective Idealism can seem especially delectable. One of the most famous of the modern political and intellectual predators in whose writings this idea was manifested was the German existentialist philosopher Martin Heidegger. Heidegger's personal brand of political predationism was German Nazism—he was a high level Nazi academic administrator as well as a philosophical champion of Hitlerian Nazism.

Heidegger was immediately influenced as a philosopher by the "Phenomenology" of the Austrian/German philosopher Edmund Husserl. Phenomenology, as the term has come to be used within the province of academic philosophy, is a sort of brand-name for a late nineteenth and early twentieth century philosophical movement which promulgated the basic ideas of Subjective Idealism. When Heidegger wrote that "the fundamental question of philosophy....must be treated phenomenologically,"[31] what he was saying was that he was a subjective idealist, and that like all subjective idealists, believed that everything was created by human consciousness, was human consciousness, and could be understood merely by examining the contents of human consciousness.

And like many, if not most subjective idealists, Heidegger believed that everything was and everything happened as an effect of *his* human consciousness. "Just as I am Nature, so I am history,"[32] Heidegger noted in his turbid treatise *Being and Time*. And if nature, and all human history, was Martin Heidegger, then people, and everything that people did, must be Martin Heidegger as well. Writing is his *Introduction to Modern Existentialism* Ernst Breisach noted the implication of this for all of the people in the world who were *not* Martin Heidegger.

"Western philosophy, with a few exceptions, has always viewed man as being in the world...." Breisach observed:

> Against this stands Heidegger's being-in-the-world. *Dasein* [33] and world are joined. They do not exist apart from each other....Only the whole man understood in total interdependence with his world provides a correct point of departure for philosophical thinking....With the total interdependence between man and his world accepted as fundamental fact, man relates himself in new ways to both things and persons. Things, for example, are then not just there, as they are for an observer, but assume the quality of tools....[34]

For with all things subjectively dependent for their existence on a man—or upon groups of men or women as is the case with Social Subjectivism—all things may then be viewed as the "tools" of, or as the property of, or as the parts of the person or persons who subjectively create these things. This goes not only for things in the world which are inanimate, such as pens and desks and mountains; but for aspects of the world which are living human beings as well. Hence we may justifiably relate to other human beings as the god of the Bible says that He relates to the people whom He creates: as "pots" made for noble or for common use. In other words, we may relate to people as though they had the "quality of tools."

And it is this right to use people as though they were pots or tools that Heidegger was asserting when he wrote in *Being and Time* that "We are ourselves the entities to be analysed. The Being of any such entity is *in each case mine*" [italics Heidegger's].[35] Being, then, and all other human beings, are "mine" for Heidegger because he *is* these entities to be analyzed. And because Heidegger is all things and all people he has a right to use all things and all people as though they were merely his personal "tools." Heidegger personally popularized this notion among people who used human beings as though they were tools—the Nazis—and passed it along to one of his students who would later become the principal advocate of such ideas in the post-Nazi-German period: the French existentialist philosopher Jean-Paul Sartre.

Jean-Paul Sartre, like his Nazi teacher, considered that Subjectivism constituted the essence of Existentialism. Of existentialists generally he said that "[w]hat they have in common is that they think that...subjectivity must be the starting point."[36] And also like his teacher Sartre considered that metaphysical Subjectivism, or Subjective Idealism, allowed him to claim that because his consciousness created all things that he therefore owned all things—and had a right to control all things because all things were really just aspects of himself. Sartre expressed these notions in a series of abstruse passages near the end of his turgidly prolix *Being and Nothingness*. Although furtively obscurantist the sinister drift of these excerpts is nevertheless unmistakable.

"In knowing, consciousness attracts the object to itself and incorporates it in itself. Knowledge is assimilation," Sartre wrote:

> The known is transformed into *me*; it becomes my thought and thereby consents to receive its existence from me alone....[T]he known object...is entirely within me, assimilated, transformed into myself, and it is entirely *me*....
>
> ....
>
> In fact the internal relation...effects the unification of the possessor and the possessed. This means that the possessor and the possessed constitute ideally a unique reality. To possess is to be united with the object possessed in the form of appropriation; to wish to possess is to wish to be united to an object in this relation....[A]nd the appropriation in each case was marked by the fact that the object appeared simultaneously to be a kind of subjective emanation of ourselves....
>
> ....
>
> To have is first to create. And the bond of ownership which is established then is a bond of continuous creation....But the original, radical relation of creation is a relation of emanation, and the difficulties encountered by the Cartesian theory of substance are there to help us discover this relation. What I create is still me—if by creating we mean to bring matter and form to existence. The tragedy of the absolute Creator, if he existed, would be the impossibility of getting out of himself, for whatever he created could be only himself. Where could my creation derive any objectivity and independence since its form and matter are from me?...I must sustain it in existence by a continuous creation.

Thus to the extent that I appear to myself as *creating* objects by the sole relation of appropriation, these objects are *myself.* The pen and the pipe, the clothing, the desk, the house—are myself. The totality of my possessions reflects the totality of my being. I *am* what I have. It is I myself which I touch in this cup, in this trinket. This mountain which I climb is myself to the extent that I conquer it; and when I am at its summit, which I have "achieved" at the cost of this same effort, when I attain this magnificent view of the valley and the surrounding peaks, then I *am* the view; the panorama is myself dilated to the horizon, for it exists only through me, only for me.

But creation is an evanescent concept which can exist only through its movement. If we stop it, it disappears. At the extreme limits of its acceptance, it is annihilated; either I find only my pure subjectivity or else I encounter a naked, indifferent material-ity which no longer has any relation to me. *Creation* can be con-ceived and maintained only as a continued transition from one term to the other....This is what we believe that we are realizing in possession. The possessed object as possessed is a continuous creation....Possession is a magical relation; I *am* these objects which I possess....In so far as possession is a continuous creation, I apprehend the possessed object as founded by me in its being. On the other hand, in so far as creation is emanation, this object is reabsorbed in me, it is only myself....it is not-me, it is myself facing myself....[37]

And it is not only desks and houses and mountains that are just so many objects magically emanating from the consciousness of Sartre. People, too, are dependent for their existence on Sartre, are created by Sartre, and are aspects of Sartre. Following the epis-temological and metaphysical logic of the German Idealists, and especially that of Kant and Hegel, Sartre says that people are merely the "perceptible manifestations" of his own awareness, which have no "separate existence" independent of himself. "This woman whom I see coming toward me, this man who is passing by in the street, this beggar whom I hear calling before my window, are all for me *objects*—of that there is no doubt," Sartre says:

> But we have seen that if this relation of object-ness is the funda-mental relation between the Other and myself, then the Other's existence remains purely conjectural....The classical theories are right in considering that every perceived human organism *refers* to something....Their mistake lies in believing that this reference in-dicates a separate existence, a consciousness which would be be-hind its perceptible manifestations as the noumenon [the actual thing] is behind the Kantian *Empfindung* [the sense-perception of a thing; italics Sartre's].[38]

And if people are merely objects which have no "separate ex-istence" from himself then Sartre can do with people as he pleases. One of the things he wanted to do with them was knead them into ideal subjects of an authoritarian state. He did this by using his "magical" subjective powers to change the nature of people in a manner that was consistent with his own political ideology. As we've noted throughout this study the power to change the metaphysical nature of people confers the power to change the nature of political morality.

"[L]et us at once announce the discovery of a world which we shall call inter-subjectivity; this is the world in which man decides what he is and what others are,"[39] Sartre wrote in his *Existentialism*. Sartre expressed the notion that he could subjectively decide what other people are through the use of the phrase "*existence precedes essence*."[40] By "existence precedes essence" Sartre meant that a per-son at first exists without having any nature—an instance of Hera-cliteanism—and "[o]nly afterward...will have made what he will be."[41]

Although at first this sounds as though Sartre is merely expressing the benign notion that a person can decide for itself what its own psychological and moral character will be—can be a moral "self-made man," so to speak—what he is actually asserting is that a person can subjectively determine what human *metaphysical* nature will be. "What they have in common," Sartre wrote of the existentialists, "is that they think that existence precedes essence, or, if you prefer, that subjectivity must be the starting point...."[42]

> What is meant here by saying that existence precedes essence? It means that, first of all, man exists, turns up, appears on the scene, and, only afterwords, defines himself. If man, as the existentialist conceives him, is indefinable, it is because at first he is nothing. Only afterword will he be something, and he himself will have made what he will be. Thus, there is no human nature, since there is no God to conceive it. Not only is man what he conceives himself to be, but he is also only what he wills himself to be after this thrust toward existence.
>
> Man is nothing else but what he makes of himself. Such is the first principle of existentialism. It is also what is called subjectivity....But if existence really does precede essence, man is responsible for what he is....And when we say that a man is responsible for himself, we do not only mean that he is responsible for his own individuality, but that he is responsible for all men....In fact, in creating the man that we want to be...our acts...at the same time create an image of man as we think he ought to be....[T]he image is valid for everybody, for our whole age. Thus our responsibility is much greater than we might have supposed, because it involves all mankind.[43]

And because Sartre was an authoritarian—he was specifically a Marxist—we shouldn't be surprised that he used his subjectivity to create an image of all mankind which could provide a basis for his Marxist ideology: "Our subjectivism allows for certainties on the basis of which we can join you in the field of the probable," Sartre said to the French Marxist writer and activist Pierre Naville in an interview published in the 1947 edition of Sartre's *Existentialism*:

> If you do not define truth, how is Marx's theory to be conceived otherwise than as a doctrine which appears, disappears, is modified, and has only the value of a theory? How is a dialectic of history[44] to be established if one doesn't begin by setting up certain rules? We can find them in the Cartesian *cogito*; we can find them only by placing ourselves on the grounds of subjectivity. We've never argued the fact that man is constantly an object for man, but reciprocally, to grasp the object as such, a subject is needed....[45]

And "man is constantly an object" for Sartre because Sartre's Subjective Idealism grasps man as a mere emanation of Sartre's psyche—a part of Sartre which he can use as an organism uses a part of its body. The reader should note that this sociopathic—one might even say psychopathic—doctrine is fundamentally consistent with Karl Marx's objectification of man by representing people as merely being "cells" in the "organic whole"[46] of society conceived of as a single being. Indeed, it may be said that Sartre's Marxism is simply a psychopathological projection of his solipsistic metaphysics and sociopathic ethics into the realm of political philosophy— and that Marxist dogmatism is born of the subjectivity of sociopathologies like Sartre's.

And hence the predatory ethics of the masters is seen to lead logically to the authoritarian politics of the tyrants. For it is out of the darkness of the hearts of predators that such phantasmagorical rationalizations for tyranny emerge. Five hundred years before the beginning of the Christian takeover of Rome the Greek Sophist philosophers were explaining to themselves why they could do whatever they wanted to their fellow human beings, morality be damned. And in modern times, beginning especially with Kant and the German Idealists, and segueing into the philosophies of the phenomenologists, existentialists, and later the so-called postmodernists and deconstructionists,[47] the philosophic heirs of this tradition lead the worst of men to, in Nietzsche's words, "the immovable faith that to a being such as 'we are' other beings have to be subordinate by their nature, and sacrifice themselves to us."[48]

CHAPTER THIRTEEN

EGALITARIANISM

With the completion of the discussion of the authoritarian tradition of ethics we are now ready to move on to the concluding sections of this survey, which evaluate the nature of the institutions which propagate authoritarian ideas, and which also introduce the opposite tradition of ideas—those which underpin liberal rather than authoritarian societies. However, before we proceed it may be advisable to examine one last tangent of authoritarian moral argument—one which has historically been a less influential aspect of this tradition but which has recently become more prominent. This theory is known contemporarily as *Egalitarianism*, although most commonplace definitions of this term do not exclusively denote the concept we are about to consider.

The word Egalitarianism refers to doctrines of equality in human relationships. In the arena of political philosophy theories of equality include the conventional notion that most adult human beings are approximately equal in their native capacities and therefore have essentially equal rights, as well as what might be referred to as the *distributive theory of equality* which says that everyone is of equal moral stature and therefore deserves exactly the same amount of the things which people value. The former hypothesis establishes a premise for political Liberalism by smashing the racist, classist, and sexist dogmas which underpin authoritarian elitism; the latter doctrine, however, is based on classically conservative premises and provides logical jumping-off points for arguments which can be used to subvert a free society. It is the latter conception of Egalitarianism with which we are here concerned.

The distributive theory of Egalitarianism can be used to subvert free societies by subverting individuals' authority over the values of property and person. It does this by stating or implying that because individuals do not really produce or otherwise earn such values that they therefore have no moral claim to them. Since individuals have no special claim to values there is no reason why one person should have more of any value than does another person, this theory says; so "fairness" requires that values be redistributed equitably from those who have more to those who have less. Because, as a practical matter, only the state can accomplish such a redistribution, this argument effectively transfers all authority over everything from individuals to the state.

The ideas which provide the foundations for the argument that individuals do not produce values are the classic authoritarian metaphysical doctrines which have been examined throughout this survey. The religious and secular versions of Idealism state that values are produced by, or simply are, God, or some secular version of God. The doctrine of Materialism states or implies that human productivity is simply an automatic natural process, like the production of rain by clouds, for which no one is responsible. And the doctrine of Heracliteanism suggests that there is no causal relationship between the cause of human effort and the effect of the production of finished goods, and/or the acquirement of ability and talent. Egalitarian theories which call for the redistribution of values are all based on variations of one or more of these doctrines.

The great modern statement of the distributive notion of Egalitarianism is Harvard philosopher John Rawls' opus *A Theory of Justice*. In this tome Professor Rawls based his call for the equitable redistribution of values chiefly upon the premise that since the present, unfair distribution results from the "arbitrary"[1] allotment of "natural assets,"[2]—talents and other advantages—that what he called "justice as fairness"[3] required the reapportionment of values so that everyone has approximately the same amount of most things. Rawls' argument that anyone who has more is unjustly advantaged and that anyone who has less deserves "redress"[4] was thus founded primarily on the Heraclitean notion that events occur arbitrarily, that is, without cause, and the materialist idea that the possession of "natural" talents and other advantages such as family background automatically causes a person to attain wealth. Hence anyone who has more is the beneficiary of a combination of blind luck and deterministic mechanics, and anyone who has less is the victim of these same impersonal forces. This theory completely eliminates the notions of volitional effort and aspirational striving as factors in determining whether or not someone actually deserves and has a right to the good things which they have. In *A Theory of Justice* Rawls writes of the need to prevent:

> [T]he distribution of wealth and income to be determined by the natural distribution of abilities and talents….[whereby] distributive shares are decided by the outcome of the natural lottery; and this outcome is arbitrary from a moral perspective. There is no more reason to permit the distribution of income and wealth to be settled by the distribution of natural assets than by historical and social fortune….The extent to which natural capacities develop and reach fruition is affected by all kinds of social conditions and class attitudes. Even the willingness to make an effort,

to try, and so to be deserving in the ordinary sense is itself dependent upon happy family and social circumstances....and therefore we may want to adopt a principle which recognizes this fact and also mitigates the arbitrary effects of the natural lottery itself.[5]

So since even the ability "to try" is "dependent" on the luck of the natural and family "lottery" the individual cannot be credited with any moral virtue whatsoever. Nor does Rawls think there is any reason to acknowledge a person's right to income and wealth which, after all, simply fell into their lap as a result of a fortunate accident. Because he believes that income is essentially a naturally occurring phenomenon that is not attributable to the efforts of anyone Rawls advocates that such a natural resource be regarded as a "common asset" like air or sunlight, which no one has a special right to and none may justly be denied. However, since some have arbitrarily come into possession of more of this naturally occurring wealth than others income must be redistributed to make sure that everyone has equal access to the fruits of luck and nature:

> We see then that the...principle represents, in effect, an agreement to regard the distribution of natural talents as a common asset and to share in the benefits of this distribution whatever it turns out to be. Those who have been favored by nature, whoever they are, may gain from their good fortune only on terms that improve the situation of those who have lost out. The naturally advantaged are not to gain merely because they are more gifted....[6]

But a doctrine which views wealth as a natural resource which the lucky have undeservedly acquired and the unlucky are unjustly being denied will necessarily require that the institutions of justice—the government—intervene to force the lucky to share with the less fortunate. Hence Rawls' regressive version of Egalitarianism is inherently favorable to the state control of wealth and hostile to private property and economic liberty. Because the redistribution of income represented as a gift of nature and fortune unavoidably requires that ultimate authority over wealth be taken away from private individuals and placed in the hands of the state Rawls' prescription is intrinsically authoritarian in practice. It is intrinsically authoritarian in theory because it is based on the assumption that private individuals are not responsible for the production of wealth and therefore have no right to it.

IDEALISM AND EGALITARIANISM

Rawls' *A Theory of Justice* emphasizes the use of materialist and Heraclitean doctrines in providing premises for its call for the redistribution of wealth; but as we noted a few pages earlier metaphysically idealist philosophies can also be used for this same purpose. By claiming that God or some secularized representation of God is responsible for the creation of all values egalitarians can overturn human individuals' claims on values and thereby clear the way for the argument that wealth should be redistributed equitably. Let us now consider how both the religious and the secular versions of metaphysical Idealism can be used to underpin egalitarian doctrines by examining first a Christian and then an early Marxist argument.

The Christian Gospels offer several examples of egalitarian doctrines which are established on the idealist concept that there is a God who produces all values and who therefore has a right to determine how values are apportioned. Of these none more clearly addresses the issue of equality of distribution than does *The Parable of the Workers in the Vineyard* in the Gospel According To Matthew. Although this passage is often interpreted as simply meaning that God is equally as welcoming to those who convert later to Christianity as He is to those who convert earlier, the principles affirmed in the allegory are as applicable to economic relationships as they are to the criteria of religious conversion.

In *The Parable of the Workers in the Vineyard* in Matthew Jesus offers an allegorical rationale for Egalitarianism in a Christian society. The kingdom of heaven is said to be like a landowner who hires men in the morning to work in a vineyard, agreeing to pay them a denarius a day. The landowner, allegorically the kingdom, then goes into a market and hires more workers who start to work as much as several hours later. At the end of the day the kingdom pays all the workers a denarius, but the workers who started to work earliest protest that the "men who were hired last worked only one hour ...and you have made them equal to us who have borne the burden of the work and the heat of the day." The kingdom/landowner then responds to this complaint by stating "I am not being unfair to you. Didn't you agree to work for a denarius....Don't I have the right to do what I want with my own money?" (Matt. 20:12, 13, 15, NIV).

The logic of this response can seem perplexing because the allegory of the vineyard obscures the critical context of who owns values in a Christian kingdom, and because it equates a state, a "kingdom," with a person, the landowner. A human landowner might well have the right to pay his workers as Jesus describes, but where does a Christian state, the "kingdom of heaven," get "the right to do what I want with my own money?" In a liberal society wealth is owned by the private individuals who produce it, or who otherwise acquire it legitimately from those who produce it, so the state has no right to impose egalitarian wage schemes upon workers. But in a Christian theocracy everything is owned by the God who creates everything, and this divine "landowner" would indeed have the right to pay everyone equally.

MARXIST EGALITARIANISM

Jesus gives expression to his religious version of redistributive Egalitarianism by saying "[s]o the last will be first, and the first will be last," (Matt. 20:16, NIV) but centuries later Karl Marx voiced a secular variant of this idea with the phrase "From each according to his abilities, to each according to his needs!"[7] And just as Jesus' "landowner" asserted his moral justification for the equal distribution of wealth by asking "[d]on't I have the right to do what I want with my own money?" so Marx referred to his justification by asserting, in his essay *The Criticism of the Gotha Program*, that "equitable distribution'….assumes a society in which the means of labor are common property…."[8]

Like those of Rawls and Jesus Marx's justification for the redistribution of wealth requires establishing that those who seem to produce wealth don't really produce it. In *A Theory of Justice* Rawls primarily employs materialist and Heraclitean doctrines to accomplish this while the Gospels, obviously, utilize idealist. As a young man Marx at first experimented with a secular version of Jesus' idealist premises, and then, in his mature philosophy, renounced Idealism and embraced a rationale that was closer to Rawlsian Materialism. Let us review how Marx at first employed idealist doctrines as grounds for robbing individuals of credit for the production of wealth, and then, in his later work, used materialist.

In the chapter of our study entitled *Metaphysics* we examined Marx's early doctrine of the "species-being" who "intellectually, in his consciousness" produces both "himself" and the "whole of nature" in the manner of a god creating the universe. This "species-being," please recall, was Marx's youthful conception of humanity as a single social organism which psychically creates the *"objective world"* according to the principles of the social version of Subjective Idealism. The species-being doctrine subverts the individual's claims on property because if it is man as a species-being who creates the universe then indeed "the means of labor are common property." And if the means of labor are common property, then " 'equitable distribution' " would be entirely justifiable.

But Marx did not restrict himself to idealist premises in his efforts to overthrow the intellectual supports of income distribution based on the prerogatives of private ownership. A practicing philosophic pragmatist, he never hesitated to switch metaphysical sides if he thought that doing so might work as a means to his ends. As we mentioned earlier Marx was just as happy to employ the materialist doctrines he is famous for as he was idealist concepts if he thought that this would be practical. So when he saw it to his advantage Marx was more than willing to ascribe human productivity to the mechanical forces of materiality, just as was Rawls.

Perhaps believing that the rise of science and the debunking of religion in nineteenth century Europe made a "scientific socialism" more palatable than a secular version of Christ's heavenly vineyard Marx decided to turn his earlier Idealism "right side up" and began representing his system as a technical analysis of natural law as it applied to human society. In the preface to the second edition of his *Das Capital* he renounced Idealism like a spurned lover and embraced a materialist explanation of the "iron laws" which determine society's development and function. But as in his idealist period Marx in his materialist system continued to represent society as an organism—except that now human individuals were depicted as parts of an organism which was physical rather than spiritual.

So loosely following the ideas of the German idealist philosopher Georg Hegel, but couching them in materialist terms, Marx in *Das Capital* and *The Communist Manifesto* depicted society as a living physical organism which uses economic forces to regulate human culture and evolve itself into higher states of social development. These economic forces, according to Marx and his intellectual collaborator Friedrich Engels, advance society through a Darwinistic clash of economic classes, determining "intellectual life generally"[9] and governing the production of material goods through a "social process of production"[10] in which "workmen are parts of a living mechanism."[11] Because the entire intellectual and material production of society "is a collective product,"[12] not a "personal"[13] one, Marx in the *Manifesto* asserts that "capital is converted into common property, into the property of all members of society..."[14] And, of course, a society in which capital is the common property of all the members of society has every right to redistribute wealth "[f]rom each according to his abilities, to each according to his needs!"

But here the question may arise: why would an authoritarian philosopher propagate egalitarian doctrines in the first place? After all, isn't the purpose of authoritarian ideology to reapportion wealth away from the common people and to a privileged class? This question needs to be answered if we are to avoid the mistake, so often made in the case of Marx and Jesus, of attributing benevolent motives to people who in fact profoundly mean us ill. So let us give some further consideration as to how egalitarian ideas can subvert a liberal society and advance the interests of a conservative elite.

The reason why authoritarian philosophers propagate egalitarian doctrines is to persuade great numbers of ordinary people to get on board the authoritarian cattle train. Once large masses of people have been convinced that it is in their interest to abandon the principles of a free society and embrace those of an authoritarian state it is relatively easy for an autocratic elite to prevail politically. In a society such as ours, which is still relatively free, this tactic can serve to move society by increments in the direction of authoritarianism; and in a society which is already authoritarian a cannily managed strategy of economic reapportionment can help sustain the delicate psycho-political balance which permits an exploitative and otherwise despicable regime to exist.

Large masses of people can be persuaded to embrace Egalitarianism by convincing them that doing so is both just and profitable. Persuading a significant proportion of society that Egalitarianism can be profitable is relatively easy because in any society at least half of the people can readily be represented as proportionately disadvantaged and so deserving of compensation. But persuading large numbers of people that Egalitarianism is just requires drenching the society in this doctrine's philosophic premises. These premises, most significantly, are the idealist, materialist, and Heraclitean metaphysical doctrines we are already familiar with.

Drenching society in the premises of Egalitarianism, however, has a cultural effect that is likely unforeseen by the average person—although not, in all probability, by the intellectuals doing the drenching. For the same idealist, materialist, and Heraclitean premises which provide the grounds for egalitarian doctrines also, as we have noted, provide the premises for the elitist dogmas upon which authoritarian states are established. What's more, because egalitarian arguments for redistribution establish that the reapportionment of values is justifiable only because no mortal individual really has a right to values, the identical arguments which undermine the productive individual's right to values can also be used to take away *everyone's* right to values. By a subtle trick of logic, then, all those who reach out to grab the fruits of egalitarian redistributionism find that they have surrendered themselves to the authoritarian philosophic Mephistopheles.

We began this study with the warning that if you could not recognize the ideas upon which authoritarian states are established you would not be able to protect yourself against those ideas—and with the promise that if you read this book you would be able to identify and thereby defend yourself from both the flowers of philosophic evil and those who offer them to you. With this discussion of the doctrine of Egalitarianism we have identified what is surely authoritarian ideology's slipperiest and most insidious intellectual trick, and as a result you should now be well prepared to protect yourself against both this as well as the other arguments which represent the authoritarian ideological tradition's doctrinal stock-in-trade. But although we have identified the ideas and the intellectual traditions which provide the foundations of authoritarian political institutions we have thus far paid far less attention to the kinds of *intellectual* institutions which have historically propagated these ideas. To further prepare readers to defend themselves against those who use ideas as instruments of political evil we will now give greater scrutiny to this issue.

CHAPTER FOURTEEN

THE GARDENERS OF EVIL

CONCERNING A STATE-INTELLECTUAL PLEXUS

With the exception of certain very modern developments in philosophy most of the ideas with which this survey has been concerned may seem to belong to the past, even to the very distant past; and contemporary readers might well be excused for wondering why they should bother to immerse themselves in their study. Why should we worry about the beliefs which dominated medieval Europe, or which underpinned forms of authoritarianism which were militarily defeated two or three generations ago, when we ourselves seem well-insulated from the political effects of these ideas by enlightened institutions of legal procedure and sturdy Constitutional guarantees? But this study was prepared in the belief that authoritarian ideas still represent a present, if not entirely clear, danger to liberal societies. This is so because it is not only established authoritarian states which have an interest in promoting destructive philosophic doctrines: any individual or institution which has an interest in violating basic human rights will have an interest in promulgating ideologies which can be used to subvert our belief in those rights. But now the contemporary reader may wonder: are there really any individuals or institutions within our modern, relatively liberal societies which have such interests?

Obviously, a common criminal has an interest in subverting humanity's basic rights and liberties. But to determine whether or not there are any truly influential individuals or institutions in our midst which share a common criminal's interests we should first give thought to what those rights and liberties are. One way to do this is to remind ourselves of what some of the basic tenets of authoritarian political philosophy say; for the purpose of these tenets is to subvert the rights and liberties upon which progressive societies are established.

Major tenets of authoritarian philosophy say that individuals have no right to control their own lives because they are not really individuals, but merely parts of one greater Individual. And they say that because individuals owe their lives and livelihoods to this great Individual that they are duty-bound to serve this Individual and have no right to serve their own interests. With regard to property, the tenets of authoritarian philosophy say that because all property is part of or is created by some great, divine or quasi-divine Individual that only this Being and no empirically apparent, objectively independent individual has any rights over property. Because the claims of authoritarian states rest on such tenets it stands to reason that the opposite assumptions constitute the premises of liberal societies. And indeed this is exactly the case: liberal societies are based upon the actual, objectively real independent individual's right to control itself and the property in which it has volitionally invested its labor.

This means that any institution which has an interest in abrogating the individual's right to control itself and its property may also have an interest in promoting authoritarian ideas. But can you think of any institutions within our modern liberal democracies which have such interests? During the recent economic crisis you as a citizen were compelled by your government to make involuntary loans to Wall Street banks and Detroit automobile companies. Were these loans consistent with your right to control yourself and your property? Do Wall Street banks and Detroit automobile companies have an interest in promoting authoritarian ideas?

And what about small businesses which receive loans from the Small Business Administration, or Midwestern farmers who receive subsidies from the United States Department of Agriculture? You are compelled to make these loans and provide these subsidies whether you want to or not, without your personal consent as an individual. Do government subsidized small businessmen and farmers have any interest in supporting the ideas upon which free societies are based? Are the loans and subsidies they receive consistent with your right to control yourself and your property?

And what about so-called "nationalized" businesses—businesses which were once private but have been taken over by the government—"Amtrak," the national passenger railway service, for instance, or some of the ferry systems in certain parts of the country? Or what about agencies which seem to have little to do with the government's core function of protecting our rights but which were founded as government enterprises in the first place—government agencies such as our cities' municipal bus systems and our regional airports and national air traffic control agencies—and in the United States, that granddaddy of all government enterprises, the U.S. Postal Service. Do the people who manage and work for such organizations have any reason to support your rights as an individual?

In a liberal society certain government agencies like the military and the courts are established as "public"—that is, as publicly subsidized, because if they weren't supported by every citizen they would have no reason to refrain from serving only the interests of the minority of people from whom they received their money. Can you imagine a court system which was responsive only to the interests of a small number of wealthy patrons from whom it received financial support? Out of regard for this concern, and out of a need to concentrate society's use of force in a few institutions which can be easily monitored by the people and the press, we make an exception for those who are in the business of forcibly protecting our rights and allow them to monopolize this business and to forcibly compel all of us to contribute to their maintenance.

But why are we compelled to support bus drivers and farmers and Wall Street bankers and Detroit automakers? Are these not precisely the sort of people which liberal governments are established to protect us from being compelled to support? And if the people in these professions have no right to live off public subsidies do they then have a reason to subvert the principles upon which liberal societies are based? Do they then have a reason to support the spread of the opposite principles—authoritarian principles?

But have you ever heard an executive of General Motors or the owner of a Small Business Administration assisted bicycle shop or a manager at Amtrak espouse the principles of authoritarian dogma? Perhaps they have and do but how effective would such people be at promoting these abstruse and sophisticated arguments? Not many people, after all, are likely to pay much attention to the philosophical pronouncements of big businessmen or small business owners or minor state and municipal employees. But is there any really large and influential institution interested in subverting liberal rights which people might *have* to pay attention to?

One which touched the hearts and minds of almost everyone in our society, or at least enough people to have a significant impact on our social and political culture?

What about the public schools?

But ah, you say, the public schools are legitimately part of the state—like the legislature or the military or the courts. They would have no financial interest in subverting liberal rights because they are rightfully subsidized by the state. But is this really true? Are schools and teachers legitimately subsidized by the state? In a liberal society are not the only people rightfully permitted state subsidies those who protect us from having to subsidize anyone else—protect us from being financially enslaved by our fellow citizens, so to speak? How do letter-carriers, small businessmen, Wall Street bankers and Detroit auto executives protect us from being enslaved? How do public school teachers?

And if public school and public university instructors are not in the business of protecting us and have no more right than Amtrak employees or Wall Street bankers or Midwestern farmers to compel us to subsidize them do they then share these other professions' presumable financial interest in subverting our liberal rights and freedoms? And if they do would they not, as instructors in the high schools, and state colleges and subsidized "private" universities throughout the land be in a splendid position to subvert these rights in the minds of large numbers of impressionable young people? The French totalitarian philosopher Auguste Comte said that "ideas govern the world, or throw it into chaos...all social mechanism rests upon opinions."[1] Who is in a better position to spread opinions about the ideas which govern our world—including philosophical ideas—than the teachers who govern our schools?

Many people in the liberal West today look upon the steady encroachment by the state upon individual rights and liberties and wonder about the "social mechanism" which is driving this governmental incursion. Given that the benefits of liberty are historically well-established and otherwise almost self-evident, why are so many people electing to deprive themselves of more and more of their own freedoms—and why would their elected officials seem so blithely willing to assist them in doing so? This seeming conundrum very reasonably invites speculation that some very influential apparatus of social manipulation is driving very large numbers of people to do what is manifestly not in their best interest. Might we not reasonably speculate that this apparatus may be our own schools?

In a June, 2012 article published in the Opinion/Editorials pages of the *New York Times*[2] University of Chicago professor Luigi Zingales bemoaned what he referred to as the "undue subsidy" of colleges and universities by federal and state governments. He pointed out that what he called academic "crony capitalism" helps "keep afloat" the "most subsidized industry of all: higher education." If these subsidies are indeed "undue"—presumably meaning *unjust*—would not those whom Professor Zingales refers to as a "privileged class (professors like myself)" have an interest in using the departments of their schools, including the philosophy departments, to promote ideas which can be used to justify injustice? And if they do would we not have reason to fear the spread of such ideas in our society?

Of course, the ideas we have been studying enjoy many ports of entry into our society. Churches, mosques, synagogues, and temples purvey the scriptures of the Bible, Koran, Torah, Bhaga-vad-gītā and other religious texts; and Adolf Hitler's *Mein Kampf* and Karl Marx's *Das Kapital* are available from any public library. But who taught you to reflexively revere secular philosophers like Socrates, Plato, and Descartes—to be dazzled, rather than disgusted by, the names of Kant, Hegel, Heidegger, and Sartre? Were you taught to admire these philosophers during your local church's Sunday service? Were their maxims quoted to you appreciatively by a trusted friend or mentor? Did you read their books yourself?

Perhaps you acquired your esteem for these philosophers through a kind of intellectual osmosis—a cultural process by which socially acceptable notions are subliminally communicated through popular media such as the arts, journalism, and the proselytizing of politicians. But even ideas which come to us through such media must have some societal point of origin. Religions have their own theologies and theologians which they are concerned to promote; and artists, journalists, and politicians don't usually spend their days with their heads buried in Plato's *Dialogues* or Kant's *Critique of Pure Reason*. So who's inculcating the artists, journalists, politicians, and you, with a reverence for the secular philosophers whose ideas can be used to subvert Liberalism and justify the various forms of "crony-capitalism?" Is it not reasonable to assume that it is, at least in part, the professorial "privileged class" of the "most subsidized industry of all: higher education"?

And indeed, contemporary university and college philosophy textbooks typically tender the most respectful introductions to the philosophers and philosophies we have been studying without ever even mentioning, with occasional exceptions for Plato, that these savants and their ideas are representative of—indeed *are*—the authoritarian tradition of thought.[3] Usually these volumes solicitously canvass these doctrines and thinkers in a manner which leaves the reader with the complacent impression of these philosophers' disinterested moral earnestness and high-minded probity. It is almost unheard of for one of these books to bluntly warn its readers that in perusing these doctrines they are entering the Boschian intellectual landscape of Adolf Hitler's Third Reich or Joseph Stalin's "gulag archipelago." Should we be concerned that this ambiguity represents an effort to trick us into entering this landscape ourselves?

But probably most of these books are written and published with no such evil intent. That said, however, what is all but certainly occurring is that the subsidized academic philosophers in our colleges and universities are trying to protect their own undue financial privileges by legitimizing the ideas which justify *all* undue privileges. And because the ideas which justify a petty injustice— undue subsidies for philosophy professors for instance—are logically the same ideas which justify the grossest of injustices, these academic crony-capitalists are compelled by philosophic logic to ally themselves with the ideas which underpinned Nazi Germany and Marxist Russia or be forced to abandon these arguments altogether. Because these professors know of no way—for there is none—of logically restricting the application of evil ideas to the defense of their own narrow financial interests without logically legitimizing the application of these ideas everywhere, the doctrines they release into their classrooms to protect these interests spread like intellectual Ebola viruses into every corner of society.

We promised you at the outset of this study that we would inoculate you against evil ideas by teaching you to recognize them. But the course of our discussion has introduced us to the necessity of discussing something else which we must learn to recognize if we are ever to be entirely safe from tyranny. This something else is a type of intrinsically evil institution which is dangerous to Western Liberalism precisely because it has a pecuniary interest in promoting evil ideas, as well as a means of promoting them. If we are not able to recognize this type of institution and its interests we will never be free from evil concepts, even if we are able to identify and refute them.

For want of a better term we will call this type of institution a *state-intellectual establishment.* A state-intellectual establishment is exactly what it sounds like: a state or state-subsidized body of persons who are in the business of developing and/or promulgating ideas.

Such people may be educators, philosophers, scientists, artists, or journalists—and most significant historically they have been priests. What state-intellectuals all have in common is the illegitimately subsidized businessman's interest in undermining free societies—and remember what Comte said: "*ideas govern the world.*"

Ideas govern the world because of the peculiar influence that the cognitive constructs we call concepts—which are abstract intellectual models of the world—have on creatures such as human beings. Unlike animals, human beings' bodies are not adequately adapted to the environment, so human beings cannot deal with the environment as animals do: through physical force exerted by their bodies. Human beings must therefore deal with their environment by using knowledge—not the simple, perceptual-level knowledge of sight and sound to which animals are restricted—such knowledge would be inadequate for human beings. Rather, human beings must deal with reality through the kind of knowledge which allows people to know all kinds of things which they couldn't possibly know if they couldn't think in abstract terms: knowledge in the form of ideas, expressed in the form of symbols, such as words.

Because people are so dependent on ideas those who are the masters of ideas have an overwhelming influence on society. When these masters of ideas become corrupt, as happens when they are unduly subsidized, they will try to destroy that political antithesis of corruption which is political and economic Liberalism. Because most of the West's intellectuals—especially that most influential type of intellectual which is a teacher—are now subsidized—the West's intellectual establishment is now working overtime to destroy liberal society. This leads us to the obvious conclusion that in order to defend liberal society we are going to have to destroy the contemporary state-intellectual establishment.

Destroying a state-intellectual establishment in a theocracy—

that is, in a society ruled by priests—means simply separating church and state. But in a secular society such as ours it means, first and foremost, legally prohibiting the direct and indirect subsidy of school teachers and university professors. It also means banning subsidies to any other type of intellectual, such as an artist, a scientist, or a journalist. Consistent with this imperative, in the United States of America, such a ban should take the form of an Amendment to the Constitution because in the United States Constitutional law is the sturdiest, most broadly applicable species of law. Advisable also is a clause incorporated into this Amendment which would more specifically and explicitly prohibit the indirect or direct subsidy of religion, because historically subsidized religious intellectuals—theologians, priests, and "prophets," etc.—have represented the gravest of all dangers to a free society.

And since we have touched once more upon the danger presented to free societies by religion let us take a moment to further elaborate upon this important subject. For particularly in the United States of America among all the nations of the liberal world there is a large number of well-intentioned but profoundly misinformed people who mistakenly believe that religion, and specifically Christianity, is a friend, rather than the bitterest enemy of, the Western concept of individual freedom. Throughout this study we have noted how religions use ideas to subvert liberty, and in the last few paragraphs we have explained why a subsidized priest has the same financial incentive as does any other type of subsidized intellectual to subvert a free society. But at this point it would be worthwhile to review the *institutional* role which religion has historically played in the subversion of liberty so that the reader will be less likely to make the mistake which so many American Christians have made in believing that their freedoms would be more secure if church and state were legally reattached.

At the dawn of humanity's political life most civilizations have been dominated by the more violent and unscrupulous people living within them, because it is enormously difficult to discover and institutionalize the philosophic principles and legal procedures upon which just societies are established. Because of this early human societies have almost always been ruled by brutal political authoritarians, who having once achieved power were understandably reluctant to surrender it. But just because a ruler dominates a society through brute strength does not mean that such a ruler is unintelligent. Despots are often very intelligent and it is usually not very long before the insight occurs to them that clever lying is a much safer and more economical means of controlling a population than is sheer violence. From this surmise lying as an instrument of political control is born.

Unsurprisingly, the first thing that a despot is concerned to lie about is the subject of who has a right and who has a duty to do what. Because the tyrant wants to manipulate his victims into believing that he has a right to do whatever he wants and his victims have a duty to do whatever they're told, everything the dictator says about right and duty—about morality in the realm of human relations—is meant to serve this purpose. The first doctrines developed to accomplish this were religious.

We have already discussed the specific arguments which religions use to buttress tyranny, so there is no reason to again review these tenets in detail. But to briefly recap, the tyrant, who often as not historically has also been a priest, has usually asserted something to the effect that he has met some Great Spirit on a mountaintop and that this Great Spirit has told him that He has chosen the tyrant to administrate all His property here on earth. The tyrant relates that because this Great Spirit, "God," is the creator of the earth and everything on it, that He therefore owns everything on earth, and so may rightfully confer upon the tyrant control of all things. A variation of this theme—the pantheistic—says that because the tyrant is the part of God which God uses to control those other parts of Himself which are the earth and human society, that everyone must obey the tyrant. Both of these doctrines have historically been used by political religion—including Judaism and Christianity—to strip all right to property and self away from individual human beings and bestow it upon the despots who are the viceroys of God.

Thus institutional religion has its beginning as the original state-intellectual establishment. But occasionally, such as long ago in Greece, there have been successful intellectual rebellions against these establishments and brave philosophers have postulated that everything in the universe is created by natural forces, not by some God. And they have proclaimed that everything which exists is a distinct entity, not part of some monistic Being. These hypotheses, which are the foundations of science, undermine the doctrines of Creationism and Pantheism, and even invalidate Theism itself—the idea that there is a God; and thus they crack the institutional pillars of theocratic authoritarianism.

Authoritarian intellectuals have typically countered such developments by concocting philosophies which advance religious logic behind the prestige and impressive terminological conventions of science. In ancient Greece political reactionaries like Plato formulated systematic dogmas of scientificalized theology which became the templates for most of the secular authoritarian ideologies developed since. Professionally, this sort of intellectual often succeeded in making a living as Socrates, Descartes, and Hegel did—by making themselves useful to the authoritarian power-elites of their eras. In periods dominated by theocratic authoritarianism such intellectuals usually had their institutional bases in the temples, churches, and monasteries of state-affiliated religions. But as the influence of religion was supplanted by more secular forms of authoritarianism they increasingly were employed in state-owned schools and universities which had originally been established to prepare young authoritarian elites for the responsibilities of governance.

These universities prepared the young elites to govern by, among other things, indoctrinating them in philosophic arguments which support the authoritarian state's right to rule and which undermine the ideas upon which free societies are established. But beginning in the late eighteenth century, as the influence of courageous liberals such as John Locke eroded the power of autocratic governments, many of the states which originally founded these universities were swept away by war or revolution. The state universities themselves, however, remained intact as state-supported institutions because progressive social reformers failed to grasp the danger that state-subsidized education represented to the newly liberalized European societies. As a result, in European universities today, the academic heirs of the tradition of the state-subsidization of education have continued to work to undermine liberal principles and institutions—not in support of the explicitly authoritarian governments which were their original patrons, but because these principles and institutions represent an eternal danger to their financial interests as members of an unduly subsidized class.

And in America, because the liberal political activists who founded the new nation also failed to recognize the danger represented by a subsidized educational establishment, a similar class of reactionary state pedagogues became entrenched in the vast plexus of American state universities, state-subsidized "private" colleges, public high-schools, middle-schools, and elementary schools. The intellectually vulnerable young people these schools educate then go on to become U.S. Supreme Court justices, Majority Leaders of the United States Senate, Speakers of the U.S. House of Representatives, and the editors of the editorial pages of every newspaper in the country. They become Hollywood scriptwriters and film directors, novelists and songwriters, producers of television news and entertainment programs—and Princeton University professors who become Presidents of the United States. And wherever they go and whatever they do they spread the authoritarian intellectual bacilli which they pick up in the subsidized schools. To stop this infection these schools, like the unduly subsidized churches and monasteries before them, must be abolished.

CHAPTER FIFTEEN

THE GARDEN OF GOOD

THE PREMISES OF A LIBERAL SOCIETY

At the dawn of that mighty period of cultural liberalization which was the Italian Renaissance a great liberal political activist and philosopher found himself chased out of politics by a reactionary theocratic establishment which was very far from receptive to his forward-thinking ideas. This ground-breaking political and philosophic progressive was Dante Alighieri, who had begun a career in Florentine civil service before being forced out of government and driven into exile by forces allied to the Catholic Papacy. During his enforced retirement from Florentine politics Dante set out to express his politically and philosophically radical conception of the world in the form of an allegorical epic poem. That poem was the *Divine Comedy*.

The *Divine Comedy* is sub-divided into three sections, or canticas. These sections are the *Inferno*, the *Purgatory*, and the *Paradise*. The *Inferno* is a description of hell; the *Purgatory* of a sort of divine reform school for sinners; and the *Paradise* is a depiction of the heavenly rewards of the virtuous. The epic's narrative sees Dante guided through Hades by the ghost of the Roman poet Virgil, who, after first giving him a tour of the regions of the damned, leads him up a hidden stairway toward the realm of the blessed. Analogically, it is now time for us to end our exploration of the dominions of damned ideas and damnable institutions and look upward toward, if not to exhaustively explore, the blessed sphere of the ideas which comprise the liberal tradition of political thought.

To understand the liberal tradition of thought the first thing we need to appreciate is that it is fundamentally distinguished from the authoritarian tradition by its fealty to the facts of reality. The authoritarian tradition of thinking, as we have seen, is based on chimerical metaphysical dogmas which distort reality in order to provide premises for authoritarian theories of politics. We've learned that these distorting dogmas are the authoritarian metaphysical theories of Idealism, Materialism, and Heracliteanism; so let's contrast these authoritarian metaphysical doctrines with their liberal counterparts in order to clarify our understanding of the liberal heritage of philosophy.

By contrast to Idealism the metaphysical ideas which underlie Liberalism do not say that reality is made out of spirit or thought. The metaphysical premises of liberal politics say that reality is physical or material, not immaterial, in nature. This means that the facts which pertain to political theory are detectable by the faculties which we use to detect the physical and the material—the faculties of the senses, such as the eyes. Because liberal political theoreticians say that reality is based on the physical they reject political theories which are based on ideas that have no perceptible references; and they base their own suppositions concerning political morality and political rights primarily on premises which can be verified perceptually, or empirically.

Idealist metaphysicians say that reality is spiritual and immaterial so they can replace physical reality with baseless dogma. This, ultimately, is what one of the most famous metaphysical idealists in history, Immanuel Kant, meant when he said that he intended to "deny *knowledge*, in order to make room for *faith*." The most historically significant dogma that idealists have purveyed is the creationist doctrine which says that reality is created by some mind, providing a premise for the assertion that a supernatural Creator has the right to claim all values. In contrast to Creationism, liberal theories of reality say that all things are either created by the mechanical forces of nature or by human beings themselves, and therefore that real values may rightfully be claimed by individual people.

And liberal theories of reality insist that individual human beings *are* individuals. Idealist theories of reality, by contrast, usually say that because all things are supernatural emanations from the mind of one great individual that this great individual therefore *is* all things, including all of the seeming individuals we perceive around us. Because idealist doctrines say that all individuals are this one great individual most political theories that are based on Idealism say that only this one individual has rights, and that all the rest of the world's individuals have no rights. Liberal theories of reality, by comparison, say that each of the apparent individual human beings we see around us is a *real* individual, and therefore has real rights.

But just because liberal metaphysical theorists believe that reality is exclusively material and not spiritual does not mean that these theorists are "materialists" in the sense that authoritarian metaphysicians are materialists. For although authoritarian philosophers usually represent their use of the word Materialism as referring to the theory that reality is exclusively material what they are primarily referring to is a theory about human nature and not about nature generally. This theory says that human behavior, and especially human intellectual functioning, is mechanistically determined by the cause-and-effect mechanics which govern the actions and reactions of the processes of crude matter. Historically, this theory has been used to justify political doctrines which say that because human behavior is determined by mechanical forces, and not by a conscious fealty to morality and truth, that only the brutish machinery of authoritarian statism can provide the social controls necessary to ensure human progress and sustain a benevolent society.

But Liberalism, by contrast, does not say that human beings are mechanistically governed by the mindless cause-and-effect processes which govern crude matter. For although liberal theories are metaphysically materialist in the sense that they say that nature generally and human nature specifically are exclusively material, they also say that the physical structure and processes of the human brain permits the generation of that facility of consciousness which is known as free will. Because liberal theory says that human beings have free will it further says that they can consciously direct their thoughts to remain true to the facts of reality, and so can discover the truth about nature and morality. Liberal doctrine moreover says that human beings can voluntarily act on the truths they discover because not only their minds but also their bodies are subject to their faculty of free will. So in contradistinction to the classically conservative, or authoritarian, intellectual tradition, classically liberal philosophers say that human beings can govern themselves and do not need the lash and the club of the authoritarian state to direct their behavior.

And because liberal theory is based on such categorical interpretations of human nature it is in total disagreement with the authoritarian metaphysical doctrine known as Heracliteanism. Heracliteanism, remember, says that nothing has any particular nature because reality is a state of whirling, chaotic flux. This idea is used by authoritarians to prepare the way for moral Relativism and ethical Subjectivism by getting rid of objective standards of identity. Liberal metaphysical theory, by contrast, says that because human beings have a specific natural identity that only specific ethical codes and particular theories of political morality and political rights are applicable to them.

And liberal metaphysical theory disagrees with the implication of Heracliteanism which suggests that because nothing has any particular identity that human beings are unable to understand the world around them. By suggesting that it is impossible for people to earn a living in an inventive and productive manner this notion undermines popular support for a free society. But liberal theory says that because everything in reality is something specific, that "A is A" as Aristotle put it, that people can understand and so successfully meet the challenges to their existence. There is therefore no justification for the violence and predation which characterizes authoritarian politics, liberal theory attests.

And liberal theory also opposes the implication of Heraclitean doctrine which suggests that because reality is a chaotic flux that everything that happens occurs as the result of luck or fortune. If this surmise was true then no one would deserve the fruits of their labor and no one could be blamed for living an irresponsible life. In a society based on this idea it would be perfectly justifiable for the state to seize the wealth of anyone who had it and redistribute it to anyone who did not. But the metaphysical philosophies that free societies are based on imply that under liberal economic protocols personal initiative rather than blind luck is the primary cause of a person's economic status, and that therefore it would be unjust for the state to arbitrarily seize private wealth.

But it is not only in the realm of metaphysics that the authoritarian and the liberal traditions of philosophy diverge. Liberal theory is distinctly different from the authoritarian in the province of epistemological philosophy as well. Epistemology, recall, is the branch of philosophy which seeks to define what knowledge is and how we should go about getting it. Authoritarian methods of acquiring knowledge are faith-based, or subjectivity-based, because authoritarian dogma is established upon fantasies which cannot be substantiated through the use of the eyes and the ears and the other senses. But Liberalism is built on physical facts which can be apprehended by the senses, so liberal epistemological methodology counsels reliance on sense-perception as the foundation of valid knowledge.

But a reliance on sense-perception is not the only characteristic which distinguishes liberal epistemological methods from authoritarian. Because liberal theory is based on physical fact it needs to employ methods of abstract thinking which are consistent with physical fact, rather than faith-based thinking which is perverted by irrational impulses. The method of thinking which is consistent with physical fact, as well as with itself, is known as logic; and although the authoritarian epistemological philosophy referred to as Rationalism advocates logical deduction from unquestioned premises as a means to knowledge, the contradictory nature of authoritarian metaphysical premises—Idealism, Materialism, and Heracliteanism—means that authoritarian thinking is unavoidably illogical as well.

And just as Liberalism and authoritarianism diverge in the realms of epistemological and metaphysical philosophy so they diverge in the sphere of moral philosophy also. Moral philosophy pertains to both ethics, which is concerned to discover and prescribe the general ways in which people go about their lives; and politics, which specifically addresses what is rightful and just in our relationships with other people. Authoritarian moral philosophers prescribe moral dogmas which instruct people to live their lives and relate to others as though we all lived in the fantasy lands of authoritarian theories of reality. In contrast, liberal moral philosophy assumes that we live in the world of the physical facts about human nature and the natural world around us.

The physical facts of the natural world dictate that human beings must find or produce food, clothing, and shelter, or perish. The facts of human nature dictate that human beings employ methods of accomplishing these ends which exceed the unaided capacities of the human body, because human bodies are not adequately adapted to the physical environment, as are the bodies of animals. So liberal ethical philosophy teaches people to use that distinctive human faculty which is high intelligence to invent new ways of finding resources and producing consumable goods. But authoritarians are not interested in inventing or producing anything, so authoritarian ethical philosophy practically ignores the virtues of inventiveness and productivity in its moral prescriptions.

The reason that authoritarians are not interested in inventing or producing anything is because authoritarians are political and economic predators; so authoritarian ethical philosophy was developed to facilitate predation. To authoritarians themselves authoritarian ethicists prescribe ethical doctrines which explain why preying on people is a perfectly reasonable and moral thing to do; and to the victims of this predation these philosophers preach ethical doctrines which have the effect of making the victims easier to prey upon. We noted the various aspects of these ethical doctrines in the section of this book entitled *The Ethics of the Slaves and The Ethics of the Masters*. Let's review these doctrines and contrast them with their liberal counterparts.

The ethics of the slaves emphasize an ethic of duty and service to the great Being of which all human beings are part, and from whom they receive everything they value. Religionists refer to this great Being as God, while secular authoritarians usually describe it as Society, or the State, or Humanity conceived of as a single, supernatural organism. Because every value which human life depends on is created by this great Being authoritarian ethics say that individual human beings have both a practical need and a moral obligation born of gratitude to serve and obey this Being. These ethics further say that because all of the people we think of as individual human beings are really just parts of this one great Being that they have a duty to serve the interests of this Being rather than their own interests.

But liberal ethics are based on a theory of reality which says that every value in the world is created either by mechanistic natural forces or by individual human beings themselves, not by a God or by some supernatural societal Creator. So liberal theory says that individual human beings are under no ethical obligation to serve God or society conceived of as a single organismic Self. And liberal ethics are further based upon a theory of human nature which says that each individual is a distinct and real individual, and not part of some greater individual. So liberal ethics say that there is no moral requirement that individuals serve the interests of a greater individual, and may ethically serve their own interests instead.

Authoritarian ethicists also prescribe an ethic of poverty and appetitive repression in order to prepare people to live under the authoritarian yoke and lash. These ascetic ethics teach people to eschew the material values authoritarians intend to confiscate and to abstain from earthly pleasures which distract from service to the greater Being. Ascetic ethicists make use of the authoritarian metaphysical theory of Idealism in order to convey that the material and the earthly are an illusion and that a concern for the physical is a sinful vanity. In contrast to this, liberal ethical theory is based on a metaphysical doctrine which says that the material world is the only world which exists—the legitimate theory of Materialism—and that therefore a concern for the material should be paramount and the pursuit of material values and earthly pleasures respected.

Authoritarian ethicists also promulgate a subspecies of ascetic ethical attitudes known widely as Quietism in order to effect their political purposes. Quietist ethical doctrines, recall, advise passivism as a response to life's hardships—both executive passivism, "turn the other cheek," and intellectual passivism, "judge not that ye not be judged." Religious authoritarians typically employ quietist ethics by asserting that because every action of any state represents the will of God that the actions of states should never be resisted or questioned. Liberal ethics, by contrast, are founded on theories which say that everything in existence, including a state, is created either by people or by the forces of nature—not by some god. So liberal ethics generally do not counsel passive approaches to life's difficulties, including the offenses of authoritarian states.

But it is not only the authoritarian's ethics of the slaves which conflict with Liberalism's ethical premises; so also do the ethics of the masters. Recall that in the Western tradition of thought the first systematic expression of the ethics of the masters developed out of the metaphysically and epistemologically skeptic, ethically subjectivist, and morally relativist doctrines of the Greek Sophists. Philosophers who followed the Sophists, and some of the Sophists themselves, concluded that since there was no solid metaphysical or epistemological basis upon which to found a substantiable moral philosophy that there could be no moral basis upon which to build a peaceful society. They therefore concluded that only brute political force could secure human existence and that in the absence of objective moral standards only brute political "might" could determine what was "right."

In contrast to this, liberal ethical philosophy develops out of a metaphysical and epistemological tradition which says that because the features of nature and human nature have a consistent identity that they can therefore be reliably known by the human faculties of consciousness—the mind and the faculties of sense-perception. Liberal ethicists have concluded therefore that a demonstrable and ascertainable ethical philosophy can be discovered to serve as the basis for a just and benevolent society. Founded on their metaphysical and epistemological premises liberal ethicists have counseled an ethics of scientific discovery, technological innovation, productive labor, and voluntary economic cooperation as the individual's proper means of securing a livelihood. And they have called for the rejection of the masters' ethics and the prohibition of their politics of violence and predation.

And indeed in recent decades the world has witnessed how the rejection of the doctrines of economic and political violence and the adoption of economic and political policies based on technical innovation, productivity, and voluntary cooperation have brought peace and prosperity and reduced poverty and conflict in parts of the world which have suffered under malicious ethical and political dogmas for millennia. Unfortunately, as we have discussed, the philosophies these policies are based upon are being methodically undermined in the West itself—most certainly by a hyperconservative and archly reactionary academic intelligentsia entrenched in the West's subsidized state schools. In the long run these schools will have to be reformed, de-subsidized, and legally separated from the state in order to eradicate the incentive to use their lecture halls and class-rooms to systematically subvert liberal society. In the short run regular citizens can protect their minds from abuse by familiarizing themselves with the intellectual tactics which these schools are using against them—especially the philosophical tactics.

Toward that end this book was written, and if the reader has been a careful student of these pages he or she is now well prepared to resist the ideas which are intended to ruin his life and destroy her society. The reader is warned, however, that authoritarian intellectuals are ever concocting new ways of expressing old sophistries, for nothing prevents an unscrupulous ideologue from cooking up a new religion or giving new names to all of the old philosophies we have here discussed. The reader must learn, therefore, to recognize the basic concepts of the authoritarian ideological tradition however they are represented.

And it is just as important for the citizens of free societies to recognize and have a sturdy grasp of the metaphysical, epistemological, and ethical ideas upon which the political philosophies of liberty and Liberalism are established. For knowledge of these ideas will allow benevolently-intentioned people to reestablish their societies upon sound philosophical foundations as well as fill their hearts with the moral and intellectual self-confidence they will need to face down the malefactors who threaten their rights and may one day threaten their lives. Happily, we can leave the reader with the glad news that there is in fact a new vanguard of liberal philosophers astir in the West who have provided brilliant new arguments with which to defend the principles of freedom. Readers must search these philosophers out, study their ideas, and arm themselves intellectually for the battle to preserve the liberal world.

GLOSSARY

Altruism: The term Altruism was coined by the nineteenth century French philosopher Auguste Comte to denote his ethic of duty to the social organism which, he asserted, is "Humanity" conceived of as a single being. Proceeding from the premise that what we think of as individuals are not really individuals at all but only parts of a greater individual which is comprised of all other people, Comte advocated an ethic of service to others as a means of serving the needs of the larger being of which everyone is part. In popular usage the term Altruism has come to refer to an ethic of charitable service to the apparent individuals we see around us rather than one of mandatory duty to the one ideal individual who is everyone. From a theoretical standpoint the distinction between acts of charity and actions from duty is that duties are moral imperatives, plausibly enforceable by laws, whereas charity may be construed as elective. The word Altruism literally means "otherism."

Asceticism: In a general way the term Asceticism refers to the practice of self-denial, and to moral philosophies which advocate the repression of desire and the equanimous acceptance of physical discomfort and material privation. Ascetic ethical doctrines typically prescribe the repression of physical cravings such as the appetites for food and sex, and the stifling of material interests such as the yearning for better clothing and accommodations. Also discouraged may be psychological appetites such as professional ambition and the desire for social status, and even the longing for social satisfactions such as companionship, respect, and affection. An aspect of Asceticism which is sometimes referred to as Quietism advocates the pacification of the intellect and the faculties of judgment, as well as the adoption of an attitude of indifference to provocations such as verbal insults and physical assaults.

Authoritarianism: As the term is used in this study authoritarianism refers to political and ideological systems which demand and compel abject obedience from the individual. Feudalism, Fascism, and Communism are representative of authoritarian systems.

Cartesian: Pertaining to the ideas of René Descartes.

Causality: Refers to the relationship between a cause and its effect.

Creationism: Creationism is the belief that the whole of reality—the universe and everything in it—is supernaturally brought into and sustained in existence by God, or by a being that has god-like powers.

Deconstruction, or Deconstructionism: As a philosophic movement Deconstructionism is challenging to describe, in part because its originators insist that nothing is describable. As a result, in order to characterize Deconstructionism, students must assume that its proponents are adherents to those philosophic tenets which imply that everything is indeed indescribable. This is not unfair to deconstructionists because when occasionally they condescend to linguistic clarity everything they say indicates that they subscribe to those tenets.

In the realm of metaphysics both Heracliteanism and Subjective Idealism imply that everything is indescribable because existing things have no objective identity. It is safe for critics to suppose, therefore, that behind their ambiguity deconstructionists are metaphysical Heracliteans and/or Subjective Idealists. In the province of epistemological philosophy Skepticism implies that nothing is describable because human faculties of knowledge automatically distort what we are aware of, so we may comfortably presume that deconstructionists are skeptics. Because deconstructionists refuse to make any positive statements about what they themselves believe and confine themselves to denigrating the beliefs of others we may reasonably deduce that Deconstructionism is primarily a movement of intellectual nihilism. And given the history of intellectual nihilism we can therefore expect that once the deconstructionists are through annihilating everyone else's beliefs they will seek to impose on society some surreptitiously held beliefs of their own.

Deduction: Deduction is the method of reasoning which allows new knowledge to be attained by considering the logical implications of knowledge we already have. For instance, if we know that Socrates is a man, and that all men are mortal, we may deduce that Socrates too is mortal by considering the logical implications of the statements from which this deduction was derived. Deduction is sometimes described as the method by which one reasons from the *general*, "all men are mortal," to the *specific*: "Socrates is mortal."

Deontology: Deontology is the study of concepts and theories of the ethic of duty. Deontological ethics represent the fulfillment of duty as a person's only moral obligation, abrogating all other moral considerations. The principal modern proponent of such doctrines was Immanuel Kant. (See glossary entry *Duty*).

Determinism: Determinism is the theory that all events are caused by prior events in time, like the cause-and-effect processes which determine the functions of machinery. When applied to the functioning of human psychology and mentality this theory implies that human thoughts and emotions are mechanistically determined by forces which are beyond a person's control, thus invalidating the notion of free will. As such, Determinism is closely related to, but not synonymous with, the metaphysical theory of Materialism as it is most commonly represented in modern philosophy. Modern philosophic definitions of Materialism also say that all events, including the processes of human consciousness, are mechanistically determined by prior events in time; but additionally they say that everything in the universe is of the nature of the material rather than the spiritual. Determinism, on the other hand, is a comment on the causal nature of events, rather than on the qualitative nature of reality.

Dialectical Materialism: A technical term denoting the philosophy of Karl Marx. Many of the available definitions of Dialectical Materialism are virtually incomprehensible, and Marx himself was much clearer in his philosophic statements than his interpreters usually are in explaining them. The highlights of Marxist philosophy, frequently expressed in his own words, are related at various points in this study.

Dogmatism: Dogmatism in practice is the unquestioning belief in an idea or body of ideas without any objective evidence that the ideas are true. As an epistemological method Dogmatism advocates blind, unthinking belief, usually in an established and authoritative ideology, as a means of attaining knowledge.

Dualism: Dualism is primarily but not exclusively a metaphysical theory which says that reality has two different and incompatible natures, those of spirit and those of matter. When applied to human beings this theory suggests that people themselves have two completely different natures, the spiritual and the physical, which pull them in morally irreconcilable directions.

Duty: Duty refers to concepts of moral obligation. The most common concepts of duty that religious and philosophic ethicists have prescribed are those of obedience and service to God and/or society. Such prescriptions have usually been represented as taking moral precedence over the individual's concern for its own happiness and even over its elemental well-being. Radical theories of duty, such as those of Immanuel Kant, assert that duty defined as self-sacrificial obedience and servitude is the only moral obligation and the exclusive moral good. Such theories say that any concern for self-interest is immoral.

Egalitarianism: The word Egalitarianism is usually employed to denote one or both of two principal doctrines of equality as a consideration in theories of social, political, and economic justice. On the one hand the term refers to a doctrine which says that because all people are of equal moral stature they should all receive an equal amount of the things which people value; and on the other it signifies a doctrine which says that because most people have fundamentally equal capabilities they should also have equal political rights. The former doctrine has been used as a premise for demands that all values be redistributed equally among all people; while the latter merely says that all people should be treated equally under the law.

Empirical/Empiricism: Philosophically, the term Empiricism is used in a variety of ways, many of them poorly defined. But essentially Empiricism refers to methods of attaining knowledge which are based on sense-experience rather than faith, intuition, or pure logic. An "empirical fact," then, is one which can be verified by reference to the testimony of the senses, such as the eyes.

Epistemology: Epistemology is one of several major branches of philosophy which also include metaphysics, ethics, politics, and esthetics. Epistemology is the particular branch of philosophy which is concerned with the subject of knowledge, and specifically with how knowledge is attained and what constitutes valid knowledge.

Ethical Naturalism: Refers to any theory of ethics or morality that is based on natural principles or natural law. Can but does not necessarily refer to moral theories that attempt to impose the survival-of-the-fittest, might-makes-right principles that govern the behavior of animals on human beings.

Ethics: Ethics is the branch of philosophy which is concerned with morality and moral values. More precisely, ethics is the philosophic discipline which is charged with discovering the general moral values which human beings ought to pursue, and with prescribing the general but not the specific methods by which people ought to pursue them.

Existentialism: Existentialism may reasonably be described as the modern manifestation of the ancient Greek philosophy of Sophism. This modern version of Sophism was reinvigorated as a major philosophic movement principally by the nineteenth century philosophers Sören Kierkegaard and Friedrich Nietzsche, and reached its twentieth century zenith of influence through the impact of Martin Heidegger and his student Jean-Paul Sartre. Like Sophism, Existentialism is metaphysically and morally nihilistic, insisting that reality has no objective identity (Heracliteanism) and that morality has no basis in fact. Like Sophism, Existentialism is at once skeptic and subjective in the realm of epistemology, proposing that reality is unknowable and yet advocating a reliance on highly subjective interpretations of reality as a dependable source of knowledge. Influenced by eighteenth century German Idealism Existentialism is metaphysically idealist when it is not metaphysically nihilistic, asserting that the individual can create its own reality out of the contents of its own consciousness. And basing subjective interpretations of morality on subjective recreations of reality Existentialism insists that valid moral conclusions may be arrived at merely by consulting the contents of consciousness, especially as guided by the emotional faculties. In the late twentieth and early twenty-first centuries Existentialism has been superseded by the postmodernist and deconstructionist philosophic movements, which are based on similar principles and which come to much the same conclusions. These movements may be interpreted as extensions of the existentialist movement, or as merely a rebranding or renaming of it.

Hedonism: In ethics, the theory that pleasure is the only measure of value and is always valuable no matter how it is attained.

Heracliteanism: Heracliteanism refers to the philosophy of the ancient Greek philosopher Heraclitus of Ephesus. Heraclitus is most famous for his metaphysical doctrine which says that everything is in a constant state of flux or change, but that regulating this change is an immutable source of cosmic law called *Logos* which itself never changes. Although Heraclitus's doctrine of the *Logos* or Reason is fundamentally an idealist concept his name has nevertheless become synonymous with the aspect of his philosophy which says that everything is constantly changing. The term Heracliteanism is most often used to refer to this dictum.

Idealism: In the realm of technical philosophy the term Idealism is primarily used to refer to a metaphysical concept which says that reality is the product of a mind or minds and is fundamentally mental or spiritual in nature. Because this concept closely parallels or is in some instances identical to religious conceptions of reality religion is usually categorized as being metaphysically idealist. Also metaphysically idealist are the metaphysical philosophies of such thinkers as Plato, Berkeley, Kant, and Hegel, although these philosophers de-emphasize the religious implications of Idealism and represent their doctrines as secular or semi-secular interpretations of the nature of reality.

Immaterialism: Immaterialism is a metaphysical theory, or theory about the nature of reality, which says that matter does not exist and that only mental phenomena and the minds which generate them exist. This theory may be said to be the reverse expression of the concept of metaphysical Idealism, which says that only minds and the psychic phenomena generated by minds exist, and that nothing which exists is material.

Induction: Induction is a method of acquiring conceptual knowledge of reality by inferring ideas from reality's directly observed particulars. For instance, if we observe that water flows downhill and not uphill we can attain conceptual knowledge of reality by inferring (formulating, inventing) the concept *water flows downhill* from observing this fact with our eyes.

Innatism: Innatism refers to the theory that there are "innate" ideas implanted in the human mind prior to a person's first conscious thought or experience of reality. These "a priori" ideas are usually described as acting something like a computer program installed in the mind before birth, or before a person's first conscious awareness. This "program," the theory says, forces a human being's thinking along predetermined lines, or at least introduces human beings to ideas which they might not otherwise have considered. Examples of innate ideas, and of Innatism, include the supernatural "Forms" which Plato said people are exposed to before they are born, and the "categorical" ideas which Kant asserted are intrinsic aspects of human consciousness.

Liberalism: In the province of technical political philosophy the term Liberalism has a different meaning than it does in the vernacular of the practical politics of the twentieth and twenty-first century United States. As a technical philosophic term Liberalism refers to a politics of individual liberty and to the economics of commercial and entrepreneurial freedom. In the realm of the practical politics of the contemporary United States, however, the term Liberalism has come to refer to the politics and economics of what might most fittingly be referred to as welfare-statism. This species of statism places significant but far from absolute constraints upon individual liberty.

Although they share the same name philosophical Liberalism and welfare-state Liberalism are essentially opposites with regard to their fundamental metaphysical assumptions, and opposites also regarding the conclusions they come to about political rights and political morality. Political philosophers occasionally remark that the Liberalism of modern welfare-statism is based on the same philosophical premises as are the authoritarian political doctrines outlined in this book, and is ultimately indistinguishable from them in its political philosophy. It might be said that the political struggle between these two definitions of Liberalism is the defining social struggle of our time, and that the outcome of this struggle will determine whether or not civilization continues in its experiment with individual liberty or slips backward into graver and grosser manifestations of authoritarianism. Because this study is a discussion of technical political philosophy it employs the term Liberalism to denote the politics of personal, political, and economic freedom, rather than the politics and economics of welfare-statism.

Materialism: As a philosophic term Materialism refers to a metaphysical doctrine which says that everything that exists is material in nature, and that all events are physical events which ultimately have physical causes. These concepts provide a philosophical premise for science by eliminating the idealist notion of a universe which is immaterial and/or spiritual in nature, where everything which occurs does so as the result of acts of will by gods or other supernatural agents. In modern times, however, the word Materialism has come to denote not this broad definition of the term, but rather certain narrow and one might even say perverted applications of its definition. The word now refers primarily to the notion that everything in the universe, *including especially the human mind*, is ruled by the cause-and-effect physical forces which govern the actions of crude matter. In essence, then, the modern usage of the term Materialism has devolved to denote merely the notion of Determinism; especially the kind of mental Determinism which says that human beings lack intellectual free will. (See Glossary entry *Determinism*.)

Metaphysics: Metaphysics is one of several major branches of philosophy which also include epistemology, ethics, politics, and esthetics. It is the specific branch of philosophy which studies the general nature of reality as distinct from the special sciences such as chemistry which focus on narrow aspects of existence. Is reality immaterial, like a spirit? Is it material, like a stone? Or is it dualistic, having both material and spiritual attributes? These are metaphysical speculations in that they hypothesize about the underlying nature of reality. The reader should note that the word *ontology* is often defined as synonymous with metaphysics.

Mind/Body Dichotomy and Mind/Body Dualism: See Soul/Body Dualism.

Monism: The term Monism is most frequently used to denote the metaphysical theory that everything in the universe is just one thing and that this one thing has only one metaphysical nature. Although this term can be employed to specify the idea that the universe is just one material thing it is more often used to refer to the notion that it is one omnipresent spirit such as a pantheistic god. Monism may be contrasted with metaphysical Dualism, which says that reality has two natures, those of matter and of spirit; and with Pluralism, which says that reality is many things and has many natures (See Glossary entries *Dualism* and *Pluralism*).

Mysticism: Broadly, Mysticism refers to an epistemological theory which says that human beings have available to them some mysterious source of knowledge which may be accessed without the use of normal faculties of knowledge such as the senses and cognition. More narrowly, Mysticism is the theory that knowledge may be attained by passively submitting one's consciousness to the consciousness of some divine or otherwise supernatural mind and simply allowing knowledge to flow into one's mind from this higher mind.

Nominalism: Essentially a skeptical doctrine, Nominalism is a theory about the status of ideas. This theory says that because all our knowledge about the general nature of things is false that our ideas and the words we use to refer to them can never truthfully designate the general characteristics which classes of things have in common. According to this doctrine the idea "man" can credibly refer only to the narrow details of a definition of the word "man," or to a particular man, but never to the general characteristics which all beings with man-like qualities share. Because Nominalism assumes that our ideas about general characteristics are false its proponents assert that the words we use to refer to such characteristics are merely meaningless "names" which have no corresponding referents in reality. The reader may note that the term Nominalism itself contradictorily refers to a theory which insists that all ideas have a certain characteristic in common.

Organicism: In the domain of metaphysical philosophy Organicism refers to the notion that the whole of reality is a giant organism. Pantheistic theologies which say that reality is the supernatural organism that is God and subjective idealist doctrines which say that reality is an extension of human consciousness are both similarly organismic. In the literature of modern political philosophy the term Monism is frequently used to refer to ideologies which employ organicist metaphysical theories as foundations for organic theories of the state. This study employs the term Organicism for that purpose, however, because the term Monism can also refer to theories of reality which are not organismic.

Pantheism: Pantheism is a theory about the nature of God which says that God is everything and that everything is God. As such, Pantheism is as much a metaphysical theory about the nature of reality as it is a theological theory about the nature of the Deity. As a theory of reality Pantheism is metaphysically organicist (See Glossary entry *Organicism*) in that it says that reality is the supernatural organism which is God, and metaphysically monist in that it says that reality is just one thing (See Glossary entry *Monism*).

Phenomenology: Phenomenology is the study of the subjective phenomena of consciousness, on the assumption that the world outside our consciousness can never itself be known or does not even exist. Based on the philosophy of Immanuel Kant Phenomenology asserts that because all we are aware of is the processes of our own mental functioning that only the contents of our own minds and not the "real" world outside needs to be investigated. A species of Subjective Idealism, Phenomenology asserts that everything which exists is merely a manifestation of human consciousness and that therefore truth can only be found by looking within one's own mind or the mind of someone else. Closely associated with Existentialism, Phenomenology is frequently represented as having provided the twentieth century proponents of that philosophy with their subjectivist metaphysical and epistemological approaches.

Pluralism: The term Pluralism is used in a metaphysical sense to refer to theories of reality which say that there are many or an infinite number of different and diverse types of realities. This doctrine may be contrasted with Monism, which says that there is only one type of reality, and with Dualism, which says that there are two types of realities. As a metaphysical term Pluralism is often ambiguously defined but is most frequently characterized as applying to theories of reality which are highly subjective and/or Heraclitean in nature, such as those associated with Sophism, Pragmatism, and Existentialism.

Positivism (1): The name given by Auguste Comte to his "new religion" of "Humanity." See Index entries under *Positivism*. **(2):** Beyond denoting Comte's religion of humanity Positivism refers to an epistemological theory, also identified with Comte, which says that only what is empirically observable may be known. According to this doctrine all metaphysical principles and moral maxims are merely specious speculations because they cannot be verified by sense-perception. Because they only concede the validity of knowledge which is directly supported by empirical evidence "positivists" attempt to understand everything, including human beings and human societies, without making any metaphysical or moral assumptions. And because they believe that reality has no essential nature they assert that all moral theories are subjective and relativist in nature.

Positivist epistemological methods are represented as scientific in that they restrict knowledge to the empirically observable. But because it rejects all metaphysical theories about the fundamental nature of reality the epistemology of Positivism is ultimately skeptical, relativist, and subjective, even about scientific law.

Postmodernism: In the domain of philosophy Postmodernism refers to a skeptic, relativist, and subjectivist tendency among contemporary theorists. Postmodernists generally reject the metaphysical idea that there is a concrete, objectively actual reality underlying existence, and at the same time embrace the Kantian notion that the reality we are aware of is a manifestation of our own consciousness. As such, postmodernists are at once Heracliteans and subjective idealists in their metaphysics.

In the realm of epistemological philosophy postmodernists derive their beliefs about the nature of knowledge from their metaphysical theories. Human beings have no way of attaining objective knowledge about the real world, postmodernists believe, either because a Heraclitean universe in inherently unknowable, or because the world we think we know is really just a projection of our own conscious faculties. Yet at the same time postmodernists are usually agreeable to the subjectivist notion that we can acquire useful knowledge about the world we are aware of by simply referring to the contents of our own consciousness, since our consciousness actually begets the world.

As a consequence of their metaphysics and epistemology postmodernists are both relativists and subjectivists in their ethics. Believing that there is no objective basis for certain knowledge about morality postmodernists skeptically conclude that morality is merely a projection of the subjective preferences of different people, and as such is relative to a particular person or demographic group. But given that there is no objective reason to reject any particular theory of morality postmodernists conversely believe that they are perfectly justified in intuiting any theory of morality they prefer, thus complementing their moral Skepticism and ethical Relativism with a contradistinctive ethical Subjectivism.

As seems obvious Postmodernism is a manifestation of the philosophic tradition that begins with the ancient Greek Sophists and culminates in modern Existentialism and Deconstructionism. Postmodernism is so called because it rejects the belief in a definite, tangible reality and the validity of human knowledge which provide the foundations of the modern post-Enlightenment world. Ultimately, as a consequence, Postmodernism rejects the notion of an absolute political morality and the absolutely "inalienable rights" which provide the premises of modern Liberalism. As such, postmodern philosophies may reasonably be identified as classically conservative, or "reactionary."

Pragmatism: Pragmatism is primarily an epistemological philosophy about the meaning of concepts and about what constitutes truth. It contends that the meaning of concepts, or ideas, is not their corresponding referents in reality, but rather, their "practical" effects. If, for instance, the practical effect of the idea that the unemployment rate is six percent is that of convincing voters that unemployment is being reduced then the idea that unemployment is six percent means that voters believe unemployment is declining, not that unemployment is actually six percent.

Respectively, the pragmatic theory of truth says that the word "truth" refers not to a corresponding or consistent relationship between a statement and the facts of reality, but rather to whether the idea "works" as a means of achieving a desired end. If, for example, lying to voters about the rate of unemployment works as a means of achieving the desired end of convincing them that unemployment is declining then the idea that the unemployment rate is six percent is "true."

Quietism: In the realm of ethics Quietism is a doctrine which advises intellectual, emotional, and executive passivity as a route to the moral life. Quietism is an aspect of ascetic ethics and is associated with Stoic philosophy.

Rationalism: As it is popularly understood the term Rationalism refers to an epistemological method which employs reason as a means of attaining knowledge; but this is not how modern philosophic scholarship usually defines this word. For if reason may technically be described as the application of inductive and deductive logic to the particulars of reality then Rationalism as the term is used academically has nothing to do with reason. The present technical use of the term primarily refers to an epistemological philosophy which completely ignores the particulars of reality and says instead that knowledge may be attained only through logical deduction from preconceived premises without reference to the evidence of sense-perception. As such Rationalism is an epistemological method which traps the human mind in a realm of ideas deduced from unexamined assumptions and refuses to allow it to peek outside at the world testified to by the senses. Rationalism of this sort is historically associated with the so-called "Continental Rationalists": Descartes, Leibniz, and Spinoza.

Realism: Realism is another one of those terms which have a completely different and one might even say contradictory meaning within the province of philosophy than in the popular argot. As a philosophic term Realism refers primarily to a theory about the metaphysical status of ideas which says that ideas are "real" entities existing outside and independent of the human mind. The best known form of Realism, Platonic Realism, says that supernatural ideas called "Forms" exist in some purely spiritual dimension and cause the objects we see around us to come into existence by beaming their reality-creating power throughout the universe. Another well-known theory of Realism, Aristotelian Realism, says that ideas are inherent in material things and somehow cause those things to become the objects we associate with particular ideas. A tree, for instance, becomes a tree because of the idea "tree" which exists within it.

Both Platonic and Aristotelian Realism can seem theoretically bizarre to the modern mind, and it might be said that a more "realistic" theory of ideas would simply propose that ideas exist *within the human mind* as abstract symbols of the things which we create the ideas to represent.

Reason: Reason may be defined as the epistemological method which logically conceptualizes the information provided by the senses and then applies the resultant concepts to the things we sense in order to understand them in the abstract. Reason, then, is inductive and deductive logic, applied to the world we apprehend through sense-perception.

Relativism: Relativism is a term which is used to refer both to epistemological theories about the status of knowledge and the properties of truth, and to ethical theories about the standing of moral doctrines. As an epistemological theory Relativism says that because each person or type of person perceives the world through the lens of their own subjectivity that knowledge is not absolute, but is relative to the person or people cognizant of it. This theory leads logically to the notion that knowledge of morality, and ultimately morality itself, is also relative to particular people—the theory of Ethical Relativism.

Skepticism: As an epistemological philosophy, or philosophy of knowledge, Skepticism (or Scepticism) is a doctrine which asserts that no knowledge is possible. Skeptics assert this either on the assumption that human faculties for attaining knowledge don't work, or on the supposition that reality itself is intrinsically unknowable. Proponents of Skepticism have frequently advocated systematic doubt, or the deliberate suspension of the willingness to believe, as an attitude toward the prospect of knowing.

Social Darwinism: Social Darwinism is a political philosophy which says that society and humanity can evolve into higher and better states of existence by imposing the natural laws which govern the relationships between sub-human species on human political and economic relationships. The resulting survival-of-the-fittest competitions naturally select the best human types and eliminate the weaker, resulting in social and biological advancement, Social Darwinism says.

Solipsism: As a metaphysical philosophy Solipsism says that the self alone exists and that everything which exists is the self. Epistemological Solipsism, as a consequence, says that to attain knowledge one need merely look within the self because everything one is aware of is the self. Solipsism is closely associated with the metaphysical philosophy known as Subjective Idealism and with the epistemological philosophy that is similarly known as Subjectivism.

Sophists: The Sophists were professional educators prominent in Greece in the fourth and fifth centuries B.C. Among their most notable representatives were Protagoras of Abdera, Gorgias of Leontini, and Thrasymachus of Chalcedon. The earlier Sophists, men such as Protagoras, were associated with a philosophy of epistemological Skepticism which led logically to subjectivist and relativist moral doctrines. In the absence of the moral absolutes implied by these doctrines some of the later Sophists embraced a might-makes-right political ideology which presaged the Social Darwinism of the nineteenth and twentieth centuries.

Soul/Body Dualism: Terms such as Soul/Body Dualism, Soul/Body Dichotomy, Mind/Body Dualism, and Mind/Body Dichotomy are variously used to designate theories of human nature which say that people have two opposite natures: one physical and the other spiritual. The soul or mind, these theories aver, is entirely spiritual, while the body is exclusively material; and the two aspects of human nature have no physical connection to each other. Such theories frequently say that the soul and the body are driven by and subject to entirely different and contradictory appetites and laws, which pull a person in morally irreconcilable directions.

Stoicism: Designates the ideas of the ancient Greek Stoic philosophers. In the realm of ethics Stoicism advocates repression of the passions and appetites and indifference to suffering as the primary moral virtues. As such Stoicism is representative of or is synonymous with ascetic ethics.

Subjective Idealism: Subjective Idealism is a metaphysical theory, or theory about the nature of reality, which says that reality is, and is created and sustained in existence by, the conscious states of human subjects or selves. According to this theory, what we think of as real is actually just our awareness of the functioning of our own perceptual and cognitive faculties, not something which exists independent of us. A tree, for instance, is simply the way in which our eyes process light, and light itself is just a by-product of the functioning of our visual faculties. Nothing is real except the reality our consciousness produces, this theory says, and what we think of as reality is nothing but our consciousness.

Subjectivism: Subjectivism is a term which refers to a wide variety of doctrines in the disparate fields of metaphysical, epistemological, and ethical philosophy. These doctrines are called subjectivist because of their emphasis on the significance of the self, or selves. Subjectivist theories may be sub-divided into doctrines which emphasize the significance of the private, or individual self, and those which stress the relevance of the collective or group self. These theories are sometimes referred to as "simple" or "personal" Subjectivism on the one hand, and as "social" Subjectivism on the other.

Metaphysical Subjectivism refers to theories of metaphysics, or theories of reality, which say that reality is a product of the conscious states of an individual self, or of groups of selves, and is nothing but these conscious states. The most common representation of this theory, known as Subjective Idealism, says that because all we are aware of are the processes of our own mental functioning that what we think of as reality is in fact created by our own minds. The epistemological implication of this is *Epistemological Subjectivism*, which says that all we need to do to know reality is consult our own thoughts about it, since reality can never be anything except what we think it is. In the realm of ethics this theory implies that whatever we think about morality must be correct because there is no standard of truth other than the thoughts of the private self—or in the social version of the theory, society as a whole. These latter doctrines are representative of *Ethical Subjectivism*.

Theism: The theory that there is a God.

Theocracy: The political rule of society by God or by God's representatives.

Utilitarianism: Utilitarianism is an ethical doctrine which combines Hedonism and Altruism. Developed and popularized in the eighteenth and nineteenth centuries by British philosophers Jeremy Bentham, James and John Stuart Mill and others, Utilitarianism obliges the individual to seek "the greatest happiness of the greatest number."

Voluntarism: In the province of metaphysical philosophy Voluntarism is the theory that reality is the manifestation of an unreasoning, unpredictable, supernatural will, and that everything which happens occurs as the result of the power of this will. In ethics Voluntarism is the theory that human will, as opposed to reason, is the appropriate faculty to consult when making moral decisions. Since will is essentially desire or aversion coupled with the urge to act, Ethical Voluntarism amounts to making moral decisions based on irrational, emotional, or appetitive impulses.

NOTES AND CITATIONS

Chapter One: A Disease of Ideas

1. Hume, David, "Of the First Principles of Government," in *Hume: Political Essays*, ed. Knud Haakonssen, pp. 16-19 (Cambridge, UK; New York: Cambridge UP, 2003), p. 16.
2. Marx believed that people were conditioned by the material and cultural circumstances of their economic class to automatically hold opinions which were supportive of the financial interests of that class. This justified the political use of brute force against "class enemies" as a means of changing society because people whose thoughts were mechanically determined by class interest could not be influenced by appeals to reason. As J. Lucien Radel observed, "...Marx also opposed the evolutionary Socialist tendency to moralize. Morals had nothing to do with a change in society since he conceived of a violent change resulting from the outcome of the struggle between two forces, capital and labor. In other words, Marx looked for power relations to decide the change in morals, or justice." Radel, J. Lucien, *Roots of Totalitarianism* (New York: Crane, 1975), p. 188.

Chapter Two: Authoritarian Theories of Reality

1. The Gospels are replete with assurances that faith—that is, belief alone—can alter reality. For instance, the Gospel of Matthew relates that "a woman who had been subject to bleeding for twelve years came up behind him [Jesus] and touched the edge of his cloak. She said to herself, 'If I only touch his cloak, I will be healed.' Jesus turned and saw her.

'Take heart, daughter,' he said, 'your faith has healed you.' And the woman was healed from that moment" (Matt. 9:20, 21, 22, NIV). Later in Matthew Christ identifies himself to Peter by permitting Peter to walk on water. But when Peter "saw the wind, he was afraid and, beginning to sink, cried out, 'Lord, save me!' " Christ thereupon admonishes Peter that it is his failure of faith that is causing him to sink, saying, "You of little faith...why did you doubt?" (Matt. 14:30, 31, NIV). Elsewhere in Matthew Christ assures his followers that "if you have faith as small as a mustard seed, you can say to this mountain, 'Move from here to there' and it will move. Nothing will be impossible for you." (Matt. 17:20, NIV).

2. A. L. Basham, " 'The Greater Vehicle' of Mahāyāna Buddhism," in *The Buddhist Tradition in India, China, & Japan*, ed. William Theodore de Bary, pp. 73-109 (New York: Modern, 1969), p.100.

3. Ibid., p. 100, cited as "From *Ratnamegha Sūtra, Śikṣāsamuccaya*, pp. 121-122."

4. The *Dhammapada*, trans. J.R. Carter and M. Palihawadana (New York: Oxford UP, 1987), pp. 42-43, 45, 49-51.

5. Bosker, Ben Zion, trans. and Ben Zion Bosker and Baruch M. Bosker, eds. *The Talmud: Selected Writings* (New York: Paulist, 1989), p. 8.

6. *Everyman's Talmud*, rev. ed., trans. and ed. Abraham Cohen (New York: Schocken, 1995), p. 29.

7. *Bhagavad-gītā As It Is*, abr. ed., ch. 8, txt. 20, trans. A.C. Bhaktivedanta Swami Prabhupāda (New York: Bhaktivedanta, 1975), p. 148.

8. Ibid., p. xxx.

9. Ibid., ch. 15, txt. 16, p. 232.

10. The *Koran*, sura lvii, trans. Lane, Edward W., Stanley Lane-Poole and A.H. G. Sarwar (New York: Crescent, n.d., ISBN: 0-517-138964), pp. 219-220.

11. While many general reviews of philosophy decline to discuss the economic, social, and political backgrounds of the major philosophers those that do provide some invaluable insights into the nature of philosophic ideas. For a doctrine which on the surface seems entirely detached from the concrete may be revealed as sensibly practical if the political and economic interests of a philosopher are known. Among the philosophic overviews which persistently indicate the social status and political associations of philosophers is Eduard Zeller's *Outlines of the History of Greek Philosophy*. Zeller says of Anaximander that, "he was of distinguished family [and]...led a Milesian colony to Apollonia on the Black Sea" (p. 28). Of Heraclitus Zeller mentions that he was "a born aristocrat" who "was a member of the noblest family in which the royal office of sacrificial priest to the Eleusinian Demeter was hereditary" (p. 44). Parmenides is described as "a man of noble and rich family, who gave his native city an excellent [legal] constitution..." (p. 49). And Aikin's *General Biography: Or Lives, Critical and Historical, of the Most Eminent Persons of All Ages, Conditions, and Professions* relates of Philolaus that he "fell a sacrifice to political jealousy, for aiming, or for being suspected of aiming at the possession of despotic power in the government of his country." Zeller, Eduard, *Outlines of the History of Greek Philosophy*, 13th ed., (New York: Dover, 1980). Aiken, John, et al., *General Biography: Or Lives, Critical and Historical, of the Most Eminent Persons of All Ages, Conditions, and Professions, Arranged According to Alphabetical Order....Volume The Eighth* (London: G. G. and J. Robinson, 1813), p. 152, Web, 25, Aug., 2013, http://books.google.com/books?id=lEMDAAAAYAAJ&pg=PA152&lpg=PA152&dq=Philolaus+biography#v=onepage&q=Philolaus%20biography&f=false.

12. Perhaps no philosophers are more widely misunderstood by the general public than are Socrates and Plato. For the average

citizen of the modern Western democracies thinks vaguely of these two ancient Athenian giants as among the philosophic founding fathers of the West's tradition of democracy and liberal republicanism. But in fact if these philosophers were alive today they would be among the bitterest enemies of what are contemporarily referred to as free societies, and would ally themselves with the worst of these societies' adversaries. As Chester C. Maxey notes in his *Political Philosophies*, "[w]ere he alive to-day Plato would be the reddest of reds, and would no doubt hasten to [Soviet] Russia with the same expectant enthusiasm he displayed in answering the call of the ancient tyrant of Syracuse [Dionysius]" (p. 55). Socrates was similarly retrograde, and Anton-Hermann Chroust, in his *Socrates: Man and Myth*, relates that he "appears to have been favourably impressed with the aristocratic or oligarchic governments of Crete and Sparta....In this manner he gradually acquired the reputation of being a 'reactionary' or perhaps the intellectual leader of the 'anti-democratic reaction' in Athens.... [H]e... surround[ed] himself with such notoriously 'aristocratic' or 'reactionary' men as Charmides.., Adeimantus, Alcibiades, Plato, and others" (p. 168). Together, Socrates and Plato were the twin literary co-authors of Plato's misleadingly titled *Republic*, which despite its name is a philosophic template for a totalitarian state. The contemporary popular reverence for Socrates and Plato undoubtedly reflects the hostility that many modern Western intellectuals, particularly academics, bear toward liberal political and economic values generally—a hostility which all but certainly has its roots in the financial interests of state-subsidized academics as a class and which is discussed in detail toward the end of this study. Maxey, Chester C., *Political Philosophies*, rev. ed. (New York: Macmillan, 1959). Chroust, Anton-Hermann, *Socrates: Man and Myth: The Two Socratic Apologies of Xenophon* (Notre Dame, IN: U of Notre-Dame P, 1957).

13. Will Durant relates in *The Story of Philosophy* that "Schopenhauer thought it 'not the least merit of [Prussian dictator] Frederick the Great, that under his government Kant could develop himself, and dared to publish his *Critique of Pure Reason*. Hardly under any other government would a salaried professor' (therefore, in Germany, a government employee) [parenthetical remark Durant's] 'have ventured such a thing'… It was in appreciation of this freedom that Kant dedicated the *Critique* to Zedlitz, Frederick's far-sighted progressive Minister of Education" (p. 340). "The close relationship between minister and philosopher continued throughout the remaining years of Frederick the Great's reign," T. J. Hochstrasser observed in his *Natural Law Theories in the Early Enlightenment*. "Zedlitz was indeed the dedicatee of the *First Critique* – one of the few cases, perhaps, where we can be fairly sure that a minister of education not only read but approved a work of systematic philosophy dedicated to him" (p. 195). And with the support of Frederick's government "[t]he 'critical philosophy' was soon being taught in every important German-speaking university…. In some cases the German government even undertook the expense of their support," notes the *Great Books* edition of Kant's "critiques" of "Reason" and "Judgment" (p. vi). But Durant's comment that Frederick's education minister Zedlitz was "progressive" should not be taken as meaning that Kant's Hohenzollern patrons were in the classical sense "liberal." Although Frederick is reputed to have loosened the reins of state power after inheriting the throne from his draconian father his rule was nevertheless characterized in Desmond Seward's *Napoleon and Hitler* as a "terrifyingly dynamic compound of militarism and State service, of discipline, and precision" (p. 11). Writing of the roots of German militarism in his *The Rise and Fall of the Third Reich*, William L. Shirer related that "the Hohenzollerns managed to create a Spartan military

state whose well-drilled army won one victory after another and whose Machiavellian diplomacy…brought constant additions to its territory….There thus arose quite artificially a state born of no popular force nor even of an idea except that of conquest, and held together by the absolute power of the ruler, by a narrow-minded bureaucracy which did his bidding and by a ruthlessly disciplined army….And the state, which was run with the efficiency and soullessness of a factory, became all; the people were little more than cogs in the machinery. Individuals were taught not only by the kings and the drill sergeants but by the philosophers that their role in life was one of obedience, work, sacrifice and duty. Even Kant preached that duty demands the suppression of human feeling, and the Prussian poet Archibald Alexis gloried in the enslavement of the people under the Hohenzollerns. To Lessing, who did not like it, 'Prussia was the most slavish country in Europe' " (p. 93). Durant, Will, *The Story of Philosophy: The Lives and Opinions of the Great Philosophers* (New York: Pocket, 2006). Hochstrasser, T. J., *Natural Law Theories in the Early Enlightenment* (Cambridge, UK: Cambridge UP, 2006), p. 195. Web, 28, July, 2014, http:// books.google.com/books? id=1PnZ_FuYLnsC&pg=PA195& lpg=PA195&dq=Frederick%27s+minister+of+education+zedl itz&source#v=onepage&q=Frederick's%20minister%20of%20 education%20zedlitz&f=false. *Great Books of the Western World*, vol. 39, ed. in chief Mortimer J. Adler (Chicago: Britannica, 1996). Shirer, William J., *The Rise and Fall of the Third Reich* (New York: Simon, 1960).

14. Marx, of course, is most famous for his "materialist conception of history," not for the idealist conception that was the metaphysical basis of his early forays into political thought. But it wasn't until he wrote the famous preface to the second edition of *Das Capital*, first published in 1873, that he formally renounced his earlier Idealism and made plain his commitment

to the metaphysical Materialism which was the hallmark of his "mature" philosophizing. It is nevertheless important to keep Marx's youthful Idealism ever in mind because a crucial aspect of the materialist system he outlined in *Capital*, its Organicism, is difficult to reconcile with the facts of material reality which were ostensibly the concern of "scientific socialism." Indeed, without reference to the hocus-pocus of idealist systems it is all but impossible to compelling represent human society as part of one great organism.

15. Mussolini, Benito, *The Doctrine of Fascism* (New York: Fertig, 2006), pp. 7-8.

16. Hitler, Adolf, *Mein Kampf*, trans. Ralph Manheim (Boston: Houghton, 1971), pp. 379, 380, 381.

17. Marx, Karl, "Letter to His Father: On a Turning-Point in Life," in *Writings of the Young Marx on Philosophy and Society*, trans. and ed. Loyd D. Easton and Kurt H. Guddat, pp. 40-50 (Garden City, NY: Anchor, 1967), p. 46.

18. Over time this notion of man as a single collective being has devolved into group-identity ideologies which represent humanity as comprised of various racial, national, sexual, or class collectivities, each one considered as a single individual, rather than as a collection of individuals. This sub-dividing of "man" became the basis for group-identity movements such as Nazism and Marxism, which divide people into Aryan and Jew, proletarian and bourgeoisie.

19. Marx, Karl, "Estranged Labor," in *Economic and Philosophic Manuscripts of 1844*, Web, 24, Aug., 2013, https://www.marxists.org/archive/marx/works/1844/epm/1st.htm#s4.

20. Tucker, Robert C., *Philosophy and Myth in Karl Marx*, 2nd ed. (New York: Cambridge UP, 1972), p. 130.

21. Marx, Karl, "Contribution to the Critique of Hegel's Philosophy of Right," in *Karl Marx: Early Writings*, trans. and ed. T. B. Bottomore, pp. 41-60 (New York: McGraw, 1964), p. 44.

22. Tucker, op. cit., p. 22.

Chapter Three: Creationism

1. Ullmann, Walter, *Principles of Government and Politics in the Middle Ages* (New York: Barnes; Frome and London: Butler, 1961), p. 21.
2. Luther, Martin, *Martin Luther: Selections From His Writings,* ed. John Dillenberger (Garden City, NY: Anchor, 1961), pp. 208-209.
3. Ibid., "Secular Authority: To What Extent It Should Be Obeyed," pp. 363-402, pp. 377-378.
4. Ibid., p. 399.
5. Lesser, Jonas, *Germany: The Symbol and the Deed* (New York: Thomas Yoseloff, 1965,), pp. 106-107.
6. The *Koran*, sura lxxvi, trans. Lane, Edward W., Stanley Lane-Poole, and A. H. G. Sarwar (New York: Crescent, n.d., ISBN: 0-517-138964), p. 35.
7. Ibid., sura vii, p. 135.
8. The Koran alleges that God is authoring the Koran through His "illiterate" messenger, Mohammed. In sura xxxvi God says "We have not taught Mohammed poetry, nor would it befit him. It is only a warning and a plain Koran...." In fact, however, as this passage makes obvious, Mohammed is writing the Koran himself, and calling himself "illiterate" to make it less apparent that he is naming himself the authority over all creation by having his Koran appoint him the Creator's representative here on earth. Mohammed's calling himself "illiterate" is a clumsy dodge, since he could not have written even "a plain Koran" were he not literate. Ibid., p. 43.
9. *Bhagavad-gītā As It Is*, abr. ed., ch. 10, txt. 7, trans. A.C. Bhaktivedanta Swami Prabhupāda (New York: Bhaktivedanta, 1975), p. 166.

10. Ibid., ch. 10, vs. 8-9, pp. 166-167.
11. Ibid., ch. 4, vs. 13, p. 74.
12. In the *Introduction* to his translation of the *Śrī Īśopaniṣad* Hindu scholar A. C. Bhaktivedanta Swami Prabhupada offers that "[t]here are four divisions of society....This is called *varṇāśrama*. It is stated in the *Bhagavad-gītā*, 'These divisions are everywhere because they are created by God.' The divisions of society are brāhmaṇa, kṣatriya, vaiśya, śūdra. Brāhmaṇa refers to the very intelligent class of men, those who know what is Brahman. Similarly, the kṣatriyas, the administrator group, are the next intelligent class of men. Then the vaiśyas, the mercantile group. These classifications are found everywhere. This is the Vedic principle, and we accept it," [the śūdra are the laboring class]. *Śrī Īśopaniṣad*, trans. A.C. Bhaktivedanta Swami Prabhupāda (New York: Bhaktivedanta, 1975), pp. i-ii. The online Hindi-English dictionary *Shabdkosh* defines "Brahman" as a member of the most elite of the four Hindu varnas or social divisions, and specifically a member of the sacerdotal or priest class. Web, 31, Aug., 2013 http://www.shabdkosh.com/hi/translate ?e=brahman&l=hi.
13. *The Rabbis' Bible: The Torah*, Solomon Simon and Morrison David Bial (New York: Behrman, 1966), p. 197, (Deut. 8:11-14, 17, 18).
14. Ibid., p. 7, (Gen. 1:1).
15. Ibid., pp. 8, 10-11, (Gen. 1:11, 20, 24, 26).
16. Ibid., p. 10.
17. Ibid., pp. 197-198, (Deut. 10:12, 13, 14).
18. The terms "right wing" and "left" or "left wing" are rendered in quotation marks in this study to communicate their dubiousness as instruments for conveying abstract political principles. These terms have been rendered semantically useless for that purpose by their commonplace employment as instruments for denoting concepts and political movements

which are fundamentally dissimilar in their character. The term "left wing," for instance, is routinely used to refer both to the position that a woman has an individual right to abort her fetus as well as to doctrines (Marxism, Socialism, Communism, etc.) which say that only society and never the individual has any rights at all. Similarly, the term "right" and "right wing" are employed to denote both Fascist and Nazi doctrines as well as their absolute theoretical opposites: "classical" Liberalism and Libertarianism. Because these two semantically adulterated terms can be manipulated to communicate opposite meanings they can be utilized by the intellectually unscrupulous to sabotage rational political discourse—specifically by equating a political principle with its antithesis. Philosophers, editorialists, and political journalists, therefore, are ethically prohibited from using these terms, and they appear in quotation marks in this survey to remind the reader of this.

19. Mussolini, Benito, *The Doctrine of Fascism* (New York: Fertig, 2006), pp. 11-13, 27.

20. Ibid., p. 9.

21. Ibid., p. 13.

22. Ibid., pp. 12, 13, 29.

23. *The Speeches of Adolf Hitler*, vol. 1, trans. and ed. Norman H. Baynes (New York: Fertig, 1969), p. 662.

24. Ibid., Himmler, quoted by Baynes, p. 175.

Chapter Four: Monism, Pantheism, and Organicism

1. Cf. Angeles, Peter A., *The HarperCollins Dictionary of Philosophy*, 2nd ed. (New York: HarperPerennial, 1992), p. 216.

2. Gregor, James A., *Contemporary Radical Ideologies* (New York: Random, 1968), p. 305.

3. Mussolini, Benito, *The Doctrine of Fascism* (New York: Fertig, 2006), pp. 10, 13, 27.

4. Mussolini, Benito, *Fascism: Doctrine and Institutions* (New York: Fertig, 1968), p. 133.
5. Rosenberg, Alfred, *The Myth of the Twentieth Century*, trans. Vivian Bird (Newport Beach, CA: Noontide, 1993), pp. 383, 415.
6. Chamberlain, Houston Stewart, *Foundations of the Nineteenth Century*, vol. I, trans. John Lees (New York: Fertig, 1968), p. 320.
7. Boguslavsky, B. M., Karpushin, Rakitov, Chertikhin, Ezrin, *ABC of Dialectical and Historical Materialism*, trans. Lenina Ilitskaya (Moscow: Progress, 1978), pp. 354-355.
8. Ibid., p. 443.
9. Marx, Karl, "On the Jewish Question," in *Karl Marx: Early Writings*, trans. and ed. T. B. Bottomore, pp. 1-40 (New York: McGraw, 1964), p. 31.
10. Ibid., Marx, "Alienated Labour," pp. 120-134, p. 126.
11. Marx, Karl, *Capital*, reprinted in *Great Books of the Western World*, vol. 50, trans. Samuel Moore, Edward Aveling, Marie Sachey, and Herbert Lamm, ed. Friedrich Engels, pp. 1-411 (Chicago: Britannica, 1996), p. 6.
12. Ibid., p. 169.
13. A.C. Bhaktivedanta Swami Prabhupāda, purport of the invocation of his translation of the *Śrī Īśopaniṣad* (New York: Bhaktivedanta, 1975), pp. 3-4.
14. *Bhagavad-gītā As It Is*, complete ed., ch. 4, txt. 35, trans. A.C. Bhaktivedanta Swami Prabhupāda (New York: Collier, 1974), p. 261.
15. *Śrī Īśopaniṣad*, mantra 1, trans. A.C. Bhaktivedanta Swami Prabhupāda (New York: Bhaktivedanta, 1975), pp. 4-5.
16. Noss, John B., *Man's Religions*, rev. ed. (New York: Macmillan, 1960), p. 230.
17. Ibid., pp. 138-139.
18. Lyon, Quinter M., *The Great Religions* (New York: Odyssey, 1957), p. 158.

19. *The Essential Kabbalah*, trans. Daniel C. Matt (Edison, NJ: Castle, 1995), p. 72.
20. Ibid., pp. 81-82.
21. *Everyman's Talmud*, rev. ed., trans. and ed. Abraham Cohen (New York: Schocken, 1995), p. 6.
22. Ibid., p. 184.
23. See note eleven in chapter two.

Chapter Five: Materialism

1. Flew, Antony, Jennifer Speake, and Sarah Mitchell, eds. *A Dictionary of Philosophy*, rev. 2nd ed. (New York: St. Martin's, 1984), p. 222.
2. Susser, Bernard, *Political Ideologies in the Modern World* (Boston: Allyn, 1995), p. 31.
3. Luther, Martin, *Martin Luther: Selections From His Writings*, ed. John Dillenberger (Garden City, NY: Anchor, 1961), pp. 369-370.
4. Ibid., p. 139.
5. Hitler, Adolf, *Mein Kampf*, trans. Ralph Manheim (Boston: Houghton, 1971), p. 338.
6. Marx, Karl, and Friedrich Engels, *Manifesto of the Communist Party*, reprinted in *Great Books of the Western World*, vol. 50, trans. Samuel Moore, ed. Friedrich Engels, pp. 415-434 (Chicago: Britannica, 1996), pp. 427-428.
7. Hitler, op. cit., pp. 383-384.
8. Marx and Engels, op. cit., p. 419.
9. Ibid., Engels, Friedrich, preface, p. 416. Engels' statement to the effect that a Marxist revolution will lead to the "emancipating [of] society at large from all exploitation, oppression, class distinctions and class struggles" may seem to contradict the idea that Marxism is a socially Darwinistic doctrine which advocates class struggle as a means of elevating

society to higher states of social evolution. But Marxists and Marx always insisted that, unlike natural evolution, social evolution would end and all class struggle cease after the natural forces of social progress had lifted society to a state of proletarian perfection. In other words, Social Darwinism— brute force—until *we* are in power; then all political struggle must stop.

10. Lenin, V. I., *State and Revolution* (New York: International, 1943), p. 70.

11. Boguslavsky, B. M., V. A. Karpushin, A. I. Rakitov, V. Y. Chertikhin, and G. I. Ezrin, *ABC of Dialectical and Historical Materialism*, trans. Lenina Ilitskaya (Moscow: Progress, 1978), pp. 310-311.

12. *The Speeches of Adolf Hitler*, vol. 1, trans. and ed. Norman H. Baynes (New York: Fertig, 1969), p. 17.

13. Hitler, *Mein Kampf*, op. cit., p. 303.

14. Tucker, Robert C., *Philosophy and Myth in Karl Marx*, 2nd ed. (New York: Cambridge UP, 1972), p. 112 fn.

15. Marx, Karl, "On the Jewish Question," in *Writings of the Young Marx on Philosophy and Society*, trans. and eds. Loyd D. Easton and Kurt H. Guddat, pp. 216-248 (Garden City, NY: Anchor, 1967), pp. 243-244.

16. Hitler, *Mein Kampf*, op. cit., pp. 80, 84-85.

17. Ibid., p. 104.

18. It is important for students of Marxian theory to remember that both Marx and Marxists go back and forth between, on the one hand, attributing the processes of human intellectual functioning to the mechanics of materialist economic forces, and, on the other, to the will of society conceived of as a single, volitional organism. The passage cited, when it is perused in its entirety, illustrates this inconsistency, which is ultimately attributable to the logical quandaries resulting from advocating both materialist and idealist metaphysical positions simultaneously. Indeed,

depending on how this passage is parsed, it may be used to illustrate either of these two contradictory positions, rather than just one of them. Here it is edited to illustrate the materialist position because this section of the study concerns Materialism. When unredacted, however, the passage provides an excellent example of philosophers attempting to speak out of both the materialist and the idealist sides of their mouths at the same time. See index entries under the heading *Dualism* for further insights into this issue.

19. Boguslavsky, B. M., et al., op. cit., p. 442.
20. Ibid., p. 443.
21. Ibid., p. 442.
22. Marx, Karl, *Capital*, reprinted in *Great Books of the Western World*, vol. 50, trans. Samuel Moore, E. Aveling, M. Sachey, and H. Lamm; ed. Friedrich Engels, pp. 1-411 (Chicago: Britannica, 1996), p. 165.

Chapter Six: Heracliteanism

1. Mussolini, Benito, *Fascism: Doctrine and Institutions* (New York: Fertig, 1968), p. 10. Mussolini did not here elaborate on what he meant by "eighteenth century materialism" or "economistic literature." But given Fascist philosophical perspectives it is reasonable to assume that by "eighteenth century materialism" he meant that form of Newtonian scientific materialism which ascribes predictable causes to physical events, rather than the authoritarian theory of Materialism which insists that human behavior is mechanistic. And by "economistic literature" he seems to have been alluding to the liberal economic hypotheses of eighteenth century theorists such as Adam Smith, which promised a wide-spread and general prosperity if the feudalist and mercantilist practices of earlier centuries were laid aside in favor of free-market policies. Both Newtonian science and liberal

economics heralded a bright future for Western civilization—a future which the Fascists were certainly opposed to.

2. Ibid., pp. 37, 39, app.
3. Ibid., pp. 25, 26, 27.
4. Heraclitus, web, 26, Sept., 2013, http://www.goodreads .com/author/quotes/77989.Heraclitus.
5. Heraclitus, web, 26, Sept., 2013, https://www.goodreads .com/author/quotes/77989.Heraclitus?page=2.
6. Spengler, Oswald, *The Decline of the West*, vol. I, trans. Charles Francis Atkinson (New York: Knopf, 1929), p. 118.
7. Ibid., p. 424.
8. Sartre, Jean-Paul, *Existentialism*, trans. Bernard Frechtman (New York: Philosophical, 1947), p. 18.
9. Ibid., pp. 18, 19, 20, 21.
10. Breisach, Ernst, *Introduction to Modern Existentialism* (New York: Grove, 1962), pp. 102, 103.

Chapter Seven: Authoritarian Philosophies of Knowledge

1. As opposed to subjective reality, objective reality may be defined as that which exists external to and independent of our experience of it. Absolute epistemological Skepticism says that no knowledge of anything we experience, either subjectively—that is, within ourselves—or objectively—meaning outside or independent of ourselves, is possible. But historically, and as a general rule, epistemologically skeptical arguments are directed against our knowledge of the objective—the independent and externally existing—not the subjective. The reasons for this are discussed throughout the section concerning epistemological philosophy.
2. Angeles, Peter A., *The HarperCollins Dictionary of Philosophy*, 2nd ed. (New York: HarperPerennial, 1992), p. 104.
3. *The Speeches of Adolf Hitler*, vol. 1, trans. and ed. Norman H. Baynes (New York: Fertig, 1969), p. 224.

4. Rosenberg, Alfred, *The Myth of the Twentieth Century*, trans. Vivian Bird (Newport Beach, CA: Noontide, 1993), p. 383.

5. *The Speeches of Adolf Hitler*, vol. 1, trans. and ed., Norman H. Baynes, Baynes quoting Himmler (New York: Fertig, 1969), p. 175.

6. Hitler, Adolf, *Mein Kampf*, trans. Ralph Manheim (Boston: Houghton, 1971), p. 380.

7. *The Speeches of Adolf Hitler*, trans. and ed. Norman H. Baynes, op. cit., p. 901.

8. Angeles, op. cit., p. 75.

9. Joseph Goebbels quoted in N. Gangulee, ed., *The Mind and Face of Nazi Germany*, reprint (New York: AMS, 1982; originally published London: Murray, 1942), p. 123.

10. Pachter, Henry M., "National-Socialist and Fascist Propaganda for the Conquest of Power," printed in *The Third Reich*, an anthology published under the auspices of the International Council for Philosophy and Humanistic Studies, pp. 710-741 (London: Weidenfeld, 1955), pp. 726, 727.

11. Hitler, op. cit., pp. 458, 459, 460.

12. Diesel, Eugen, *Germany and the Germans*, trans. W. D. Robson-Scott (New York: Macmillan, 1931), pp. 153, 191, 192.

13. Descartes and Leibniz were ambitious, upper-crust 17th century court philosophers who plied their intellectual wares among the political elites of pre-French Revolution Europe. Descartes' background was that of a well-off member of the lower echelons of French nobility who rose to cap his philosophic career as the intellectual courtesan of Queen Christina, the monarch of Sweden. Leibniz was also born into auspicious circumstances and spent most of his life hustling a variety of aristocratic court appointments, most notably within the court of Hanover. Benedict (Baruch) Spinoza, on the other hand, was something of an ascetic—he made his living as a lens-grinder and frequently found himself in trouble with the more

backward-looking elements of Europe's intellectual classes. The usefulness of his ideas, however, was recognized by the autocrats and aristocrats of the period who saw the need to replace the crude theological underpinnings of European tyranny with more compelling, quasi-scientific arguments. One of these autocrats, German Prince Charles Louis (Karl Ludwig), offered Spinoza a chair of philosophy at the University of Heidelberg—at a time when such universities were little more than the indoctrinational arms of the authoritarian states which established and subsidized them. Spinoza declined Charles Louis's offer, but not, so far as the record indicates, because he had any moral qualms about serving in the employ of the regime which had made it; rather, he seems to have feared that as Charles Louis's hireling he might have had to surrender his intellectual autonomy.

14. Macridis, Roy C., *Contemporary Political Ideologies*, 3rd ed. (Boston: Little, Brown, 1986), p. 184.

15. Spengler, Oswald, *The Decline of the West*, vol. I, trans. Charles Francis Atkinson (New York: Knopf, 1929), p. 102.

16. Gregoire, F., "The Use and Misuse of Philosophy and Philosophers," printed in *The Third Reich*, an anthology published under the auspices of the International Council for Philosophy and Humanistic Studies, pp. 678-709 (London: Weidenfeld, 1955), pp. 689, 670.

17. As early as the late nineteenth and early twentieth centuries the subjugation of Western philosophic thought by Kantian and German Idealism was apparent to major philosophic scholars. In the supplementary materials offered in Paul Carus' 1909 translation of Kant's definitive *Prolegomena* Alfred Weber noted that "[w]e see that the subjectivity of time and space is the most original and, on the whole, the most fruitful of Kant's teachings....It is the mind which prescribes its laws to the phenomenal world....In short, the three [Kantian] *Critiques*

culminate in absolute spiritualism. Kant compared his work to that of Copernicus: just as the author of the *Celestial Revolutions* puts the sun in the place of the earth in our planetary system, so the author of the *Critique* places the mind in the centre of the phenomenal world and makes the latter dependent upon it. Kant's philosophy is, undoubtedly, the most remarkable and most fruitful product of modern thought. With a single exception, [Weber's footnotes indicate he means the philosophy of Auguste Comte] perhaps, the greatest systems which our century has produced are continuations of Kantianism." And in the 1901 edition of his *A History of Modern Philosophy* the eminent philosophic scholar Wilhelm Windelband wrote that "[t]his philosophical power to master the ideal material of history dwelt within the *doctrine of Kant,* and this is its incomparably high historical importance. Kant, by the newness and the greatness of his points of view, prescribed to the succeeding philosophy not only its problems, but also the means for their solution. His is the mind that determines and controls on all sides. The work of his immediate successors, in which his new principle unfolded itself in all directions and finished its life historically with an assimilation of earlier systems, is best comprehended in accordance with its most important characteristic, under the name of *Idealism* [italics Windelband's]." Weber, Alfred, "The Critique of Practical Reason, and the Critique of Judgment," *Kant's Prolegomena,* trans. and ed., Paul Carus, pp. 250-257 (London: Open Court, 1909), p. 257. Windelband, Wilhelm, *A History of Philosophy,* vol. I (New York: Macmillan, 1901, Harper, 1958), pp. 530, 531.

18. Kant, Immanuel, *Critique of Pure Reason,* trans. Norman Kemp Smith (London: Macmillan; New York: St. Martin's, 1961), p. 26.

19. Chamberlain, Houston Stewart, *Foundations of the Nineteenth Century,* vol. II, trans., John Lees (New York: Fertig, 1968), pp. 474, 475, 476.

20. Ibid., p. 477.
21. Ibid., p. 479, 480.
22. Hegel, Georg, *The Phenomenology of Mind*, trans. J. B. Baillie (New York: Harper, 1967), p. 378.
23. Marx, Karl and Friedrich Engels, *Manifesto of the Communist Party*, reprinted in *Great Books of the Western World*, vol. 50, trans. Samuel Moore, ed. in chief Mortimer J. Adler (Chicago: Britannica, 1996), p. 427.
24. Hitler, op. cit., pp. 287, 288.

Chapter Eight: Skepticism

1. Chamberlain, Houston Stewart, *Foundations of the Nineteenth Century*, vol. I, trans. John Lees (New York: Fertig, 1968), pp. 414, 415, 416.
2. Ibid., vol. II, p. 468.
3. Kant, Immanuel, *Kant's Prolegomena*, trans. and ed., Paul Carus (London: Open Court, 1909), pp. 38, 42, 43, 45, 75.
4. H. S. Chamberlain, quoted in Roderick Stackelberg, *Idealism Debased* (Kent, OH: Kent State UP, 1981), p. 132.
5. West, Thomas G., introduction to *Four Texts On Socrates*, trans. and ed. Thomas G. West and Grace Starry West (Ithaca, NY and London: Cornell UP, 1992), p. 26.
6. Socrates, as he is represented by Plato in the latter's "Crito," published in B. Jowett's (trans.) and Louise Ropes Loomis's (ed.) *Plato* (Roslyn, NY: Black, 1942), p. 74. Readers are reminded that, because Socrates did not write anything down, Socratic philosophy is only known to us through its representation by the philosopher's colleagues and contemporaries—particularly Plato and Xenophon.
7. Popper, Karl R., *The Open Society and Its Enemies*, vol. I (Princeton, NJ: Princeton UP, 1971), p. 88.
8. Leiserson, Avery, "Citizens and the Generation of Public

Opinion," in *Government and Politics*, eds. John C. Wahlke and Alex N. Dragnich (pp. 399-426), (New York: Random, 1966), p. 402.

9. Noss, John B., *Man's Religions*, rev. ed. (New York: Macmillan, 1960), p. 111.

10. A.C. Bhaktivedanta Swami Prabhupāda, purport of the invocation of his translation of the *Śrī Īśopaniṣad* (New York: Bhaktivedanta, 1975), pp. 3-4.

11. *Bhagavad-gītā As It Is*, complete ed., ch. 13, txt. 31, trans. A.C. Bhaktivedanta Swami Prabhupāda (New York: Collier, 1974), p. 657.

12. Ibid., A.C. Bhaktivedanta Swami Prabhupāda's "purport," or exegesis of, ch. 13, txt. 31, p. 657.

13. *Bhagavad-gītā As It Is*, abr. ed., ch. 3, txts. 38-41, trans. A.C. Bhaktivedanta Swami Prabhupāda (New York: Bhaktivedanta, 1975), pp. 60, 61.

14. Noss, op. cit., p. 247.

15. "Pitṛputrasamāgama, Śikṣāsamuccaya," pp. 251-52, quoted in Theodore de Bary, *The Buddhist Tradition* (New York: Modern, 1969), p. 98.

16. De Bary, Theodore, WM., *The Buddhist Tradition* (New York: Modern, 1969), p. 79.

17. Kant, op. cit., p. 45.

18. Ibid., p. 43.

19. Nietzsche, Friedrich, *Beyond Good and Evil*, trans. R.J. Hollingdale (London: Penguin, 1990), p. 115.

20. Descartes, René, "Meditations," in *Philosophic Classics*, vol. II, 2nd ed., ed. Walter Kaufmann, pp. 22-80 (Engelwood Cliffs, NJ: Prentice-Hall, 1968), p. 28.

21. Ibid., p. 29.

22. Ibid., p. 27.

23. Kant, op. cit., pp. 108-109.

24. Dixon, Brandt V. B., introduction to *Critique of Pure Reason*, rev.

ed., trans. J. M. D. Meiklejohn (New York: Collier; Colonial, 1900), p. ix.

25. Vermeil, Edmond, "The Origin, Nature and Development of German Ideology in the 19th and 20th Centuries," printed in *The Third Reich*, an anthology published under the auspices of the International Council for Philosophy and Humanistic Studies, pp. 3-111 (London: Weidenfeld, 1955), p. 92.

26. Mosse, George L., *Nazi Culture* (New York: Grosset, 1966), pp. xxvii, xxviii.

27. Ibid., p. 265.

28. Black, Peter R., *Ernst Kaltenbrunner: Ideological Soldier of the Third Reich* (Princeton, NJ: Princeton UP, 1984), p. 288.

29. Chamberlain, Houston Stewart, *Foundations of the Nineteenth Century*, vol. I, trans. John Lees (New York: John Lane, 1912), pp. 216, 221.

30. Hertz, Frederick, *The German Public Mind in the Nineteenth Century*, ed., Frank Eyck, trans. Eric Northcott (Totowa, NJ: Rowan, 1975.), p. 50, 54.

31. The term "mystical," when used to designate a method of attaining knowledge, refers to the epistemological doctrine known as *Mysticism*. Mysticism is typically defined as averring either that, 1): knowledge may be acquired by somehow directly connecting one's own mind with that source of all knowledge which is the mind of God; or as, 2): more generally asserting that knowledge may be attained through any number of extra-rational, extra-sensory methods such as intuition, divine revelation, and faith.

32. Randall, John Herman, Jr., *The Making of the Modern Mind* (New York: Columbia UP, 1976), p. 413.

33. Lesser, Jonas, *Germany: The Symbol and the Deed* (New York: Thomas Yoseloff, 1965,), p. 107.

34. Ibid., p. 107.

35. Jones, W. T., *A History of Western Philosophy: Hobbes to Hume*, 2nd ed. (San Diego, CA., USA: Harcourt, 1969), p. 65.

36. Chamberlain, Houston Stewart, *Foundations of the Nineteenth Century*, vol. II, trans. John Lees (New York: Fertig, 1968), p. 179.
37. Luther, Martin, *Martin Luther: Selections From His Writings*, ed. John Dillenberger (Garden City, NY: Anchor, 1961), p. 128.
38. Pachter, Henry M., "National-Socialist and Fascist Propaganda for the Conquest of Power," printed in *The Third Reich*, an anthology published under the auspices of the International Council for Philosophy and Humanistic Studies, pp. 710-741 (London: Weidenfeld, 1955), p. 717.
39. Stern, Fritz, *The Politics of Cultural Despair* (Berkeley, CA, USA: U of California P, 1974), p. xiv.
40. Mosse, George, *The Crisis of German Ideology* (New York: Grosset, 1964), p. 40.
41. Anstett, Jean-Jacques, "Paul de Lagarde," printed in *The Third Reich*; published under the auspices of the International Council for Philosophy and Humanistic Studies, pp. 148-202 (London: Weidenfeld, 1955), p. 171.
42. Heidegger, Martin, "The Self-Assertion of the German Universities," in *German Existentialism*, trans. Dagobert D. Runes (New York: Wisdom, 1965), p. 19.
43. Ibid., quoting *Freiburger Studentenzeitung*, "Analysis and Synthesis," p. 52.
44. Rosenberg, Alfred, *The Myth of the Twentieth Century*, trans. Vivian Bird (Newport Beach, CA., USA: Noontide, 1993), p. 449.
45. Chamberlain, op. cit., p. 242.
46. Spengler, Oswald, *The Decline of the West*, vol. II, trans. Charles Francis Atkinson (New York: Knopf, 1928), p. 12.
47. Maxey, Chester C., *Political Philosophies*, rev. ed. (New York: Macmillan, 1959), p. 657.
48. Chamberlain, op. cit., vol. I, p. 576.
49. Maxey, op. cit., p. 657.
50. Gregoire, F., "The Use and Misuse of Philosophy and Philosophers," printed in *The Third Reich*; published under the auspices of the International Council for Philosophy and Humanistic Studies, pp. 678-709 (London: Weidenfeld, 1955), p. 685.

51. Radel, J.-Lucien, *Roots of Totalitarianism* (New York: Crane, 1975), p. 8.
52. Ibid., p. 19.
53. Ernest Renan quoted in Benito Mussolini's *The Doctrine of Fascism* (New York: Fertig, 2006), pp. 22, 23.
54. Numerous sources concerning Russell's political attitudes are available online. Some, but not all of these make note of his ambivalence regarding authoritarian systems. Typical are comments found on *The European Graduate School* website: "During the First World War Russell, shifting from liberalism to socialism, engaged in anti-war protests....In 1920, Bertrand Arthur William Russell visited the Soviet Union where he met Vladimir Lenin. From his experiences with Lenin and the Soviet Union in general he published, The Practice and Theory of Bolshevism (1920). In it he, rather disillusioned, makes the poignant note that "One who believes as I do, that free intellect is the chief engine of human progress, cannot but be fundamentally opposed to Bolshevism as much as to the Church of Rome. The hopes which inspire communism are, in the main, as admirable as those instilled by the Sermon on the Mount, but they are held as fanatically and are as likely to do as much harm." Web, 23, Jan., 2014 http://www.egs.edu/library/ bertrand-russell/biography/. See also the *Encyclopædia Britannica* website, 23, Jan., 2014, http://www.britannica.com/ EBchecked/topic/513124/Bertrand-Russell, and the *Spartacus Educational* website, 23, Jan., 2014 http://www.Spartacus. schoolnet.co.uk/TUrussell.htm.
55. Bertrand Russell quoted in Randall, Jr., op. cit., p. 680.

Chapter Nine: Pragmatism

1. Mussolini, Benito, *The Doctrine of Fascism* (New York: Fertig, 2006), p. 26.

2. Ibid., p. 26.
3. James, William, "What Pragmatism Means," in *Pragmatism; A New Name for Some Old Ways of Thinking*, pp. 43-81 (London, Longman's, 1911), p. 74.
4. Ibid., p. 46.
5. Ibid, "Pragmatism and Humanism," (pp. 239-270), pp. 256, 257.
6. Ibid, pp. 248, 249.
7. Philosophic historian W. T. Jones referred to James' philosophy as "oscillations...around a central tendency, and this central tendency (as James himself on occasion saw) [parenthetical remark Jones'] falls within a Kantian framework...." And William Sahakian notes in his *History of Philosophy* that John Dewey, another of the founding pragmatists, "began in philosophy as a Hegelian and Neo-Kantian...." Jones, W. T., *Kant and the Nineteenth Century*, 2nd ed., rev. (San Diego, CA, USA: Harcourt, 1975), p. 302). Sahakian, William S., *History of Philosophy* (New York: Barnes, 1968), p. 263.
8. Kant, Immanuel, *Kant's Prolegomena*, trans. and ed., Paul Carus (London: Open Court, 1909), pp. 42, 43.
9. James, "What Pragmatism Means," op. cit., pp. 51, 53, 54, 55.
10. Ibid., pp. 57, 58, 61.
11. James, "Pragmatism's Conception of Truth," op. cit. (pp. 197-236), pp. 233, 234.
12. James, William, "The Moral Equivalent of War," *International Conciliation* 27, (1910), pp. 8, 9, 11, 14, 15, 16, 17, 18, 19, 20.
13. James, William, "What Pragmatism Means," *Pragmatism; A New Name for Some Old Ways of Thinking*, pp. 43-81 (London: Longman's, 1911), p. 51.
14. Ibid., "Pragmatism's Conception of Truth," (pp. 197-236), p. 222.
15. William James, *The Will to Believe* (New York: Dover, 1956), p. 200-01, quoted in W. T. Jones' *Kant and the Nineteenth Century*, 2nd rev. ed. (New York: Harcourt, 1975), p. 310.

16. Hitler, Adolf, *Mein Kampf*, trans. Ralph Manheim (Boston: Houghton, 1971), pp. 214, 215.

Chapter Ten: Authoritarian Ethics

1. Mussolini, Benito, *The Doctrine of Fascism* (New York: Fertig, 2006), pp. 7-9.
2. *Bhagavad-gītā As It Is*, abr. ed., ch. 2, txts. 59, 62, 63, 71, 72, trans. A.C. Bhaktivedanta Swami Prabhupāda (New York: Bhaktivedanta, 1975), pp. 39, 40, 41.
3. Ibid., p. 148.
4. Ibid., Introduction by A.C. Bhaktivedanta Swami Prabhupāda, pp. xxi, xxvii, xxx, xxxi.
5. The *Dhammapada*, trans. J.R. Carter and M. Palihawadana (New York: Oxford UP, 1987), pp. 80, 81.
6. The *Koran*, sura lvii, trans. Lane, Edward W., Stanley Lane-Poole, and A.H. G. Sarwar (New York: Crescent, n.d., ISBN: 0-517-138964), pp. 219, 220.
7. *Bhagavad-gītā As It Is*, complete ed., ch. 4, txt. 20, trans. A.C. Bhaktivedanta Swami Prabhupāda (New York: Collier, 1974), p. 243.
8. Ibid., A.C. Bhaktivedanta Swami Prabhupāda's "purport," or exegesis of, ch. 4, txt. 20, pp. 243, 244.
9. *Bhagavad-gītā As It Is*, abr. ed., op. cit., ch. 2, txt. 47, p. 35.
10. Ibid., ch. 5, txt. 10, p. 94.
11. Ibid., ch. 5, txt. 12, p. 95.
12. Ibid., ch. 17, txts. 11, 13, 14, p. 249.
13. Ibid., ch. 2, txts. 17-19, 20, 25, 30-33, 37, 38, pp. 26, 27, 29, 32.
14. Ibid., ch. 5, txt. 20, p. 99.
15. Ibid., A. C. Bhaktivedanta Swami Prabhupāda's purport of ch. 5, txt. 20, p. 99.
16. Mussolini, op. cit., p. 9.
17. A. C. Bhaktivedanta Swami Prabhupāda, introduction to *Bhagavad-gītā As It Is*, abr. ed. (New York: Bhaktivedanta, 1975), pp. xxiv, xxv.

18. Ibid., ch. 5. txts. 26-29, p. 101.

19. "[T]he state is a national organism and not an economic organization," Hitler says in *Mein Kampf* (p. 151), and later in the same volume writes of his desire to found "a state...which represents, not an alien mechanism of economic concerns and interests, but a national organism," (p. 329). On page 534 of *Mein Kampf* he extols "the effort to erect an organic folkish [racial] state in place of the present senseless state mechanism." Hitler, Adolf, *Mein Kampf*, trans. Ralph Manheim (Boston: Houghton, 1971). In his speeches Hitler makes this same point: "What is the State?" he asked in an address given after the abortive 1923 Beer Hall Putsch in Munich: "To-day the State is an economic organization, an association of persons, formed, it would seem, for the sole purpose that all should co-operate in securing each other's daily bread. The State, however, is not an economic organization, it is a 'volkic' organism," (p. 85). And in a speech at a convention of the NSDAP in Nuremberg in 1937 Hitler spoke of the need to immunize "the organism of our people" from what he referred to as "Bolshevist poisons" (p. 694). *The Speeches of Adolf Hitler*, vol. 1, trans. and ed. Norman H. Baynes (New York: Fertig, 1969).

20. Hitler, Adolf, *Mein Kampf*, trans. Ralph Manheim (Boston: Houghton, 1971), pp. 297, 298.

21. Mussolini, op. cit., pp. 7, 8.

22. *Bhagavad-gītā As It Is*, abr. ed., ch. 9, txt. 24, op. cit., p. 157.

23. Ibid., ch. 2, txts. 48-52, p. 36.

24. Ibid., ch. 5, txts. 21-24, p. 100.

25. Ibid., A. C. Bhaktivedanta Swami Prabhupāda, purport of ch. 6, txts, 13-15, pp. 107, 108.

26. *Śrī Īsopaniṣad*, mantra 6, trans. A.C. Bhaktivedanta Swami Prabhupāda (New York: Bhaktivedanta, 1975), p. 28.

27. *Bhagavad-gītā As It Is*, abr. ed., op. cit., ch. 6, txts. 7-9, p. 106.

28. *The Essential Kabbalah*, trans. Daniel C. Matt (Edison, NJ: Castle, 1995), p. 72.

29. Ibid., p. 83.
30. Noss, John B., *Man's Religions*, rev. ed. (New York: Macmillan, 1960), p. 576.

Chapter Eleven: Duty

1. Jones, W. T., *Kant and the Nineteenth Century*, 2nd rev. ed. (New York: Harcourt, 1975), p. 70.
2. Jones, W. T., *The Classical Mind*, 2nd ed. (New York: Harcourt, 1970), p. 174.
3. Luther, Martin, *Martin Luther: Selections From His Writings*, ed. John Dillenberger (Garden City, NY: Anchor, 1961), pp. 208, 209.
4. Paul the Apostle, paraphrasing Isaiah 29:16 and 45:9, in Romans 9:21, NIV.
5. Luther, op. cit., p. 399.
6. St. Augustine, *The City of God*, reprinted in *Great Books of the Western World*, vol. 18, trans. Marcus Dods, ed. in chief, Robert Maynard Hutchins (Chicago: Britannica, 1952), p. 379.
7. Ibid., p. 387.
8. *Bhagavad-gītā As It Is*, abr. ed., ch. 4, txt. 35, trans. A.C. Bhaktivedanta Swami Prabhupāda (New York: Bhaktivedanta, 1975), p. 84.
9. Ibid., A. C. Bhaktivedanta Swami Prabhupāda's purport, p. 90.
10. Ibid., A. C. Bhaktivedanta Swami Prabhupāda's purport, p. 104.
11. Ibid., ch. 5, txts. 10, 12, pp. 94, 95.
12. *The Essential Kabbalah*, trans. Daniel C. Matt (Edison, NJ: Castle, 1995), p. 72.
13. Rosenberg, Alfred, *The Myth of the Twentieth Century*, trans. Vivian Bird (Newport Beach, CA., USA: Noontide, 1993), p. 383.
14. Hitler, Adolf, *Mein Kampf*, trans. Ralph Manheim (Boston: Houghton, 1971), p. 151.
15. *The Speeches of Adolf Hitler*, vol. 1, trans. and ed. Norman H. Baynes (New York: Fertig, 1969), p. 837.

16. Nazi party philosopher H. S. Chamberlain, whose *Foundations of the Nineteenth Century* was hailed by the Nazis as the "gospel of the Nazi movement," referred to the Hindu religion admiringly in that tract as one in which "the individual no longer believed that he lived and died for himself alone but for the whole world; hence the feeling of all-embracing responsibility. The one stood for all...." Web, 6, Dec., 2013 http://coelsblog .wordpress.com/2011/11/08/nazi-racial-ideology-was -religious-creationist-and-opposed-to-darwinism/#sec3 Chamberlain, Houston Stewart, *Foundations of the Nineteenth Century*, vol. I, trans. John Lees (New York: Fertig, 1968), p. 438.

17. In *The Critique of Judgement* Kant writes of "the teleological estimate of nature," meaning nature as goal-oriented, or alive, "as a system of which man is a member" (p. 560). The ethical significance of this statement is outlined a few pages earlier when he describes such living systems as constructs in which "every part is thought as *owing* its presence to the *agency* of all the remaining parts, and also as existing *for the sake of the others* [italics Kant's] and of the whole, that is as an instrument, or organ" (p. 557). Kant, Immanuel, *The Critique of Judgement*, reprinted in *Great Books of the Western World*, vol. 42, trans. James Creed Meredith, ed. in chief Robert Maynard Hutchins (Chicago: Britannica, 1952).

18. Ibid, p. 557, fn. 2.

19. Kant, Immanuel, *Critique of Practical Reason and Other Works on The Theory of Ethics*, 6th ed., trans. Thomas Kingsmill Abbott (London: Longmans, 1954), p. 228.

20. Rosenberg, Alfred, *The Myth of the Twentieth Century*, trans. Vivian Bird (Newport Beach, CA., USA: Noontide, 1993), p. 412.

21. Kant, op. cit., pp. 13, 14.

22. Ibid., p. 16.

23. In the pages leading up to and following the cited passage Kant

frequently uses the terms "law" or "laws" to refer to "practical law," "moral law," "universal law," "laws of experience," and "laws of duty," etc. Because he normally qualifies his phrasing through the employment of adjectives and context it is usually clear that on these pages Kant is using the term "law" to refer exclusively to philosophic principles rather than to legal statutes. However, in the paragraphs and footnotes immediately prior to, within, and immediately after the cited passage Kant does not unambiguously indicate how he wishes the reader to interpret his use of such phrases as "law of itself," "law in itself," "law in general," and "any particular law," etc., leaving the reader to interpret these phrases as he or she habitually will unless the phrases are precisely defined: to include the statutes of the state. Given Kant's philosophy of the individual's relationship to the state—he says in *The Science of Right* that "[i]t is the duty of the people to bear any abuse of the supreme power, even then though it should be considered to be unbearable. And the reason is that any resistance of the highest legislative authority can never but be contrary to the law," (p. 440) there can be little doubt that he intends the reader to interpret the cited passage as averring that morality consists at least in part in a duty to obey *any law of government*, regardless of its nature. Kant's ambiguity in this passage, however, would permit him, or his defenders, to deny that he has any such crassly immoral intent. Kant, Immanuel, *The Science of Right*, reprinted in *Great Books of the Western World*, vol. 42, trans. W. Hastie, ed. in chief Robert Maynard Hutchins, pp. 397-458 (Chicago: Britannica, 1952).

24. Kant, Critique of Practical Reason and Other Works on The Theory of Ethics, 6th ed., op. cit., pp. 16-18.

25. Heidegger, Martin, quoted in *German Existentialism: Martin Heidegger*, trans. Dagobert D. Runes (New York: Wisdom, 1965), pp. 37, 38.

26. *The Speeches of Adolf Hitler*, vol. 1, trans. and ed. Norman H. Baynes (New York: Fertig, 1969), pp. 543, 544.

27. Because these would be actions motivated by inclination rather than actions in accordance with duty.

28. Jones, W. T., *Kant and the Nineteenth Century*, 2nd rev. ed. (New York: Harcourt, 1975), p. 77.

29. Augustine, op. cit. p. 379.

30. *The Essential Kabbalah*, trans. Daniel C. Matt (Edison, NJ: Castle, 1995), p. 72.

31. *Bhagavad-gītā As It Is*, abr. ed., ch. 2, txt. 47, op. cit., p. 35.

32. Ibid., ch. 3, txt. 30, p. 57.

33. A.C. Bhaktivedanta Swami Prabhupāda's purport of ch. 3, txt. 30, ibid., p. 58.

34. *Śrī Īśopaniṣad, Invocation*, trans. A.C. Bhaktivedanta Swami Prabhupāda (New York: Bhaktivedanta, 1975), p. 1.

35. Ibid., Mantra One, pp. 4, 5.

36. Ibid., purport of the *Invocation* of the *Śrī Īśopaniṣad*, A.C. Bhaktivedanta Swami Prabhupāda, pp. 3, 4.

37. Kant, Critique of Practical Reason, op. cit., p. 167.

38. Ibid., p. 353.

39. Ibid., p. 61.

40. Ibid., p. 215.

41. Mussolini, Benito, *The Doctrine of Fascism* (New York: Fertig, 2006), p. 10.

42. Mussolini is basing this statement on Heraclitean, rather than idealist, metaphysical premises.

43. Changing his metaphysical tack again, Mussolini seems to be founding this objection to self-interest on the idea of Social Darwinism, a Materialist argument, rather than upon Heracliteanism, or upon Organicism, which is usually metaphysically idealist. Mussolini's willingness to switch metaphysical theories—theories about the basic nature of reality—is not unusual among authoritarian ideologues, and is a

reflection of their epistemological Pragmatism. Mussolini is quoting Ernest Renan in this passage.

44. Mussolini, op. cit., pp. 21, 22, 23. Mussolini is quoting Ernest Renan on pages 22 and 23.

45. Ibid., p. 8.

46. Hitler, *The Speeches*, op. cit., p. 867.

47. Hitler, *Mein Kampf*, op. cit., p. 534.

48. By "self-preservation" Hitler means, not the preservation of the private, individual self, but the higher, organic, social "self" which he elsewhere refers to as "collective egoism."

49. Ibid., pp. 297, 298.

50. *The Encyclopedia of Philosophy*, vol. II, Paul Edwards, ed. in chief (New York: Macmillan, 1967), p. 176.

51. See the sub-heading "Secular Idealism" in Chapter Two.

52. *Encyclopædia of Religion and Ethics*, vol. X, ed. James Hastings (New York: Scribner's, 1956), p. 1956.

Chapter Twelve: The Ethics of the Masters

1. Nietzsche, Friedrich, *Beyond Good and Evil*, trans. Helen Zimmern (New York: Macmillan, 1907), p. 227.

2. Grenzmann, Wilhelm, "Nietzsche and National-Socialism," printed in *The Third Reich*; published under the auspices of the *International Council for Philosophy and Humanistic Studies*, pp. 203-242 (London: Weidenfeld, 1955), p. 204.

3. Nietzsche, Friedrich, *Daybreak*, eds. Maudemarie Clark and Brian Leiter, trans. R. J. Hollingdale (Cambridge UK: Cambridge UP, 1997), pp. 75, 76.

4. Ibid., p. 73.

5. Nietzsche, *Beyond Good and Evil*, op. cit., pp. 113, 114.

6. Nietzsche, Friedrich, *Beyond Good and Evil*, trans. R. J. Hollingdale (London: Penguin, 1990), pp. 53, 54.

7. Nietzsche, *Daybreak*, op. cit., p. 60.
8. Nietzsche, Friedrich, *Beyond Good and Evil*, trans. Helen Zimmern (New York: Macmillan, 1907), pp. 51, 52.
9. Ibid., pp. 58, 59.
10. Nietzsche is giving voice here, as he does frequently, to that classical authoritarian meme, the organic theory of the state.
11. Ibid., pp. 225, 226.
12. Readers should note that Nietzsche's equation of human beings with animals is essentially a metaphysically Materialist argument, asserting as it does that human beings are driven by the mechanistic forces of nature which ostensibly govern the behavior of animals. We earlier observed that the basis of the subjectivist epistemological methods Nietzsche employs in arriving at such conclusions are themselves based on metaphysically Materialist arguments which say that subjectivity is unavoidable because human faculties of knowledge physiologically distort reality.
13. Nietzsche himself issued from a line of Prussian clergyman in a society where authoritarian power had historically been facilitated by the church. Nietzsche's own father was a Lutheran minister who had been employed as a tutor to members of Prussia's royal family. See *Thus Spake Zarathustra*, trans. Walter Kaufmann (New York: Modern, 1995), p. v.
14. Nietzsche, Friedrich, *The Genealogy of Morals*, trans. Horace B. Samuel, ed. T. N. R. Rogers (Mineola, NY: Dover, 2003), pp. 22, 23.
15. Ibid., p. 58.
16. Nietzsche, *Daybreak*, op. cit., p. 67.
17. Nietzsche is referring to the "executions, tortures," and burnings-at-the-stake which he represents as part of the entertainments offered by aristocratic households during wedding feasts and "national festivals." See *The Genealogy of Morals*, op. cit., p. 42.

18. Nietzsche, *The Genealogy of Morals*, op. cit., pp. 41, 42.

19. Nietzsche, Friedrich, *Beyond Good and Evil*, trans. R. J. Hollingdale (London: Penguin, 1990), p. 159.

20. The epistemological philosophies of Skepticism and epistemological Subjectivism are themselves based primarily on the metaphysical philosophies of Materialism and Heracliteanism.

21. See endnote 17, Chapter 7.

22. See endnote 3, Chapter 8.

23. Hegel, Georg, *The Phenomenology of Mind*, trans. J. B. Baillie (New York: Harper, 1967), p. 267.

24. Ibid., p. 503.

25. Hegel, Georg, *The Philosophy of Right*, reprinted in *Great Books of the Western World*, vol. 46, trans. T. M. Knox (Chicago: Britannica, 1952), pp. 116, 117.

26. Ibid., p. 116.

27. Hegel, *The Phenomenology of Mind*, op. cit., 504, 505.

28. Nietzsche, Friedrich, *Beyond Good and Evil*, trans. R. J. Hollingdale (London: Penguin, 1990), p. 183.

29. Hegel, *The Philosophy of Right*, op. cit., p. 119.

30. Nietzsche, *Daybreak*, op. cit., p. 74.

31. Heidegger, Martin, *Being and Time*, trans. John Macquarrie and Edward Robinson (New York: Harper, 1962), p. 50.

32. Ibid., p. 453. Heidegger is quoting Count Yorck von Wartenburg.

33. Heidegger, who famously stated that, "[m]aking itself intelligible is suicide for philosophy," was never consistently clear in his use of the German word "Dasein." The term is variously translated as meaning life, state of being, living, existence, state of existing, etc.

34. Breisach, Ernst, *Introduction to Modern Existentialism* (New York: Grove, 1962), pp. 84, 85.

35. Heidegger, op. cit., p. 67.
36. Sartre, Jean-Paul, *Existentialism*, trans. Bernard Frechtman (New York: Philosophical, 1947), p. 15.
37. Sartre, Jean-Paul, *Being and Nothingness,* trans. Hazel E. Barnes, (New York: Washington Square, 1956), pp. 739, 740, 751, 753, 754, 755.
38. Ibid., p. 340.
39. Sartre, *Existentialism*, op. cit., p. 45.
40. Ibid., p. 18.
41. Ibid., p. 18.
42. Ibid., p. 15.
43. Ibid., pp. 18, 19, 20, 21.
44. Sartre is here using the phrase "dialectic of history" to refer to an aspect of Marxist theory.
45. Ibid., pp. 86, 87.
46. Marx, Karl, *Capital*, reprinted in *Great Books of the Western World*, vol. 50, trans. Samuel Moore, Edward Aveling, Marie Sachey, and Herbert Lamm, ed. Friedrich Engels, pp. 1-411 (Chicago: Britannica, 1996), p. 6.
47. The best-known of the postmodernist and deconstructionist philosophers are the French philosophers Michel Foucault and Jacques Derrida, whose existentialist influences are well-documented.
48. Nietzsche, Friedrich, *Beyond Good and Evil*, trans. R. J. Hollingdale (London: Penguin, 1990), p. 204.

Chapter Thirteen: Egalitarianism

1. Rawls, John, *A Theory of Justice* (Cambridge, MA: Belknap), p. 74.
2. Ibid., p. 74.

3. Ibid., p. 3.
4. Ibid., p. 100.
5. Ibid., pp. 73, 74.
6. Ibid., p. 101.
7. Marx, Karl, "The Criticism of the Gotha Program," *Capital, The Communist Manifesto, and Other Writings*, ed. Max Eastman, pp. 2-7 (New York: Modern, 1932), p. 7.
8. Ibid., p. 3.
9. Marx, Karl, *Capital*, reprinted in *Great Books of the Western World*, vol. 50, trans. Samuel Moore, Edward Aveling, Marie Sachey, and Herbert Lamm, ed. Friedrich Engels, pp. 1-411 (Chicago: Britannica, 1996), p. 36, fn. 2.
10. Ibid., p. 207.
11. Ibid., p. 207.
12. Marx, Karl, and Friedrich Engels, *Manifesto of the Communist Party*, reprinted in *Great Books of the Western World*, vol. 50, trans. Samuel Moore, ed. Friedrich Engels, pp. 415-434 (Chicago: Britannica, 1996), p. 426.
13. Ibid., p. 426.
14. Ibid., p. 426.

Chapter Fourteen: The Gardeners of Evil

1. Comte, Auguste, *Auguste Comte and Positivism: The Essential Writings*, ed. Gertrud Lenzer (New York: Harper, 1975), p. xxxiv.
2. Zingales, Luigi, "The College Graduate as Collateral," *New York Times*, June, 14, 2012, p. A35, print.
3. Although it is unusual for philosophy textbooks to plainly call attention to the authoritarian nature of much of philosophy and theology some academic writers have nevertheless made an earnest effort to raise their readers' awareness of the

relationship between what is popularly thought of as respectable philosophy and the tenets of the authoritarian ideological opus. Throughout this study reference has been made to the percipient comments of these honorable and responsible scholars.

INDEX

A

T

Made in the USA
San Bernardino, CA
20 November 2017